I0518161

INVESTING
Is the Best Thing

An introductory guide to the world of
investing for teenagers and their parents

Jamaal C. Boyce

Copyright © 2025 BY J Carmichael REI L.L.C.

All rights reserved. This publication, or any part thereof, may not be reproduced in any form or by any means, including electronic, photographic, mechanical, or by any sound recording system, or by any device for storage and retrieval of information without the written permission of the copyright owner.

Printed in the United States of America

3rd Edition Revised 2025

DEDICATION

This book is dedicated to the memory of my mother, Marlene Diana Boyce. I love you and miss you dearly. I will always remember to pray for peace.

CONTENTS

PREFACE

As a teacher of economics and investing for the past several years, I have been amazed by how many of my students have little to no savings or investments for graduation. Whether it be to pay for college, start a business endeavor, or simply start the process of adulthood, the lack of savings and investments for 99% of my students has been troubling. My economics and investing course is taught in their senior year of high school, right as they are about to graduate. When I ask my students how they are paying for college, most have no idea; a common answer is to take out debt. When I ask them why they have no savings or investments to pay for college or to start a business, the common answer is, "I don't know."

Most say no when I ask my students if they discuss investing with their parents. Many say that their parents have no idea about investing in their future. Many parents I have spoken to have told me they don't know anything about investing, that it is confusing, and that they have no outlet to learn about investing they trust. Students AND parents seem to believe it is a complicated process they cannot do. Many are intimidated by doing something as simple as opening a brokerage account.

As an activity, I like to show my students a compound interest calculator. We would play around with it using different numbers and rates of return. Using the calculator, I like to show my students how they have wasted every person's most valuable resource. TIME. They are amazed at how much money they could have had if someone had invested for them consistently over the past 18 years. I encourage them not to waste the next 18 years of life and to start learning about investing. I never tell them what to invest in. Instead, I give them different options. What works for one person may not work for another. I encourage them not to waste THEIR children's greatest resource when they finally have children.

This book was written in combination with a high school curriculum, online course, children's book, and student activity book as part of a series titled **"Investing Is The Best Thing."** The purpose is to expose children, young adults, and their parents to the world of investing. Learning about the world of investing is a lifelong journey. You never graduate. You must consistently continue to learn about the world of investing. There are things that I continue to learn daily. The purpose of the **Investing Is The Best Thing** series is to get members of the entire family on the path to investing to build wealth for themselves and their future generations. Hopefully, in the future, when I ask my seniors how they are paying for college, starting a business, or just adulthood, they will have concrete answers and resources to do so. This is why the **Investing Is The Best Thing** series of books and courses exist.

CHAPTER ONE

THE INVESTING MINDSET

Chapter 1.1: Introduction to Investing

"Investing is laying out money now to get more money back in the future."- Warren Buffet

"If you don't find a way to make money while you sleep, you will work until you die."- Warren Buffet

There are many different definitions of the word investing. An investment or investing is when you purchase an asset(resource) with the hopes of generating future income or an increase in value(appreciation). **Investing is using a resource you currently have to acquire another resource for current and/or future benefit.** There are many different types of resources(time, energy, money for example). Appreciation is the increase in the worth of an asset through time. When a person buys an investment, the intention is not to consume the asset immediately, but rather to use it to build wealth in the future. **If you want to grow crops to eat, you should never eat the seeds that you are planting into the earth. It won't be able to grow.** Investing is the same concept. Simply put, an investment is when you purchase something now with the hopes of making more money from that purchase later.

Investing is the outflow of a resource today—time, effort, money, or another asset—with the expectation of a bigger payback later than what was first put in. An investor may make a purchase of a financial asset now with the hope that it will provide income in the future or that it can be sold at a higher price in the future.

An asset is anything of value which has the potential to provide economic benefits to the owner. When investing in any asset, you should always ask yourself these 3 questions: *How much money can I make, when will I get this money, and how sure are you that you will get it?* Of course, you won't have the exact answers at the time you purchase the asset, but these questions can help you figure out if the asset you are investing in is worth it. Some examples of assets include:

1. Financial Assets: *Cash, bank accounts, stocks, bonds, and other securities that have a monetary value and can be easily converted into cash.*

2. Physical Assets: *Tangible items such as real estate, vehicles, machinery, equipment, and other physical possessions that have value and can be used or sold to generate income*

3. Intangible Assets: *Assets that aren't physical but have value due to legal or intellectual rights. Examples include patents, copyrights, trademarks, and goodwill.*

4. Business Assets: *Assets owned by a business, including physical assets like machinery and property, as well as intangible assets like brand recognition and intellectual property.*

   There are others as well.....

Simply put, an asset is any resource that you own that puts money in your pocket. You want to invest in assets.

*Do not confuse assets with liabilities. If an asset is something that puts money in your pocket, a liability is something that takes money out of your pocket. Make sure you are investing in ASSETS, not liabilities.

Always remember this quote: Assets feed you, Liabilities bleed you.

Question:

If you lost your job, and could never work again, how long could you live off of the assets that you own? Can the assets that you own feed you and take care of you? How long would you survive if you had to live off the assets that you own in order to take care of your liabilities? The answer to these questions should either make you feel extremely good or should scare you.

How an Investment Works

The act of investing seeks to generate income and increase value over time. Any method used to generate future income may be referred to as an investment. This involves, among other things, the purchase of bonds, stocks, or real estate property. Buying a building with the intention of renting it out is an example of purchasing an investment.

Any activity made with the intention of increasing future income might be considered an investment. When a person seeks higher education, for example, the goal is often to gain knowledge. The initial investment of time in class and money for tuition could result in greater earnings throughout the course of the student's career. This too is an investment.

Because investing is focused on the possibility of future development or income, every investment carries some amount of risk. An investment may not provide any income or may lose value over time. For example, a corporation in which you have invested may go out of business. Every investment carries risk, even the safest investments

Objectives of Investing

The following are popular investing goals:

Safeguarding your Money

Investing protects your money against sudden and wasteful spending. It also assists you in protecting your money from the consequences of inflation. Unless your money is placed in an interest-earning asset, inflation erodes its value. As a result, investing will help you stay up with inflation automatically. Most people believe that the purpose of money is to spend it. That mindset will keep you poor. **The actual purpose of money is to make MORE money. You shouldn't spend the money you make; you should only spend the money your money makes. Financially educated people understand this.**

Growing your wealth

The best way to grow your wealth is to invest wisely. It allows your money to earn interest, and if you maintain the interest invested your interest will begin to earn interest as well(compounding). You can't save your way to being wealthy, but you can invest your way to become wealthy.

Building Funds for Emergencies

Everyone in life will have financial ups and downs. Sometimes you make a good income and save money, but other times you need a huge quantity of money for an emergency. Building investment pools would come in handy on the down days. Investing can help build substantial funds for emergencies that will happen in life.

Securing your Retired Life

A great retired life is one in which you do not have to worry about how you will get money to support yourself. After you've saved and invested enough money for retirement, you'll be able to enjoy the freedom that comes with it. Investing early and in the right assets(assets that generate income for life) can allow you to retire with less financial worry.

Saving on Taxes

When you invest in a stock, and it appreciates(goes up in value), and you sell it, you pay what's called capital gains tax. When you work at a job and get paid, you have to pay what is called income tax. Long term capital gains tax(after a year of holding a stock when you sell it) is lower than income tax. When you sell a stock within a year and make money on it, it is still considered income tax, so you pay a higher rate.

Let's keep it simple. Let's say you own a stock for over a year, and you sell it and make $100,000 from the sale of the stock. You will pay capital gains tax. Now let's say you work your job for a year and make $100,000 in taxable income. You will pay income tax. Income tax is taxed at a higher rate than capital gains tax. So in essence, the money you worked for is taxed more than the money you DIDN'T work for. Not to mention, if you have another stock that you owned for a year and sold it at a loss losing money, you can use that against the stock you made money on that you owned for a year, also helping to reduce your taxes. Do you see why Investing Is The Best Thing?

It could be argued that receiving a paycheck is the worst way to get money because it is taxed at a higher rate. The wealthy understand this. The middle class and poor do not. You can get rich by getting a paycheck, but in order to be wealthy you must invest. It's that simple.

Funding Bigger Life Goals

Your monthly salary may not be sufficient enough to buy your next automobile or to buy a home for your family. However, if you save and invest a tiny amount over a few years, both scenarios may be achievable.

Different Categories of Investments

Depending on the sort of asset you invest in, you may anticipate a specific level of risk and return. There are many different types of investments:

Stocks

Bonds

ETF's

Mutual Funds

Real Estate

Real Estate Investment Trusts(REITs)

Commodities

Certificates of Deposits(CD's)

Retirement Plans

Options

Derivatives

Index Funds

Cryptocurrency

Business Ownership

Intellectual Property

Forex(Foreign Exchange)

Fine Art

Cash

And many more.....

Chapter 1.2: The Importance of Time

"I made my first investment at age 11. I was wasting my life up until then."- Warren Buffet

"The wealthy invest in time. The poor invest in money."- Warren Buffet

"Time IN the market beats timing the market."- Warren Buffet

Investing might seem to be a high-risk, difficult, and fast-paced process. With an infinite number of investment vehicles to select from, it might be tough to take your first step as an investor, particularly given that all investments entail the danger of losing some or all of your money. So, what's the point?

There are several compelling reasons to include investing in your entire financial strategy. Investing may help you maintain your wealth by eliminating the impacts of inflation(rise in prices of goods and services over time), saving for long-term objectives (like retirement or your children's education), or creating passive income(income you don't actively work for). So, how can you overcome all of the disadvantages of investing and make it work for you? A good place to start is to recognize that, if you are a young investor, you have time on your side. Time is the greatest resource we all have, for the simple fact it is non-renewable. You can't get time back. Wasted time is gone forever.

Time And Luck

The Myth

There are countless stories of people who took major risks in an investment and struck it rich quick. We all love the "get rich quick" stories because we all secretly aspire to be the stars of such stories. Those success stories contribute to the myth that being a successful investor is similar to being a hotshot gambler in that you must risk everything in order to reap a worthwhile reward and that some people are born with the innate ability to predict the market, make the right moves, buy and sell at the exact right time, and strike it rich.

The Reality

The fact is that serious investment takes a significant amount of time. Investing properly requires a thorough education. If you invest in the stock market without doing your homework, you may as well be playing the lottery or gambling. You are leaving your investments up to chance. Educating oneself about the stock market is a difficult endeavor that requires continual study. It's not only about knowing how economies and global markets function; it's also about remaining informed about what's going on in our world. A wise investor closely monitors the sectors and firms in which they invest by tracking things like performance, governance, public opinion, and industry trends. Consider all of that data changing and upgrading on a regular basis. Most people don't want to put in this work which is why only the few are successful investors.

When we recognize that investing may take some time, we reduce chance investing. It's not about taking a chance, but about making informed judgments, which is a good thing since it means investing is something you can practice, investigate, and eventually improve on over time. Investing can be pretty boring. If you are having wild swings in emotion or high excitement and down swings, you may not be investing. You may be gambling. Investing to build wealth takes time. Plain and simple.

Time and Risk

The Myth

There is a horror tale for every investment success story. Acting on faulty advice, losing every single cent, and being taken advantage of by an inept financial advisor are just a few of the examples. This myth reinforces the notion that investment is too dangerous and unpredictable to be worth the time or risk. One of the common things people will ask is "isn't investing risky?" "Why waste my time?"

The Reality

Life by itself is risky. Getting behind the wheel of a car is risky. However, you can control the level of risk. If you drive 160 mph while on the phone with one eye open, that is a different level of risk than doing the speed limit with both eyes on the road. No investment is ever guaranteed, which means your money is never completely protected. Some forms of investments may be safer than others, but the danger of losing money is always there. However, your choices when investing are no different than your choices in life. Using logic and a level of common sense combined with controlling your emotions and learning more each day will set you up for success in life as well as investing.

After making sound, well-researched investment decisions, the period of time it takes for your investment to mature is your strongest defense against risk and volatility. The shorter your investing horizon, the more exposed you are to rapid and frequently unanticipated market shocks. Day-to-day adjustments in the market, on the other hand, have less impact if your investment is long-term (think decades). Furthermore, there is time to recover from market dips, which is not necessarily true for short-term investments.

To summarize, here is why time is your greatest asset when it comes to investing:

1. Compound Interest: *Time allows for the magic of compound interest to work. Compound interest is the process where your investment not only earns returns on the initial amount but also on the accumulated returns. The longer your money remains invested, the more time it has to compound, leading to insane amounts of growth over time.*

2. Long-Term Perspective: *Investing with a long-term perspective allows you to ride out the natural ups and downs of the market.*

3. Risk Management: *Time can act as a cushion against potential losses. If your investments experience temporary declines, you have the luxury of waiting for the market to recover without needing to sell at a loss.*

4. Dollar-Cost Averaging: *Investing regularly over time, known as dollar-cost averaging, benefits from market fluctuations that occur over time. By buying more shares when prices are low and fewer shares when prices are high, you can lower your average cost per share over the long term which will increase your wealth over time. Even small contributions made consistently over time can have a substantial impact on your investment portfolio.*

5. Retirement Planning: *Time is a crucial factor in retirement planning. The earlier you start saving and investing for retirement, the more time your investments have to grow, potentially ensuring a comfortable retirement. Starting early, staying disciplined,*

and taking a long-term approach can potentially lead to significant wealth accumulation and financial security.

6. Risk Tolerance: *Time also influences your ability to take on risk. Younger investors often have more time to recover from losses, allowing them to tolerate higher levels of risk in their portfolios. This is especially true for children. Investing for your children gives them more time to build wealth. Time Is a resource that children have in more abundance than adults. Time is a valuable asset in investing. Use it to their advantage.*

Chapter 1.3: Greater Fool Theory: Don't be the Greater Fool

"The stock market is designed to transfer money from the active to the patient."- Warren Buffet

The greater fool theory states that in every market, there is always a greater fool willing to purchase an asset that is overvalued. It is this "greater fool" who suffers most when financial downturns happen. To prevent becoming a greater fool in investing, one must exercise caution. For investing purposes, you must constantly analyze an asset's inherent worth. When you purchase an investment, you should always wonder if you are the greater fool at that moment.

The greater fool theory is used to create an investing strategy based on the belief that an individual can always sell an asset or security at a higher price than the purchase price to a greater fool who is willing to pay a higher price because they really don't understand what they are investing in.

The goal is to profit by betting on future price increases regardless of market circumstances. This idea is founded on the premise that there are many fools in the market rather than just one. This investing strategy estimates the chance of selling an individual's investment to others for a better price than what was paid.

This greater fool theory focuses on the formation of investing bubbles, which may eventually burst and cause a catastrophe. It's the greater fools who bought at the highest price who will suffer the most. If you invest without a basic fundamental knowledge of investing, or without a basic understanding of the asset you are investing in, consider yourself the greater fool.

Examples

Let's examine the notion of the greater fool theory using a few of the instances provided below.

Example #1

Buying an asset at an extremely higher than normal price because everyone else is doing it is something greater fools do. For example, before the 2008 financial crisis, many took out bank loans to purchase properties with the aim of selling them at a higher price later on and making significant profits. It worked for many years until the supply of greater fools ran out. The greater fools bought the homes at the highest prices and watched as the homes eventually lost value putting them in the worst position. For some odd reason, people love to buy assets as they are rising up in price with no real explanation as to why and will refuse to buy an asset as it is dropping in price even though the asset is still good. Greater fools buy assets when they are overly expensive. Intelligent investors buy assets when they are cheap.

Example #2

This principle also applies in the stock market, when many investors invest in a not-so-profitable company, expecting that it would be sold later for a bigger profit to a greater fool. Any stock investment is not undertaken on the basis of its worth and potential for better returns. Rather, it is based on the idea that someone will be there to purchase it at a greater price.

When buying a stock or an ETF, one thing you may want to look at is the 52-week high/low of the stock price. Within the last year, what is the high price of the stock, and what is the low price of the stock? If you are buying the stock at its 52-week high, you may be the greater fool. If you are buying it near its 52-week low, you may get a better return in the long run and give yourself more margin of safety(more on this in a bit). Remember nothing is guaranteed, but having rules will help you play the game better. In any market with buyers and sellers, there are always greater fools.

How to Avoid Being a Greater Fool

In financial markets with diverse stocks, commodities, and other investment options, it is critical to control your emotions..

- It is important to remember that nothing in investing is completely predictable. Markets operate on the basis of several factors, and nothing is certain. For example, the price of an asset that is greater now may inflate or fall dramatically in the future depending on market circumstances.

- Assets should be included in a portfolio depending on their historical performance and reputation.

- Before making an investment, one should perform extensive study, planning, and market analysis. Then, a suitable plan should be devised and executed. Finally, in order to avoid speculative bubbles(unreasonable rises in asset prices), one should adopt a long-term investing strategy.

- The common herd should not be followed by paying more for something just because others are investing in it. Before investing, one should make a self-decision and overcome greed and the desire to gain a lot of money quickly.

Greater fools are those who prioritize excessive financial gains and often take on excessive risk in pursuit of those gains. Their behavior is characterized by a strong desire for quick and significant profits, sometimes at the expense of rational investing practices and risk management. Below are some common traits of greater fools when investing:

1. High-Risk Appetite: *Greater fools are often willing to take on higher levels of risk than is reasonable for their financial situation or investment goals.*

2. Chasing Quick Profits: *They may constantly seek the next "hot" investment or market trend, hoping to capitalize on rapid price increases.*

3. Ignoring Fundamentals: *Greater fools might overlook the fundamental value of an asset and instead focus solely on short-term price movements.*

4. Lack of Diversification: *They may put too much of their capital into a single high-risk investment without understanding it rather than spreading it across a diverse portfolio of investments.*

5. Overleveraging: *Greater fools may borrow excessively to amplify potential gains, but this also increases potential losses in case investments decline.*

6. Ignoring Warning Signs: *They might ignore warning signs or red flags about an investment*

7. Falling for Scams: *Greater fools are more susceptible to investment scams promising unrealistic returns.*

8. Herding Behavior: *Greater fools love following the crowd without proper analysis which can lead to participating in market bubbles or panics.*

9. Emotional Decision-Making: *Greater fools often make decisions based on emotions like fear of missing out (FOMO) rather than sound analysis.*

10. Short-Term Focus: *Greater fools tend to prioritize short-term gains over long-term wealth accumulation and might buy and sell investments frequently without understanding what they are doing.*

11. Ignorance: *"The greatest knowledge one can have is the knowledge of one's own ignorance."Thomas Sowell; Greater fools lack an understanding of their own ignorance when investing, yet invest like they know what they are doing.*

Consequences of being the greater fool can include significant financial losses, stress, and damage to one's financial well-being. Intelligent investing involves thorough research, diversification, patience, and a focus on long-term goals. As an investor, you must understand your limitations and abide by them.

*When investing based on the greater fool theory, you will miss out on certain investments that will continue rising in price long term. You may miss out on good deals. However, you may miss out on bad deals as well. The best investors do not worry about missing out on fast rising assets. They worry more about losing money on poor assets but at high prices. When investing, when one opportunity is missed, eventually another will arise. Many new investors have the fear of missing out syndrome(FOMO). This is what attracts them to fraudulent investments, and gets them in trouble when investing. As a new investor, do your best not to invest based on FOMO.

Chapter 1.4: Margin of Safety: Why you Need It

"Our goal is to find an outstanding business at a sensible price, not a mediocre business at a bargain price."- Warren Buffet

The concept of "margin of safety" suggests that investors should only make purchases of assets when their current market value is well below their true value. Simply put, buy a good asset at a great price. Price always matters in investing. The lower the price you can purchase an asset in relation, the better the return. It's that simple. The margin of safety is the difference between the current market value of an asset and your valuation of its true value. A low-risk investing opportunity presents itself when this difference occurs, as investors may choose their own margin of safety according to their level of risk.

Understanding Margin of Safety

Benjamin Graham ("Father of Value Investing") and his disciples, most notably Warren Buffett, popularized the margin of safety hypothesis. Investing with a margin of safety gives protection against mistakes in your analysis of an investment. However, it does not ensure a successful investment, owing to the fact that identifying a company's "real" worth, or intrinsic value, is extremely subjective. Investors and analysts may use multiple methods to calculate value, and these methods are seldom perfect and precise. Furthermore, predicting a company's profitability or sales is notoriously difficult.

Example of Investing and Margin of Safety

Graham's philosophy was founded on basic facts, notwithstanding his intellectual background. He understood that a stock selling for $1 today may be worth $.50 cents or $1.50 in the future. He also acknowledged that the current value of $1 may be incorrect, which would expose him to undue danger. He reasoned that if he could acquire a stock at a discount to its true worth, he could significantly reduce his losses. Although there was no assurance that the stock's price would rise, the discount offered the necessary margin of safety to assure that his losses would be limited.

For example, if he determines that the value of ABC's stock is $162, which is much less than its current share price of $192(based on his analysis of the company), he may decide not to consider buying ABC stock until it hits $162. If the stock market drops, and ABC stock falls to $134 but the analysis of the stock is the same, he may buy it at $134 knowing that its true value is $162. This would give him a level of margin of safety. Price matters. The lower the price, the greater the return. If he had purchased ABC stock at $192, he would not have given himself any margin of safety. He also would have been the greater fool. When the market rebounds and ABC stock goes to $162(it's true value price), he would make a great return. If ABC stock goes back to its original price of $192, his return will be even greater. If he purchased ABC stock at $192, and it goes back to $192, then he effectively has no return. Using this scenario, he may not be able to acquire ABC stock in the near future. However, he will not care as he only cares about buying great companies at even greater prices.

Intrinsic Value in Investing

What is Intrinsic Value?

Intrinsic value is the true worth of a company's stock based on its business fundamentals, rather than its current market price. It's an important concept in investing, especially for value investors like Warren Buffett.

There are two main ways people think about how much a stock is worth:

1. *Market Value: This is the price you see when you look up a stock. It's what people are willing to pay for it right now.*

2. *Intrinsic Value: This is what smart investors think a stock is really worth based on how well the company is doing.*

Key Points:

- *Intrinsic value looks at a company's real business value, not just its stock price*

- *It's based on things like cash flow, assets, and earnings*

- *Value investors try to find stocks trading below their intrinsic value*

Why Intrinsic Value Matters

Understanding intrinsic value helps investors make smarter decisions:

- *It can show if a stock is undervalued or overvalued*
- *It helps investors avoid buying overpriced stocks*
- *It gives a more complete picture of a company's worth beyond just the stock price*

How to Calculate Intrinsic Value

There are several ways to estimate a stock's intrinsic value. Calculating the intrinsic value of a company is complicated, and is not perfect as it is based on many assumptions about the future that cannot accurately be predicted. However, it is a tool that many investors attempt to use to give them some level of **Margin of Safety.**

Example

Let's pretend someone is selling a lemonade stand for the next 10 days:

- It makes $10 every day
- We think it will keep making $10 every day for the next 10 days

We might decide the lemonade stand is worth $100 today because that's how much money it will make in 10 days based on its current revenue and our future assumptions. If the seller is selling the lemonade stand for $50 for the next 10 days, we may buy it thinking that the price is below the intrinsic value of the lemonade stand which would give us some level of margin of safety. However, if the seller is selling the lemonade stand for $125 for the next 10 days, we may value it as overpriced and decide not to buy.

The Importance of Margin of Safety

Value investors don't just buy a stock because it seems slightly undervalued. They look for a "margin of safety" a big discount to the calculated intrinsic value. This helps:

- *Protect against errors in calculations*
- *Provide a cushion against market downturns*
- *Offer greater potential returns*

*Calculating intrinsic value isn't perfect, but it gives investors a way to make decisions based on a company's fundamental worth rather than just its stock price. Knowing the intrinsic value helps investors make smart choices. If a stock's price is lower than what they think it's really worth, it might be a good time to buy!

To summarize, here's why the margin of safety is important:

3. Reducing risk: *Margin of safety serves as a buffer against uncertainties when investing. By purchasing an asset at a price lower than its value, investors reduce the risk of losses in case the unexpected happens. When investing, always remember, the unexpected will happen.*

4. Protection Against Errors: *As an investor you will make errors in your analysis or assumptions. You are a human being and we all make mistakes in judgment. A margin of safety allows for a cushion in case you make small errors in your analysis.*

5. Market Volatility: *Financial markets are unpredictable, and asset prices can be subject to sudden and substantial changes. A margin of safety helps protect against the negative impact of market volatility.*

6. Long-Term Success: *Investors who invest with a level of margin of safety seek to invest for the long term. By investing in undervalued assets, they position themselves for potentially larger gains over time as the market recognizes the true value of the investment.*

7. Flexibility: *A margin of safety provides flexibility in decision-making. It allows investors to hold onto their investments during short-term market downturns without being forced to sell at a loss.*

8. Peace of Mind: *Knowing that you've purchased an asset at a price well below its value can provide peace of mind, reducing the emotional stress associated with market fluctuations. Many investors lose sleep at night because their investments have no room for error.*

9. Value Investing: *Margin of safety is a key characteristic of value investing, a strategy that seeks to identify undervalued assets. Value investors believe that purchasing assets with a margin of*

safety increases the likelihood of generating significantly better returns over time.

10. Exceptional Investing: *Most investors do not practice a level of margin of safety. The exceptional ones do. If you are doing the same as everyone else, you are not exceptional. By investing with a level of margin of safety, over the long term your returns will outperform the crowd.*

Margin of safety is used to manage risk and improve the odds of successful investing. It emphasizes the importance of purchasing assets at prices that provide a comfortable cushion against unforeseen events and market fluctuations that will always happen.

Chapter 1.5: Rich vs Wealthy: What's the Difference

"Oprah is rich. Bill Gates is wealthy. If Bill Gates woke up tomorrow with Oprah's money, he'd jump out of a window."-
Chris Rock

Understanding Rich

What is considered "wealthy" varies from person to person. In a nation where the average per capita income is $700 per year, someone with $3,000 in the bank may be considered wealthy. However, $3,000 would barely pay one month's rent in a city like New York or San Diego here in the United States.

High Income

Consider NBA players, who made an average of $9.5 million per year in 2022-2023, according to rookieroad.com. If they lose their capacity to compete, the majority of them lack the ability to earn the same pay in another field. This might jeopardize their "wealth." Just because you MAKE a lot of money does not mean you are wealthy. If they stopped physically working, could they maintain their current lifestyle? NBA players are rich, that is for certain. However, it is the NBA OWNERS who are wealthy. What's the difference? As comedian Chris Rock once said, the guy making $9.5 million dollars is rich. The person who is signing his checks is wealthy. If the NBA were to pause for 5 seasons, the players would struggle and many would go broke. The owners would be fine. Why? They are wealthy. They own so many investments and assets that generate income WITHOUT trading time or working for it. Meanwhile, many NBA players must work or trade time in order to get that $9.5 million dollar salary. Do you see the difference between working hard for money, or letting your money work hard for you?

Rich people have extremely high incomes. As we all make more money, we automatically feel entitled to spend more money. This is what prevents us from ever becoming truly wealthy. When you make more money, you also can qualify for more debt. High earners who can qualify for more debt will then take out more debt that they have to pay back with interest. Even though they are making a high salary, they are still broke and in many cases have a negative net worth. Can you see the cycle of why so many high earners aren't necessarily wealthy?

The Real Cost of Spending

Spending unwisely will deplete your wealth. You can't build wealth if you are constantly giving your wealth away. The infusion of money might make people seem wealthier than they are. Financial mismanagement and unhealthy spending habits churn through money quicker than it can be replenished.

Those whose wages skyrocket as a result of work advancements or company success often improve their lives gradually as their financial balances grow. However, they may suffer from the trappings of their success, such as a bigger house and private school for their children. This might leave them scurrying to sustain their new lifestyle. Despite their heightened position, they are no better off financially than they were with lesser salaries.

Understanding Wealth

Wealth refers to assets that provide income rather than money itself. According to a recent Charles Schwab poll, Americans must amass $2.2 million in order to be considered "rich." But, like richness, money is relative — you need more of it to live in New York City than in Odessa, Texas.

Passive Income and Investments

Passive income and investments are common sources of wealth. Passive income is defined by the IRS as profits generated from real estate or earned without active engagement. Passive income includes rental income from real estate, stock dividends, and royalties(income from Real Estate is not as passive as it sounds, but in comparison to working a job for income it is still considered passive income). Specifically, passive income is income that you make from an enterprise you are not materially involved in. Passive Income will help make you wealthy. Active income will not. Not to say that you shouldn't work. But working by itself will not make you wealthy. The goal financially should be as wealthy as you can be. Sure you may not be a billionaire, however your goal should be to build your wealth as if you are trying to be. And you may not see the fruition of wealth in your lifetime, however who is to say that your children or grandchildren won't? Some examples of passive income include:

Dividends, Rental Income, Royalties(payments from sales of a book you have written for example) and Interest.

Financial Freedom

Passive income sources may provide financial independence, allowing you to live your preferred lifestyle whether or not you work.

Some people live frugally in order to acquire this independence. Others have amassed much more than they can possibly spend. Whatever your lifestyle, accomplishing this aim significantly decreases financial concerns and enables you to pursue non-monetary ambitions and desires.

Difference Between Being Rich vs. Wealthy

According to Robert Kiyosaki, creator of The Rich Dad Company and author of "Rich Dad Poor Dad," wealth is measured in time rather than cash. Wealth specifically evaluates how long you can sustain your current lifestyle without working.

Getting Started on the Road to Wealth

To get started, you must commit to building wealth rather than making money in order to attain your ultimate aim. Rather than having a predetermined quantity of money in mind, you should concentrate on accumulating the assets necessary to live the life you choose. When planning for retirement, instead of wondering how much money you will need to enjoy life, you may want to think about how many income generating assets you will need in order to enjoy life.

Plan for Financial Freedom

Committing to a strategy to achieve financial independence is vital to your success. You must first define financial independence. This requires deciding on a lifestyle and locating the funds to support it. Budgeting, creating the appropriate accounts, and paying off current obligations are all important.

You will also need to create an emergency fund that will cover any unforeseen needs. Because life is unpredictable, you must be prepared for such occurrences. Always enhance your financial knowledge as it will aid in the accumulation of wealth. Following that, you should invest and create multiple streams of income.

Build Passive Income

As previously stated, individuals may generate passive income through a variety of methods. Owning rental properties is just an example of a method to generate passive income. You, too, may earn while you sleep through the act of investing.

Think About Investing

A brokerage account is a gateway to wealth creation via investment. Rising stock prices have contributed significantly to this wealth. Dividends, which are cash payments delivered on a regular, generally quarterly basis for owning shares of a particular stock also help in the process of building wealth.

Dividends are considered income, so they are taxed.

You can have the dividends deposited into your brokerage account as cash.

You can also have the dividends distributed in what's known as a Dividend Reinvestment Plan(DRIP) where the cash payout automatically purchases more shares of the stock. You can set this up in your brokerage account. It's personal preference what you decide to do.

Individual stocks are preferred by certain investors. Individual shares carry greater risk, but they may potentially offer bigger rewards. Others opt to invest in mutual or index funds. Baskets of individual stocks or other assets that are professionally managed. Funds provide diversity, which reduces risk. Whichever you choose, both can help you build your wealth.

Speak With a Financial Advisor

Financial advisors can assist you in avoiding financial blunders as well as developing methods to reach financial independence. They exist in a variety of shapes and sizes, while some are more concerned with selling financial items.

Financial advisors may not be necessary for you to invest your own money. Any individual can invest their own money if they are willing to learn about investing. Financial advisors can be wrong in their assessments and many charge fees as well, depleting your wealth. However, they can be a useful tool for certain financial decisions you may need to make that will help you build your wealth. Decide on using a financial advisor based on your specific needs and situations.

Find the Right Bank Accounts

Choose a bank account or accounts that suit your needs that you are comfortable with. Finding the correct bank accounts is crucial to wealth creation. A high-yield, low or no fee savings account may help your money grow quicker and is ideal for an emergency fund to help you pay unforeseen bills. Checking and money market accounts, as well as certificates of deposit, are examples of other deposit accounts.

To summarize:

1. Rich: Being "rich" typically refers to having a high amount of income and assets, often in comparison to others. It's about having a large amount of money at a specific point in time. A person can be considered rich if they earn a substantial income, own valuable assets, or have a high net worth. However, being rich might not necessarily imply long-term financial stability or security. Rich people in general must work to continue to maintain their lifestyle. They still must trade time for money.

2. Wealthy: Being "wealthy" goes beyond just having a lot of money or assets at a particular moment. It often implies having a sustained level of financial well-being and security over time. A wealthy individual has not only accumulated substantial assets but also managed those assets well enough to ensure financial stability for the long term. The wealthy have the ability to maintain a certain lifestyle and meet financial goals consistently, rather than just having a large sum of money. In summary, someone who is "rich" has a high amount of money or assets at a specific point in time, while someone who is "wealthy" has effectively managed their financial resources to ensure ongoing stability and security over time. The wealthy can maintain their lifestyle without working for it.

There is nothing wrong with being rich. Becoming rich is fantastic. The mindset however should be to build wealth. This is where investing helps.

Chapter 1.6: Market Crashes Can Be Good

What's hot today isn't likely to be hot tomorrow."- Warren Buffet

Market crashes(a sudden drop in asset prices) may be frightening, resulting in huge financial losses and uncertainty. Investors may transform these difficult times into chances for long-term success by being prepared and smart. When the market falls, consider the following steps:

Stay Calm and Avoid Panic

It is critical to remain cool and sensible throughout a market melt-down. Emotional responses and rash decisions based on fear may often result in more losses. Market downturns are a typical part of the economic cycle, and historical evidence shows that markets tend to rebound in the long run. Maintaining a long-term perspective is critical for surviving the storm and capitalizing on the opportunities that occur. Historically, the year following a major stock market crash has typically seen the stock market begin to rebound. Market crashes create fantastic buying opportunities.

Reassess Your Financial Goals

A market meltdown is an excellent opportunity to reassess your financial objectives, risk tolerance, and investing strategy. Take a step back and consider if your objectives or risk tolerance have changed. Consider your time horizon, financial requirements, and preferred lifestyle. Based on this evaluation, you may need to change your portfolio to better reflect your current situation and goals.

Diversify Your Portfolio

Diversification is a basic financial idea that becomes even more important during market collapses. Diversifying your assets across asset classes, sectors, and geographic locations helps to mitigate the effect of a collapse on your entire portfolio. Diversification protects against losses in certain industries or equities. Consider balancing your investments by mixing stocks, bonds, real estate, and other assets based on your risk tolerance and financial goals.

Don't Try to Time the Market

Even experienced investors find it difficult to predict the bottom of a market fall. It is notoriously difficult to precisely anticipate short-term market changes. Concentrate on your long-term investing strategy and avoid making emotional judgments based on short-term market swings. Maintain a diverse portfolio that is consistent with your objectives by being disciplined and sticking to your investing plan.

Consider Buying Opportunities

Market breakdowns may generate excellent purchasing opportunities for people with a long-term outlook. During market downturns, high-quality stocks and other assets often become undervalued. Conduct extensive research to find fundamentally solid firms or investment possibilities selling at reasonable prices. Investing in these assets during a collapse positions you to gain from their potential appreciation when the market rebounds. Exercise care, though, and make sure that your investing selections are based on good fundamentals rather than short-term market emotion.

Review Your Emergency Fund

In times of financial instability, an emergency fund is essential. Make sure you have sufficient emergency money to cover your living needs for many months. This fund acts as a safety net, helping you to get through difficult economic times without having to liquidate assets at a loss. Review your emergency fund plan and make any required revisions to ensure you have enough financial reserves in the event of a market catastrophe.

Rebalance Your Portfolio

Market downturns might lead you to depart from your intended aim when investing. Review your portfolio on a regular basis and rebalance it as appropriate. To put your portfolio back in line with your goal allocation, rebalancing may entail selling some of the outperforming assets and purchasing more of the failing ones.

Avoid Speculative Investments

There may be a desire to seek rapid profits via speculative investments or hazardous bets after a market fall. However, it is critical to remain disciplined and avoid making rash judgments based on short-term market trends or excitement. Speculative investments are riskier and may not correspond with your long-term financial objectives. To increase your chances of success, stick to strong investing concepts and a well-researched, diversified plan.

Seek Professional Advice

Consider obtaining counsel from an experienced financial adviser or an investor you trust if you are unsure how to handle a market meltdown or need assistance managing your money. An expert may provide tailored advice based on your unique financial circumstances, risk tolerance, and objectives. However, make sure to do your due diligence on whoever you choose to work with.

Market crashes, while often seen as negative, can potentially have some positive aspects depending on the context and individual circumstances. To recap:

1. Buying Opportunities: *Market crashes often lead to significant declines in asset prices, including stocks and real estate. For investors with available capital, this can present an opportunity to buy assets at lower prices, potentially leading to higher returns when the market eventually recovers.*

2. Valuation Realignment: *Over time, markets can become overvalued, and a crash can help reset asset prices to more reasonable levels. This can lead to healthier and more sustainable growth in the long term.*

3. Exposing Weak Companies: *Market crashes tend to disproportionately affect companies that are weaker than others fundamentally. When the market is flying high, ALL companies look like good investments. In a market crash, the great companies survive and the weak ones fold very quickly. This is why as an investor it is important to do your research and invest in companies that can weather economic storms..*

4. Expose Bad Investment Strategies: *A market crash can expose flaws in your investment strategies. It's hard to see your weaknesses when everything is going well. A market crash can bring you to the realization that you still have a lot to learn when it comes to investing.*

5. Investor Education: *A market crash is the perfect learning opportunity. As an investor, you can learn a lot from your mistakes. It's these mistakes and learning experiences that will shape you into a better investor.*

Chapter 1.7: The Power of Compound Interest

"Compound interest is the eighth wonder of the world. He who understands it, earns it. He who doesn't, pays it."- Albert Einstein

Compound interest is the interest on savings and investments computed on both the original principal and the Interest earned over time.

The power of compound interest, or "interest on interest," will cause a sum of money to rise faster than simple interest, which is computed just on the original amount. Compounding accelerates the growth of money. The compound interest will be bigger the more compounding periods there are. Compound interest may assist your assets but make it more difficult to pay off debt.

How Compound Interest Works

Let's look at a simple example of compound interest from Forbes. com

Let's say you have $1,000 in a savings account that earns 5% in annual interest. In year one, you'd earn $50, giving you a new balance of $1,050. In year two, you would earn 5% on the larger balance of $1,050, which is $52.50—giving you a new balance of $1,102.50 at the end of year two.

Thanks to the magic of compound interest, the growth of your savings account balance would accelerate over time as you earn interest on increasingly larger balances. If you left $1,000 in this hypothetical savings account for 30 years, kept earning a 5% annual interest rate the whole time, and never added another penny to the account, you'd end up with a balance of $4,321.94.

Source- Forbes.com

Compound Interest and the Time Value of Money

The notion of the time value of money, which argues that the value of money varies depending on when it is received, provides the basis for compounding interest. Having $100 now is better than getting it in a few years because you may invest it and earn dividends and interest. That money may increase thanks to compounding. If you waited two years to get the $100, you would lose out on two years of compound interest. Once again, this proves the importance of time.

Compound Interest Results Over Time

Another approach to grasp the power of compound interest is to enter numbers into a compound interest calculator online, which illustrates how much your money may grow over time. Compound interest plays a significant role in building a large amount of wealth over time.

For example, a 20-year-old who invests $10,000 today in a safe mutual fund and earns 4% per year on average for the following 50 years would have $71,067 if the purchase is done via a tax-free account like an IRA. They would have ended up with $2,890,022 if they had invested in stocks and had a 12 percent average annual rate of return during the same period. Adding higher-yielding asset classes would result in nearly 40 times more money, owing to the power of compounding. Investor.gov is a popular website with a compound interest calculator that you may want to use, and there are several others.

CHAPTER 1:
THE INVESTING MINDSET

Quiz No: 1

Serial No	Question	Answer
1.	What is the objective of investing? A. To increase current income B. To achieve financial goals and build wealth C. To consume commodities D. To eliminate the risk of losing money	
2.	What is the primary purpose of investing in financial assets? A. To generate future income B. To consume commodities C. To eliminate risk D. To achieve immediate financial goals	
3.	How can one avoid being a greater fool in investing? A. Follow the advice of others and invest based on market trends B. Make self-decisions and overcoming greed C. Invest without performing extensive research and analysis D. Pay more for assets to ensure high returns	

4.	Who popularized the margin of safety concept? A. Benjamin Graham B. Warren Buffett C. The greater fools D. Speculators	
5.	Which of the following should be avoided in a market crash? A. Panicking and selling off all assets B. A reassessment of financial goals C. Staying calm D. Seeking professional advice	
6.	What is the difference between being "rich" and being "wealthy"? A. Richness refers to liabilities that provide income, while wealth is measured in money. B. Richness is based on the amount of money one has, while wealth refers to a high income. C. Being rich means having a lot of money, while being wealthy means having valuable assets. D. There is no difference; the terms "rich" and "wealthy" are used interchangeably.	
7.	What is passive income? A. Income earned without active engagement or involvement. B. Income earned through high-paying jobs. C. Income earned through speculative investments. D. Income earned from winning the lottery.	

8.	According to Robert Kiyosaki, how is wealth measured? A. By the amount of money one has in the bank. B. By the value of one's assets. C. By the ability to sustain a lifestyle without working. D. By the level of financial independence achieved.	
9.	What is the purpose of an emergency fund? A. To invest in high-risk assets. B. To cover living expenses during a market collapse. C. To speculate in the stock market. D. To pay off existing debts.	
10.	What is compound interest? A. The amount of money you owe in taxes B. The interest you must pay on investment income C. The interest you must pay for an investment D. The interest on savings computed on both the original principal and the interest earned over time.	

Key

1. B

2. A

3. B

4. A

5. A

6. C

7. A

8. C

9. B

10. D

CHAPTER
TWO

INVESTMENT ACCOUNTS

Chapter 2.1: Brokerage Account

"Money doesn't grow on trees; It grows in accounts."- Jamaal C. Boyce

A brokerage account is a type of investment account that is kept with a registered brokerage business. When an investor funds their brokerage account, the brokerage company executes orders for investments such as stocks, bonds, mutual funds, and exchange-traded funds (ETFs) on their behalf. The assets in investment accounts belong to the investors, who must generally disclose the account's income as taxable.

There are several kinds of brokerage accounts and brokerage companies, allowing investors to choose the model that best meets their financial needs.

Some full-service brokers demand high fees for detailed financial advice and other services. Most internet brokers, on the other hand, just offer a secure platform via which investors may place trading orders. Robo-advisors are digital platforms that provide financial planning and investing services that are powered by algorithms rather than individuals.

Types of Brokerage Accounts

Full-Service Brokerage Accounts

Investors looking for financial advice can explore full-service brokerage companies such as Merrill Lynch, Morgan Stanley, Wells Fargo Advisors, and UBS, among others. Financial advisers are compensated to assist their customers in developing investment strategies, carrying out transactions, monitoring their investments and the markets, and other tasks. Financial advisers operate on a non-discretionary basis, which requires customers to authorize transactions, or on a discretionary basis, which does not need prior client consent.

Full-service brokerage accounts may charge trading commissions or adviser fees. Many commission accounts charge a fee whenever an investment is purchased or sold, regardless of whether the advice originated from the customer or the adviser, and regardless of whether the transaction is successful or not.

Discount Brokerage Accounts

Investors who like to handle their own investing may want to use a discount brokerage. These businesses charge much less than their full-service equivalents. In fact, many charge nothing at all. However, discount brokerage firms like Charles Schwab, E*TRADE, Vanguard, Robinhood, Webull, Chase Bank and Fidelity among others provide fewer services for lower to no fees. This, on the other hand, may appeal to investors who are primarily concerned about keeping expenses low and completing transactions using simple internet trading platforms. Many brokerage accounts provide access to resources for research to help you when investing. For someone new to investing looking to keep things simple, these types of accounts will most likely suit you. In fact, these accounts are generally the most popular.

Robo-Advisor Accounts

Robo-advisors are accounts in which they, rather than the account user, choose investments using algorithms and without human intervention. They consider your personal preferences for investment and create a portfolio based on your specific needs. Robo-advisors may be suitable for both new and experienced investors who want a hands-off approach to portfolio management.

Artificial Intelligence(AI) Trading Accounts

AI trading means using innovative computer programs to help buy and sell stocks. These programs can quickly look at lots of information about the stock market and decide what stocks to trade. AI trading programs can do several things, such as

- *Look at past stock prices to predict future prices*

- *Read news articles and social media to see how people feel about different companies*

- *Buy and sell stocks automatically when certain conditions are met*

- *Analyze many different markets at once to find good trading opportunities*

Using AI for trading stocks has some advantages:

1. Saves time: AI can do research much faster than humans.

2. More accurate: Computers don't make mistakes like humans sometimes do.

3. Works 24/7: AI programs can watch the markets all day and night.

4. Find patterns: AI can spot trends in stock prices that humans might miss.

Imagine you want to buy stock in a smartphone company. An AI program could quickly read thousands of news articles, examine the company's past stock prices, and check what people are saying on social media. It might notice that the company's stock price goes up every time a new phone is released. The AI could suggest buying the stock before the new phone is announced.

While AI trading can be helpful, there are some risks to be aware of:

1. Less understanding: It can be challenging for people to know precisely how AI makes decisions.

2. Relying too much on past data: Sometimes unexpected events can change how stocks behave.

3. Big mistakes: If there's an error in the AI program, it could make many wrong trades very quickly.

4. Security worries: Hackers might try to attack AI trading systems.

Brokerage Accounts With a Regional Financial Advisor

Those who seek personal contact and a variety of services may wish to engage with a brokerage business in their local town. They might look at a regional company that is priced between full-service brokerage companies and cheap brokerage firms.

Online Brokerage Accounts

Online brokerages are a wonderful option for investors who like to choose their own investments and transactions using a website or mobile app. Many however provide research and analytical tools to assist investors in making educated judgments. Many demand a commission for each transaction. Some companies do not charge commissions. Robinhood is a commission-free online broker that trades stocks, ETFs, and options.

Cash Brokerage Accounts

To begin trading with a cash brokerage account, you must deposit funds. This account restricts your selections to the fundamentals, such as stock purchases. You cannot borrow against the funds in a cash brokerage account and you must purchase all assets in full with cash.

Margin Accounts

A margin account enables you to borrow money against your account in order to begin trading. The broker serves as a lender, and the borrowed money enables bigger transactions and more sophisticated deals, such as short-selling a stock. The investor pays interest on the borrowed money. If the value of an investor's account falls below a certain threshold owing to market activity, the brokerage may require an urgent deposit of cash. Since you are new to investing, investing on margin is highly discouraged due to its risk.

How to Open a Brokerage Account

Opening a brokerage account is a quick and easy procedure that takes just a few minutes. Once you've decided on a broker and the type of account (taxable or tax-advantaged), gather the necessary personal information: This information includes:

Your name

Social security number or taxpayer identification #

Address

Telephone number

E-mail address

Date of birth

Driver's license, passport or some form of government ID

Employment information

Annual Income

Net worth

Investment objectives

Type of investment account you are interested in

Bank account number and bank routing number

Questions regarding your financial requirements, investment objectives, investing style, and risk tolerance will be asked throughout the setup process.

After you've made your profile and opened your account, you'll need to finance it. Deposit cash into the account(you can link the account to your bank account for example for easy movement of funds or do a bank transfer), and then you can begin investing when you are ready. Just because there is cash in the account does not mean you have to buy anything. Be patient, and do your due diligence before you purchase an investment.

Chapter 2.2: Retirement Accounts

"The best investment one can make is in oneself."- Warren Buffet

There are various sorts of retirement accounts.

IRAs and 401(k)s are examples of traditional retirement plans. You may contribute pre-tax cash to an account with these tax-deferred retirement plans. You only pay taxes on your assets when you remove them from a standard IRA or 401(k). ***Tax-deferred means you pay taxes later instead of now. It does not mean tax free.***

Roth 401(k)s and Roth IRAs are non-traditional retirement plans in which you pay taxes on the money before adding it to the account. The money grows tax free and can also be withdrawn tax free.

Let's take a deeper look at some of the most popular retirement plans and their pros and cons:

IRA-Individual Retirement Account

- **Contributions:** You can contribute to a Traditional IRA using pre-tax dollars, which means you may be able to deduct the amount you contribute from your taxable income for the year. The contribution limit for 2025 is $7,000, or $8,000 if you are aged 50 or older.(Over time, these numbers will increase so make sure to stay on top of the changes)

- **Taxation:** The earnings within a Traditional IRA grow tax-deferred, meaning you don't pay taxes on the growth until you make withdrawals.

- **Withdrawals:** Withdrawals from a Traditional IRA are subject to ordinary income tax(which is a higher tax rate). If you withdraw funds before age 59½, you may also face a 10% early withdrawal penalty, unless you qualify for an exception like a first-time home purchase or certain medical expenses.

Pros:

Tax deduction: Contributions to a Traditional IRA may be tax deductible, reducing your current taxable income.

Tax deferred growth: Earnings within the account grow tax-deferred until withdrawal

Flexibility: Traditional IRA's offer a wide range of investment option including stocks, bonds, mutual funds, and ETFs

Cons:

Taxation upon withdrawal: Withdrawals from a Traditional IRA are subject to income tax, which will impact your retirement income. Income tax is taxed at some of the highest rates

Required Minimum Distributions(RMD)Starting at age 73(2023), and age 75(2033), you must take annual withdrawals from the account. This will greatly impact your taxes in retirement, as again this will count as income tax.

When you die, your beneficiaries may have to pay income tax on the money in your IRA which will affect their income tax rates as well.

Early withdrawal penalties: Currently, withdrawals taken before age 59 ½ may be subject to a 10% early withdrawal penalty, in addition to income tax.

Roth IRA

- **Contributions:** Roth IRA contributions are made with after-tax income, so you don't get an upfront tax deduction. The contribution limits for 2025 are the same as the Traditional IRA.

- **Taxation:** The earnings in a Roth IRA grow tax-free, and qualified withdrawals are also tax-free. This means that when you withdraw funds in retirement, you won't owe any income tax on the earnings.

- **Withdrawals:** Contributions to a Roth IRA can be withdrawn at any time without taxes or penalties since you've already paid taxes on that money. To withdraw earnings tax-free, you must be at least age 59½ and have held the account for at least five years.

Pros:

Tax Free withdrawals: Qualified withdrawals from a Roth IRA are tax-free, providing tax-free income in retirement

Flexible withdrawals: Contributions to a Roth IRA(not the earnings) can be withdrawn anytime without taxes or penalties

No RMDs: Roth IRAs do not require you to take RMDs during your lifetime(you already paid the taxes on the contributions), offering more flexibility in managing your retirement income

Potential for estate planning: Roth IRAs can be passed on to beneficiaries tax-free.

Cons:

No immediate tax deduction: Contributions to a Roth IRA are made with after-tax dollars, so you do not receive an upfront tax deduction

Income limitations: High income individuals may be restricted from contributing directly to a Roth IRA(check the irs.gov website or speak to your tax advisor)

Five Year Rule: Earnings in a Roth IRA must be held for 5 years to qualify for tax-free withdrawals

Early withdrawal penalties: Withdrawing earnings before 59 ½ and not meeting certain conditions may result in taxes and penalties

*IRA's may have income limits, depending on if your employer offers a retirement plan. Be sure to do your due diligence with the IRS or your accountant. ROTH IRA's have income limits. Do your homework.

401(k)

- **Contributions:** 401(k) plans are employer-sponsored retirement accounts. Contributions are made with pre-tax dollars, reducing your taxable income. The contribution limit for 2025 is $23,500, with an additional $7,500 catch-up contribution for individuals aged 50 or older. This will increase over the years.

- **Taxation:** The earnings within a traditional 401(k) grow tax-deferred, meaning you won't owe taxes on the growth until you withdraw the funds.

- **Withdrawals:** Withdrawals from a 401(k) are subject to ordinary income tax. If you withdraw funds before age 59½, you may face a 10% early withdrawal penalty.

Pros:

Employer match: Many employers offer matching contributions, which is essentially free money added to your retirement account

Higher contribution limits: 401(k) plans have higher annual contribution limits compared to IRAs

Tax deferred growth: Earnings in a 401(k) grow tax-deferred until withdrawal, providing compounding growth

Cons:

Limited investment options: 401(k) plans generally offer limited investment options, determined by the employer. Also, the fees may be high

Vesting schedules: You may need to stay with the company for a certain time period in order to fully own the contributions

Taxation upon withdrawal: Withdrawals from a 401(k) are subject to income tax, which will impact your retirement income. Income tax is taxed at some of the highest rates

Required Minimum Distributions(RMD)Starting at age 73(2023), and age 75(2033), you must take annual withdrawals from the account. This will greatly impact your taxes in retirement, as again this will count as income tax.

When you die, your beneficiaries may have to pay income tax on the money in your 401(k) which will affect their income tax rates as well.

Early withdrawal penalties: Currently, withdrawals taken before age 59 ½ may be subject to a 10% early withdrawal penalty, in addition to income tax.

403(b) and 457 plans

- **Contributions:** 403(b) and 457 plans are similar to 401(k) plans but are typically offered by educational institutions, hospitals, governmental employers and nonprofit organizations. Contributions are made with pre-tax dollars, similar to 401(k)s. These plans do not have matching contributions generally like a 401(k).

- **Taxation:** The earnings grow tax-deferred, just like traditional 401(k)s.

- **Withdrawals:** Withdrawals are subject to ordinary income tax. If you withdraw funds before age 59½, you may face a 10% early withdrawal penalty, unless you qualify for an exception.

Pros:

Higher contribution limits: 403(b) and 457 plans have higher annual contribution limits compared to IRAs

Tax deferred growth: Earnings grow tax-deferred until withdrawal, providing compounding growth

Cons:

Limited investment options: 403(b) and 457 plans generally offer limited investment options, determined by the employer. Also, the fees may be high

Taxation upon withdrawal: Withdrawals from a 403(b) and 457 plan are subject to income tax, which will impact your retirement income. Income tax is taxed at some of the highest rates

Required Minimum Distributions(RMD)Starting at age 73(2023), and age 75(2033), you must take annual withdrawals from the account. This will greatly impact your taxes in retirement, as again this will count as income tax

When you die, your beneficiaries may have to pay income tax on the money in your 403(b) or 457 plan which will affect their income tax rates as well

Early withdrawal penalties: Currently, withdrawals taken before age 59 ½ may be subject to a 10% early withdrawal penalty, in addition to income tax

Roth 401(k)

- **Contributions:** Some employers offer Roth 401(k) options alongside traditional 401(k) plans. Roth 401(k) contributions are made with after-tax dollars, so you won't get a tax deduction.

- **Taxation:** The earnings within a Roth 401(k) grow tax-free, and qualified withdrawals are also tax-free, similar to Roth IRAs.

- **Withdrawals:** Roth 401(k) withdrawals follow the same rules as a Roth IRA

Roth 403(b)

- **Contributions:** Like Roth 401(k)s, some employers offer Roth 403(b) options alongside traditional 403(b) plans. Contributions are made with after-tax dollars.

- **Taxation:** The earnings within a Roth 403(b) grow tax-free, and qualified withdrawals are also tax-free, similar to Roth IRAs.

- **Withdrawals:** Roth 403(b) withdrawals follow the same rules as a Roth IRA

Roth 401(k) and Roth 403(b) Pros:

Tax Free Withdrawals: Qualified withdrawals are tax-free, providing tax-free income in retirement

No income limits: Unlike Roth IRAs, there are no income limitations

Potential for employer match: Some employers may offer matching contributions

No RMDs: You are not required to take required minimum distributions during your lifetime, giving you more control over your retirement income

Roth 401(k) and Roth 403(b) Cons:

No immediate tax deduction: Contributions are made with after-tax dollars so you won't receive an upfront tax deduction

Early withdrawal penalties: Withdrawals of earnings before 59 ½ and not meeting certain conditions will result in taxes and penalties

Limited investment options: Investment options may be determined by your employer, and the fees may be high

*There is also a **Simplified Employee Pension Plan(SEP Plan).** It is used by employers, generally owners of small businesses for their employees.

What is a SEP Plan?

A Simplified Employee Pension (SEP) plan is a type of retirement savings plan that allows employers to contribute to traditional Individual Retirement Accounts (IRAs) for their employees. These special IRAs are called SEP-IRAs.

Key Features of SEP Plans:

- *Available to businesses of any size, including self-employed individuals*
- *Easy to set up and operate*
- *Low administrative costs*
- *Flexible annual contributions*
- *Only the employer contributes (not the employees)*
- *Contributions an employer can make to an employee's SEP-IRA cannot exceed the lesser of:*
  1. 25% of the employee's compensation, or
  2. $70,000(2025)

Eligibility for SEP Plans

To be eligible for an SEP plan, an employee typically must:

- *Be at least 21 years old*
- *Have worked for the employer for 3 of the last 5 years*
- *Have earned at least $750 in 2024 (this amount may change each year)*

Benefits of SEP Plans

- *Easy setup: SEP plans are simpler to establish than many other retirement plans.*
- *Flexibility: Employers can adjust their contributions based on their business's performance.*
- *Tax advantages: Contributions are tax-deductible for the employer, and employees don't pay taxes on the contributions until they withdraw the money.*

- *100% vesting: Employees always have full ownership of the money in their SEP-IRAs.*

Thrift Savings Plan (TSP):

The Thrift Savings Plan, or TSP for short, is a unique way for people working for the government to save money for retirement.

The TSP is for:

- People who work for the federal government
- Members of the military
- People in the Ready Reserve
- Contribution limits are the same as a 401(k)

Health Savings Accounts (HSAs)

What is an HSA?

An HSA is a special investing account for health care costs. It helps people invest money to pay for doctor visits, medicine, and other health expenses.

With an HSA, you can put money into the account before paying taxes. This means you can invest more money for health care. You can use this money anytime to cover health costs your insurance doesn't cover.

You can use HSA money for things like:

- Paying your deductible (the amount you pay before insurance starts helping)
- Copayments (the amount you pay when you see a doctor)
- Medicine
- Other health costs your insurance doesn't pay for

You don't pay taxes on the money you put in

The funds can earn interest, and you don't pay taxes on that, either

You can use the money anytime for health costs

*Mistakenly, many people believe that IRA's, Roth IRA's, 401(k)'s, 403(b)'s etc. are investments by themselves. They are not. They are accounts. You must decide what investments are purchased within the accounts. Just putting money in an IRA for example is not investing the money. Remember that. Think of an IRA or a 401(k) like a cookie jar. The cookies you choose to hold in the cookie jar are like the investments you choose to hold in the IRA or 401(k).

*The SECURE 2.0 ACT of 2022 is a law that improves the options for retirement for employers and employees. Its goal is to encourage people to invest and save more for retirement. Many of the changes associated with the SECURE 2.0 ACT started taking place in 2023 with more changes upcoming in the following years. These changes include:

- The age for required minimum distributions rises

- No more Required Minimum Distributions(RMDs) on Roth employer-sponsored accounts

- Lower penalties for missing RMDs

- Automatic enrollment and escalation in retirement plans(2025)

- Larger catch-up contributions for those over 60 years of age

- Catch-up contributions for higher earners must go into a Roth

- Employer matching can be treated as a Roth contribution

- 529 plans can be rolled over into Roth IRAs

- Hardship withdrawals from retirement plans

- Student loan 401(k) match(employers can match contributions to your retirement plan based on your student loan payments)

Please check with your employer or your accountant to find out more information on these new rules

Annuities

An annuity is a special kind of contract. It's like a promise between two people or groups. One person agrees to pay money to the other person regularly for a long time more than a year. The person who gets the money is called the annuitant.

Types of Annuities

There are different types of annuities. Let's look at some of them:

Fixed Period Annuities

- These pay the same amount of money every time
- They last for a specific amount of time
- Example: Your aunt might get $100 every month for 10 years

Variable Annuities

- The amount of money can change each time
- It might depend on things like how well investments are doing
- Example: Your uncle might get $80 one month and $120 the following month

Single Life Annuities

- These pay money to one person for as long as they live
- The payments stop when the person dies
- Example: Your grandpa might get $200 every month until he passes away

Joint and Survivor Annuities

- These start by paying one person
- After that person dies, it pays another person
- The amount might stay the same or change
- Example: Your grandma gets $150 a month. If she passes away, your grandpa might then get $100 a month

Where Do Annuities Come From?

You can get an annuity in two main ways:

1. You can buy one yourself
2. Your job might help you get one as part of your work benefits

Some special types of annuities are:

- Qualified employee annuities: These are retirement annuities that your job buys for you

- Tax-sheltered annuities: These are for people who work in public schools or some special organizations

Annuities: Advantages and Disadvantages

Advantages

1. **Regular Money**

Annuities can give people money regularly, like an allowance. This can be helpful for adults when they stop working.

2. **Money for Life**

Some annuities can give people money for as long as they live. This way, they don't have to worry about running out of money when they're older.

3. **Grows Without Taxes (for a while)**

The money in an annuity can grow without paying taxes immediately. It's like planting and letting a seed grow before picking the fruit.

4. **Safe Growth**

Some annuities promise that your money will grow by at least a certain amount. It's like having a safety net..

Disadvantages

1. **Can Be Expensive**

Annuities can cost a lot of money to buy and keep. It's like paying a high price for an object that might not be worth it. Also, the fees can be extremely high.

2. **Hard to Get Your Money Back**

Once you put money in an annuity, it can be hard to get it out if you change your mind. It's like putting your toys in a locked box and not being able to play with them for a long time.

3. **Complicated**

Annuities can be very confusing. There are lots of rules that can be hard to understand.

4. Company Problems

The company that gives you the annuity might have problems some-day. If that happens, you might not get all the promised money.

Highlights of changes for 2025

The annual contribution limit for employees who participate in 401(k), 403(b), governmental 457 plans, and the federal gov-ernment's Thrift Savings Plan is increased to $23,500, up from $23,000.

The limit on annual contributions to an IRA remains $7,000. The IRA catch-up contribution limit for individuals aged 50 and over was amended under the SECURE 2.0 Act of 2022 (SECURE 2.0) to include an annual cost-of-living adjustment but remains $1,000 for 2025.

The catch-up contribution limit that generally applies for em-ployees aged 50 and over who participate in most 401(k), 403(b), governmental 457 plans, and the federal government's Thrift Savings Plan remains $7,500 for 2025. Therefore, participants in most 401(k), 403(b), governmental 457 plans and the federal government's Thrift Savings Plan who are 50 and older generally can contribute up to $31,000 each year, starting in 2025. Under a change made in SECURE 2.0, a higher catch-up contribution limit applies for employees aged 60, 61, 62 and 63 who participate in these plans. For 2025, this higher catch-up contribution limit is $11,250 instead of $7,500.- Source: IRS.gov

Chapter 2.3: UGMA/UTMA Account

"Stop buying your kids what you never had and start teaching them what you never knew."- Myleik Teele

UTMA and UGMA accounts are custodial accounts that enable you to save and transfer funds to a child without the need for a trust. Both are held in the name of the minor but cared for by a parent or other adult relative until the child turns 18 to 21 depending on the state.

The acronyms UTMA and UGMA stand for Uniform Transfers to Minors Act and Uniform Gifts to Minors Act, respectively. Knowing the abbreviations is useful, but understanding how UTMA and UGMA accounts function, their advantages, and how they compare to 529 plans is essential before starting one.

However, there are some disadvantages to custodial accounts. UGMA/UTMA brokerage accounts are considered assets held by the minor and may have an influence on financial assistance when applying to college. Also, regardless of the kind of custodial account, the custodian must pass the account to the kid at a young age (between the ages of 18 and 21), after which the money may be used for any purpose. If your child is not financially educated when they inherit the account, they may waste the money(please read this book with them).

How Custodial Accounts Work

Brokerage accounts with an UGMA/UTMA are taxable investment accounts with no contribution limitations. These accounts provide no tax advantages at the time of contribution. A portion of profits from a custodial account may be excluded from federal income tax (up to $1,350 in 2025), and any earnings in excess of the exempt amount may be taxed at the child's tax rate, which is normally lower than the parent's tax rate. You may also move existing stocks, mutual funds, or other assets from your personal account to a custodial account. The UGMA/UTMA brokerage account allows extensive trading and a diverse selection of assets, such as stocks, bonds, mutual funds, exchange-traded funds, options, CDs, and more.

The account is opened for a particular child by the adult custodian. The adult may then deposit funds into the account and choose investments. When the kid reaches a particular age (usually between the ages of 18 and 21, depending on the state), the assets and control of the account must be transferred to them. These accounts are simple to open with a brokerage firm like the ones mentioned earlier.

Custodial accounts come in a variety of forms.

- **A Roth IRA for Kids** permits an adult to save a child's wages in a retirement account, which allows earnings to grow tax-free as long as the money remains in the account. If the money is removed before the age of 59 ½ without qualifying for an exemption, taxes, and penalties may be owed. The kid will gain possession of the account when they reach the required age in their state, as with other custodial accounts. Research more about how a Roth IRA for kids may help your child's retirement.

- **A custodial 529 account** is identical to a standard 529 plan. The main difference is that a kid on a custodial account cannot be changed. When money in a 529 plan is used for eligible educational costs, there may be tax benefits; but, if the money is used for other reasons, there may be taxes and penalties required. Custodial 529 funds are considered parent-owned assets for financial aid purposes and have no influence on financial aid calculations.

- **The Coverdell Education Savings Account (ESA)** has a maximum contribution of $2,000 per year. There is also an income restriction that may restrict who may donate to one of these accounts.

Chapter 2.4: 529 Account

A 529 plan is a tax-advantaged savings plan used to help pay for college. Initially restricted to postsecondary education expenditures, it was extended in 2017 to include K-12 education and apprenticeship programs in 2019. Following the passage of the 2019 Setting Every Community Up for Retirement Enhancement Act (SECURE Act) and SECURE 2.0 in 2022, 529s may also be used to pay off student debts and fund a Roth IRA.

Types of 529 Plans

There are several plans from which to save for college, but 529 plans are often classified as either prepaid tuition or college savings plans. Each of these plans operates as follows:

- **College savings plans:** Your after-tax contributions are invested in mutual funds or similar assets. There are various investment alternatives available under the 529 college savings plan. The value of the 529 plan account will fluctuate depending on the success of what you choose to invest in. Make sure you check your statements to see how your 529 plan is performing. When you withdraw funds to pay for college they are not taxed.

- **Prepaid tuition plans:** These options allow you to pay for all or a portion of the expenses of an in-state public college education in advance. They may also be used in private and out-of-state universities.

How to Choose a 529 Plan

Although almost every state offers at least one 529 plan, you are not confined to using the plan in your home state. Each 529 plan provides investment portfolios that are designed for your specific needs and time frame. Your account's value may rise or fall depending on the success of the investment choice you choose. Before you invest, you should think about your investing goals.

You should choose a 529 plan depending on your preferred investing strategy. However, with many 529 plan providers, you may still have a lot of say in how your account is invested. There is no advantage or disadvantage to the state in which your plan is sponsored as long as it is a national 529 plan.

When choosing a plan, the two key factors to examine are any prospective costs and the plan's track record of returns.

Chapter 2.5: Education Savings Account

A Coverdell Education Savings Account (ESA) is a tax-advantaged investment account intended to assist families in saving for educational expenditures. ESAs were established in 1997 as part of the School Savings Account Program to provide people with a way to save money exclusively for eligible education costs.

Here are some of the most important features and advantages of Education Savings Accounts:

1. **Tax Advantages:** Contributions to an ESA are not tax-deductible, but profits accumulate tax-free. Withdrawals for approved school expenditures are tax-free, which means the money may be taken without being subject to federal income tax.

2. **Qualified Education Expenses:** ESAs may be used to pay for a variety of educational expenditures, including tuition, fees, books, supplies, equipment, and even housing and board. Qualified costs may be spent at qualified primary, secondary, and postsecondary schools.

3. **Contribution Limits:** The IRS determines the maximum yearly contribution limit per beneficiary, which is subject to change. The yearly contribution maximum for an ESA is $2,000 per recipient as of the year 2025(this could always increase in future years). Contributions must be given in cash and may be contributed by anybody, including parents, grandparents, and other family members.

4. **Income Restrictions:** Contributors to ESAs are subject to income limits. Make sure to check if you qualify.

5. **Beneficiary Designation:** ESAs need the designation of a beneficiary who will utilize the money for educational purposes. The beneficiary might be a kid, grandchild, or anybody else who is under the age of 18 or has special needs.

6. **Account Control and Flexibility:** The ESA is controlled by the account holder (usually a parent or guardian) until the funds are withdrawn for approved educational costs. If the original recipient does not use all of the money or does not pursue higher education, the account might be transferred to another qualified family member.

7. **Investment Options:** ESAs provide more investing flexibility. The money may be invested in a variety of financial assets, including stocks, bonds, mutual funds, and CDs. The account user may choose investments that match their risk tolerance and financial goals.

8. **Rollover and Transfer Options:** Unused money in an ESA may be rolled over to another ESA for the same recipient or transferred to another qualifying family member's ESA. This flexibility enables savings efforts to be continued even if the initial recipient does not need the cash for educational expenditures.

It's crucial to understand that ESAs are not the same as 529 plans, which are another popular way to save for college. While both provide tax benefits for school savings, 529 plans have larger contribution limits and fewer income limitations. However, you must make sure to check the fees and investments that you are picking in a 529 plan. Also, what will you do if your child decides not to go to college or any school? If assets in a 529 plan are used for something other than qualified education expenses, you may have to pay both federal income taxes AND a 10% penalty on earnings. However, there are ways around this such as changing the beneficiary to another family member, paying off student loan debt, making yourself the beneficiary for continuing education or using the funds for apprenticeships for the child. Factor these things into your decisions on what to choose.

How To Open Education Savings Account

To establish an Education Savings Account (ESA), you should complete the following steps:

1. **Research and Choose an ESA Provider:** Begin by studying several financial institutions or investment businesses that provide ESAs. Fees, investment opportunities, customer service, and reputation are all important considerations. Look for providers that are educated about ESAs and have a track record of providing excellent customer service.

2. **Gather Required Information:** Once you've decided on an ESA provider, acquire the essential information and documentation to start the account. Personal identity information, such as your Social Security number, address, and date of birth, is often in-

cluded. You will also need the beneficiary's details if you are creating an ESA for them.

3. **Complete the Application:** Request an ESA application form from the ESA provider's website or branch office. Fill out the application form fully and properly. Fill out all of the essential information, including information about yourself and the recipient.

4. **Fund the Account:** Determine how much you wish to donate to the ESA and make the first contribution. Some service providers may need a minimum initial deposit to start an account, while others may not. Be mindful of the IRS's yearly contribution restrictions and make sure you do not exceed them.

5. **Select Investment Options:** ESA providers typically offer various investment options for the funds held in the account. Investigate and evaluate your investing options, which may include stocks, bonds, mutual funds, or CDs. Choose assets that are compatible with your risk tolerance and long-term objectives.

6. **Review and Sign the Agreement:** Examine the terms and conditions thoroughly. Examine the fees, investment possibilities, withdrawal regulations, and other account data. Sign the agreement and any relevant paperwork once you are satisfied.

7. **Provide Funding Instructions:** Describe how you plan to finance the ESA account. You may set up one-time payments or make recurring contributions through automated transactions. To send money to the account, follow the instructions given by the ESA provider.

8. **Maintain and Monitor the Account:** Once your ESA is open, you must keep track of it on a regular basis. Keep track of your contributions, the success of your investments, and any changes in the beneficiary's educational plans. Keep up to speed on any modifications or changes to IRS laws and regulations pertaining to ESAs.

Remember that the procedure of creating an ESA may differ according to the provider you choose.

Accounts for your children may impact their ability to receive financial aid or assistance for college. However, many students are already ineligible for financial assistance and if invested properly you may not need the assistance or aid to begin with. Student loans can be a major issue for a young adult starting their lives on their own. Paying for college in full and coming out of school with an education with no loans to pay back is a fantastic way to start your child on the right financial foot in their 20's.

CHAPTER 2:
INVESTMENT ACCOUNTS

Quiz No: 2

Serial No	Question	Answer
1.	What is a brokerage account? A. An investment account held with a registered brokerage business. B. A savings account held with a bank. C. A retirement account held with an employer. D. A checking account used for daily expenses.	
2.	What type of account is suitable for hands-off portfolio management using algorithms? A. Full-Service Brokerage Account. B. Discount Brokerage Account. C. Robo-Advisor Account. D. Online Brokerage Account.	
3.	Which type of brokerage account offers detailed financial advice and other services but charges higher fees? A. Full-Service Brokerage Accounts. B. Discount Brokerage Accounts. C. Robo-Advisor Accounts. D. Online Brokerage Accounts.	

4.	Which type of account allows investors to borrow money for trading? A. Cash Brokerage Account. B. Margin Account. C. Full-Service Brokerage Account. D. Online Brokerage Account.	
5.	Which retirement plan allows contributions with after-tax dollars and allows tax free withdrawals? A. Traditional IRA. B. 401(k). C. Roth IRA. D. 403(b).	
6.	Which retirement plan is employer-sponsored and allows contributions with pre-tax dollars? A. Roth IRA. B. 401(k). C. Traditional IRA. D. UGMA Account.	
7.	What is a disadvantage of Roth IRA? A. Tax-free withdrawals in retirement. B. No required minimum distributions (RMDs). C. No immediate tax deduction for contributions. D. No income limitations for withdrawals.	
8.	What type of account is held in the name of a minor and managed by a custodian until the child turns 18? A. UGMA/UTMA Account. B. Retirement Account. C. Brokerage Account. D. 457 Plan.	

9.	What is a characteristic of ESAs? A. Contributions are tax-deductible. B. Qualified withdrawals are subject to income tax. C. Account control is transferred to the child at age 18. D. Investment options are limited to CDs.	
10.	What may happen if you do not use funds from a 529 plan for educational purposes? A. You may have to pay back funds to the brokerage B. You may have to close the account C. You may have to pay taxes and a penalty on what you withdraw D. Nothing will happen	

Key

1. A

2. C

3. A

4. B

5. C

6. B

7. C

8. A

9. C

10. C

CHAPTER THREE

BASIC INVESTMENT KNOWLEDGE

Chapter 3.1: Introduction to Financial Markets

"Mr. Market is kind of a drunken psycho. Some days he gets very enthused, some days he gets very depressed."- Warren Buffet

Financial markets include any marketplace where assets are traded, including the stock market, bond market, currency market, and derivatives market, among others. Financial markets are required for capitalist economies to operate. Because they distribute resources and generate liquidity(easy cash) for enterprises and entrepreneurs, financial markets are important to the successful operation of capitalist economies. A marketplace allows buyers and sellers to exchange financial holdings and products. One example of a financial market is the stock market. When a financial market is in a **Bull Market,** that means the market is doing well and trending upwards. When a financial market is in a **Bear Market,** that means the market is struggling and trending downwards. Most people love bull markets and are fearful of bear markets. However, TRUE investors are the opposite. While they like bull markets, they LOVE bear markets. Why? Because investing in a bull market is risky. Things are going up which means you may be investing at a time where things eventually go down, decreasing your investment. However, a bear market isn't as risky a time to invest. It's actually an opportunity, because you can get investment's cheaper, and the lower they are, the more room they eventually have to rise. Wealth is created investing in **bear** markets, not **bull** markets. Bull markets make you money. Bear markets make you wealthy, as long as you continue to invest!

Types of Financial Markets

1. Stock Markets

One of the most popular financial markets is the stock market. The stock market is where corporations offer shares or pieces of ownership of the company for sale and where traders and investors may buy and sell them. Companies utilize stock markets, also known as equities markets, to obtain cash through an initial public offering (IPO), with shares then exchanged among numerous buyers and sellers in what is known as a secondary market.

An Initial Public Offering, or IPO, is when a private company first sells shares of its stock to the public on a stock exchange. This is a big step for a company, often called "going public."

Companies have IPOs for several important reasons:

To raise money: By selling shares, the company can get a lot of money to help it grow or pay off debts.

To let early investors cash out: People who invested in the company early on can sell their shares and make money.

To become more well-known: Being listed on a stock exchange can make a company more famous and respected.

2. **Over-the-Counter Markets**

An over-the-counter (OTC) market is a decentralized market (no physical locations and trading is done electronically) in which market participants sell securities directly between two parties without the need for a broker. While OTC markets may handle trading in some equities (e.g., smaller or riskier businesses), major stock exchanges handle the majority of stock trading. In general, OTC markets and the transactions that take place on them are less regulated.

3. **Bond Markets**

A bond is a security in which an investor lends money for a certain length of time at a fixed interest rate. A bond is an agreement between a lender(an investor) and a borrower. Bonds are issued by businesses, municipalities, states, and governments to fund programs. Bonds are sold on the bond market, such as notes and bills issued by the United States Treasury. The bond market is often referred to as the debt market, the credit market, or the fixed-income market.

4. **Money Markets**

Money markets typically trade in highly liquid short-term assets (less than one year) and are characterized by a high degree of safety and a relatively modest interest yield. They include money market mutual funds purchased by private investors and money market accounts created by banks. Individuals can also participate in the money markets by purchasing short-term certificates of deposit (CDs), municipal notes, or U.S. Treasury bank notes, to mention a few possibilities.

5. Derivatives Markets

A derivative is a contract between two or more parties, where the value of the contract is determined by an agreed-upon underlying financial asset (such as a stock) or collection of assets (like an index). A derivatives market rather than trading stocks directly, trades futures and options contracts, where the contract derives its worth from underlying assets including bonds, commoditles, currencies, interest rates, market indexes, and stocks

6. Forex Market

The forex (foreign exchange) market is a market in which investors can buy, sell and speculate on currency exchange rates. Because cash is the most liquid of assets, the Forex market is the world's most liquid market. The forex market is made up of banks, commercial companies, central banks, investment management firms, hedge funds, and forex brokers and investors.

Forex is the global marketplace where currencies are traded(bought and sold). It's the largest financial market in the world, with about $7.5 trillion traded daily. It operates 24 hours a day, 5 days a week, and trading happens electronically over computer networks. Anyone can participate, from big banks to individual traders. It involves buying one currency while selling another. When you trade forex, you're always dealing with pairs of currencies. For example:

- *EUR/USD (Euro/US Dollar)*
- *GBP/JPY (British Pound/Japanese Yen)*
- *USD/CHF (US Dollar/Swiss Franc)*

The goal is to predict which currency in the pair will get stronger compared to the other. If you're right, you make a profit. Let's say you believe the euro will get stronger against the US dollar. You would buy euros (and automatically sell dollars). If the euro gets stronger, you can sell it for more dollars than you started with.

There are three main types of forex markets:

1. **Spot Market:** This is where currencies are bought and sold immediately at the current price.

2. **Forwards Market:** Here, you agree to buy or sell a currency at a specific price on a future date through a private agreement, and over the counter.

3. **Futures Market:** Similar to forwards, but are traded on exchanges.

People and companies trade forex for different reasons:

1. *To make a profit: Traders try to benefit from currency price changes.*

2. *To protect against risk: Companies use forex to guard against losses from currency fluctuations.*

3. *To get foreign currency: For international trade and investment.*

While forex can be profitable, it's also risky:

- The market can change quickly due to global events

- Using leverage (borrowed money) can lead to significant losses

- It's complex and requires a good understanding of global economics

If you're interested in forex trading:

1. *Learn the basics: Understand currency pairs, market patterns, and what affects currency prices.*

2. *Practice with a demo account: Many brokers offer these free.*

3. *Start small: When ready for actual trading, begin with small amounts.*

4. *Stay informed: Keep up with global news and economic reports.*

5. *Manage your risk: Never trade more than you can afford to lose.*

7. **Commodities Markets**

Commodity markets allow producers and consumers to trade physical commodities such as agricultural products (e.g., maize, cattle, soybeans), energy products (oil, gas, carbon credits), precious metals (gold, silver, platinum), or "soft" commodities (such as cotton, coffee, and sugar).

8. **Cryptocurrency Markets**

Several years have passed since the launch and rise of cryptocurrencies such as Bitcoin and Ethereum, decentralized digital assets based on blockchain technology. Today, hundreds of cryptocurrency tokens are accessible and traded on independent online crypto exchanges throughout the world. These exchanges provide digital wallets via which traders may exchange one cryptocurrency for another or for currencies like dollars or euros.

Chapter 3.2: Functions of the Financial Markets

"Mr. Market is your servant, not your guide."- Warren Buffet

The key roles of financial markets are as follows:

1. **Puts savings into more productive use**

Financial markets put money to use, and allow wealth to be created.

2. **Determines the price of securities(investments)**

Investors want to benefit from their investments and buying these investments at the right price enables them to do so. The price of securities(investments) is set by financial markets.

3. **Makes financial assets liquid**

Buyers and sellers can swap their securities at any moment. They can utilize financial markets to sell or invest their securities as they see fit.

Importance of Financial Markets

Financial markets enable many things, including the following:

A platform for businesses, banks, investors and people to buy and sell financial assets

The growth of wealth for economies and individuals over time

Job opportunities for many people

Chapter 3.3: Common Investment Types

"Why not invest your assets in companies you like? As Mae West said, 'Too much of a good thing can be wonderful.'"-
Warren Buffet

Investing involves putting your available resources(like time or money) into something that you believe will earn money, appreciate, or provide some other advantage in the future. When you invest, you acquire assets that you hope to appreciate in value over time, provide constant income, or both potentially increasing the amount of wealth you have.

Investing has grown more popular among Americans; however, the average American has no idea what they are doing when it comes to investing.

How Does It Work

Investing is placing your available resources into something that you believe has the potential to provide a positive return to you over time, which will grow your net worth. It usually provides you with a financial stake in the asset in which you invest.

Most Common Investment Types

Stocks

To gain cash for their operations, companies sell shares or pieces of the company to the general public. Buying shares gives you a stake or ownership in the company. If the company is profitable, the value of your shares will grow, and in some cases, you may be paid a dividend(regular income). If the company collapses, you might lose money because the value of your shares lowers.

Bonds

Corporations and governments issue bonds to raise money to fund their business or government expenses. When you buy a bond, you are making a loan to the company or country from which you bought it. You will be paid interest over a set length of time. Bonds are less risky than stocks, but over time generally provide lower returns.

Commodities

Commodities include agricultural products, oil, gas, and other energy items, as well as metals, particularly precious metals such as gold and silver. Their value fluctuates according to market demand. For example, if oil becomes scarce, the price of oil rises, as does the value of your investment.

Real estate

If the value of a property or piece of land is predicted to improve over time, it might be termed a real estate investment. Real estate investments come with different levels of risk. Property values may be affected by crime rates in a certain location, as well as the housing market collapse that triggered the Great Recession. Real estate investment trusts (REITs), which are organizations that generate money from real estate, are another option. When owning rental properties, the goal is to gain consistent positive cash flow, with appreciation of the property.

Mutual funds and ETFs

Mutual funds and exchange-traded funds (ETFs) allow you to acquire various combinations of typical investments such as stocks, bonds, commodities, and real estate. When you invest in these funds, you are investing in hundreds of different assets. This can help to diversify your portfolio and reduce the chance of losing money on investments.

More Advanced and Alternative Investments

There are several innovative and alternative investments available. These usually involve significant risk or may need a significant initial commitment. Private equity funds, hedge funds, and cryptocurrency are examples of alternatives to the most common investment types.

Private Equity

Private equity assists companies in raising financing without going public. Private equity funds and other investors invest in private companies.

Derivatives

Derivatives are investments with high risk and great profit possibilities. They are financial contracts whose value is derived from another financial asset, such as a market index like the S&P 500, Dow Jones, Nasdaq, or Russell 2000. Imagine you and a friend make a bet on who will win a boxing match. You pick boxer A, and they pick boxer B. You sign a contract on the bet. The contract is based on the result of the underlying boxing match. Derivatives work in a similar fashion.

Options

Option contracts are a type of derivative contract. Options provide the buyer the right to buy or sell a security at a fixed price and within a certain time frame.

Hedge funds

Hedge funds need large minimum investments or a high net worth. To invest, you must be an accredited investor(meaning you must have a high net worth or a lot of money in most cases). Investors in hedge funds pool their cash and generally invest in high-risk investments. One technique is to buy investments using borrowed money in the hope of achieving a large profit.

Cryptocurrency

Cryptocurrencies are digital currencies with no real-world assets to back them up. The most well-known cryptocurrency is Bitcoin. They may be traded without a broker and are tracked on digital ledgers. The majority of the risks involved with this type of investing are related to cryptocurrency volatility, which causes their value to fluctuate dramatically at times.

Chapter 3.4: Saving vs. Investing

"Never spend your money before you have it."- Thomas Jefferson

"How many millionaires do you know who have become wealthy by investing in savings accounts? I rest my case."- Robert Allen

Saving is frequently meant for shortand intermediate-term goals, such as an emergency reserve for car repairs. Many people confuse saving with investing. They are both necessary for financial success, however they are very different.

Over time, investing provides the potential for higher benefits (but also increased risk). As a result, some people use investing to attain long-term goals like retirement. Savings is much safer than investing, however saving makes it much harder to build wealth(due to factors such as inflation, and low rates of return on your savings account). Saving is important, but so is investing.

	Savings account	Investment account
Where money goes	A financial institution's account, such as a bank's.	Stocks, bonds and mutual funds are examples of financial items whose values are stored in an investment account.
How money grows	Slowly but steady. In general, the greater the interest rate(money paid into the account), the larger the necessary minimum balance.	An account's value varies when investments such as stocks gain or lose value. Growth is more likely, but it is not assured. You can also sell investments for profit (or loss), or collect dividends or interest on bonds.
Risk and flexibility	Low risk, moderate flexibility, and little variation. In general, each institution is insured up to $250,000 in total. Many have transfer fees and limitations. In most cases, interest is taxed.	Purchases or additions are generally quite flexible; Early withdrawal penalties on retirement funds may apply. There is no guarantee of growth, thus there is increasing risk.

Chapter 3.5: Best Time To Start Investing

"You don't have to see the whole staircase, you just have to take the first step."- Dr. Martin Luther King Jr.

The sooner you begin investing, the bigger your chance of prospective gains. This is the effect of investing more money over a longer period of time and the power of compound wealth over time. REMEMBER TIME IS YOUR MOST VALUABLE RESOURCE. However, don't rush out today and start investing without some knowledge. You must have an idea of what you're doing, even though the process of learning about investing is for life. Here is proof as to why the earlier you begin investing for you or your child, the better.

Michaela begins investing $100 a month at age 20. She earns an average 4% annually, which is compounded monthly for 40 years. She earns $151,550 by age 65(when projecting investments, you may want to low ball the figures as to keep yourself humble and keep expectations reasonable. If the average is 10% over the same time period, clearly the earnings will be much higher). Her principal investment was only $54,100

Alonzo, her twin brother, begins investing at age 50. He STARTS with a $5,000 initial investment, then invests $500 monthly for 15 years, also averaging 4% annually, which is compounded monthly for 15 years. By age 65, Alonzo has only earned $132,147. His principal investment is $95,000.

SourceInvestopedia.com

Alonzo will have invested more money than Michaela, and earned less money when they both reach 65 years of age. Why? TIME. Michaela utilized our greatest resource in life more efficiently than Alonzo. The earlier you start investing, the better. This is especially true for children. Here is another example:

Let's look at Ben and Joey. Both will invest in an S&P 500 Index Fund, and will receive an average annual return of 11%.

Ben starts investing at 21

He invests $2400 a year

He STOPS contributing at age 30(only 9 years)

He contributes $21,600

Joey starts investing at age 30

He invests $2400 a year

He contributes until age 67(37 years)

He contributes $88,800

At age 67, Ben's investment will grow to $2.1 million. Joey's grows to $1.2 million. Why did Ben grow his investment more than Joey even though he contributed for less years? TIME. HE START-ED EARLIER.

Source- Ramseysolutions.com/compoundinterest

To be able to invest, you must first get your financial home in order so that you can free up funds for investing. Making a yearly budget, monitoring what you spend, and minimizing your debt are all necessary first steps. All of this is part of securing your financial well-being in order to take the following steps toward investing.

Signs You're Ready

Time in the market is more essential than timing the market. This is a popular saying. And starting to invest as soon as possible, even if in little quantities, may position you for future success. Here are four indicators that may assist you in making your decision.

1. **You're building a strong emergency fund.**

Life is unpredictable. To provide yourself with the margin of safety you will need to begin investing, it's a good idea to maintain an emergency fund that can cover many months of expenses. If something unexpected happens, your emergency fund will provide a buffer, allowing you to avoid tapping into assets allocated to longer-term goals.

2. **You have money left over at the end of each month.**

Your emergency money is in good shape. You pay all of your bills as well as any high-interest debt(you should pay these off as quickly as possible first before investing). You have sufficient funds to cover your expenses. Is there still some left? It does not have to be a significant chunk of money. Investing is all about starting small and gradually increasing (more on that below).

3. **You're ready to make a financial commitment.**

Investing is a trip that is more rewarding if you know where you're going. Goals give focus and direction.

4. **You are eligible for a retirement plan.**

A 401(k). A 403(b). If you can contribute to one of these employer-sponsored retirement plans, you may have already made a significant step toward investing. You can choose to have money invested from each paycheck in most employer-sponsored retirement plans.

Chapter 3.6: Investing Basics

"The most important quality for an investor is temperament, not intellect."- Warren Buffet

Compounding is another reason to leave your money alone. Compounding interest occurs when you begin earning money on money that has already been earned through your investments. It's similar to a snowball effect.

Investing earlier in life provides a great benefit. Simply by remaining involved in the market for a longer period of time, you increase your earnings.

Consider the 120 Rule, a financial guideline.

The idea is straightforward. Subtract your age from the number 120. The outcome is the percentage of your money that should be invested in stocks. The remainder is invested in bonds.

A 30-year-old, for example, might invest 90% in stocks and 10% in bonds. A 50-year-old, on the other hand, might invest 70% in equities and 30% in bonds. Again, do what works best for you in your situation. Everyone is different. This is just a guideline and is not a one size fits all. The age you plan to retire may alter this tremendously.

It is preferable to invest when you are young, but it is never too late. Even if you're in your forties or fifties, you still have alternatives, such as maxing out your yearly 401(k) plan.

Investments Which Are Right For You

Understanding why you are investing is important. Your investing objectives will determine what you invest in, how much you invest, and for how long.

Factors to consider when investing:

Your age

Your income

Your goals

Your risk tolerance

Time Frame

The majority of individuals invest with retirement in mind. Why? Simply, retirement is costly. However, it can be suggested to invest as if you will live to 150 years old. Investing now is a sensible and straightforward method to lessen the likelihood of running out of money after leaving work. It may also be beneficial to look at how many assets that you can own in retirement rather than retirement savings. Why? Assets can provide you with income for life, whereas savings will deplete over time the longer you live, ESPECIALLY if there is an ill-timed market crash when you are older.

Chapter 3.7: Amount of Money Needed to Start Investing

"Do not invest what is left after spending; Spend what is left after investing."- Warren Buffet

"The philosophy of the rich and the poor is this: The rich invest their money and spend what is left. The poor spend their money and invest what is left."- Robert Kiyosaki

How much do you need?

When you are ready to invest, there is no set amount needed to begin. Invest the amount that you can afford to invest and not miss from your daily life. You can start with $25 a month if that's all you can afford at this time. The goal is to start and stay consistent. As you make more money, instead of increasing your standard of living like 99% of people do and going into debt or buying things that lose money, you can increase what you allocate towards investing into assets that will make you money. Don't compare yourself to others. Invest what you can afford.

Investing first before spending money may help you make wiser financial decisions. You may find you have more money to invest than you previously thought. Of course you will have bills and maybe debts to pay, however if you invest first and spend what is left over, you may go out to dinner fewer times per month, or it may save you from buying another pair of shoes or another device that isn't need-ed. This could very well help you make smarter financial decisions when spending money while you grow your wealth at the same time.

New investors must be patient. Long-term investments are more likely to provide larger returns. This is because your assets will take time to grow. Contribute what you can to these assets. They will also require time to respond to market ups and downs.

Many, but not all, financial products demand a minimum deposit. However, there are plenty of options that do not.

While contributing to an employer-sponsored 401(k) plan is a ter-rific way to get started with investing, there are alternative options if you are new to investing or have limited funds.

The sooner you can begin investing, the better – even if you start with little. However, before you devote substantial quantities of money to investments, you should enhance your financial literacy. This involves learning to budget in order to significantly decrease or eliminate debt and saving for unexpected expenses. Once that is done, invest with what you can. There is no magic financial number that you need to begin investing with. Start small, and grow as you become more confident in what you are doing.

Chapter 3.8: Figure out and Set your Investment Goals

"A goal without a plan is just a wish."- Antoine de Saint-Exupery

Having goals may help you achieve financial success by giving you a clear and detailed strategy to follow. When it comes to investing, having objectives in place might help people take the first step toward something that is unfamiliar or intimidating to them.

Setting a goal allows you to plan your strategy for achieving it, including how, when, and where to spend your money, as well as how much time you have or need."

What Makes a Good Investment Goal?

The use of SMART Goals is a popular way that many investors use to create investment goals. It's an acronym that stands for the following:

SPECIFIC- *Have a precise financial plan of action*

MEASURABLE- *You should be able to monitor your financial goals and see how close you are to attaining them*

ACHIEVABLE- *Choose goals that are within your reach at that particular moment*

RELEVANT- *Your investment goals should be consistent with you personally, and nobody else*

TIME- *Include a time frame for your investment goals(short term, long term) so that you understand how you should invest your money*

How to Set Realistic Investing Goals

It's one thing to talk about the necessity of having goals; it's quite another to really take the measures required to develop and accomplish your financial objectives. Steps to correctly create realistic investment objectives are provided below.

1. **Identify Your Goal**

The first step in achieving your objectives is determining what you want to accomplish. Retirement, a child's college education, or a dream house are all common investment aspirations. Knowing your objective and making it SMART can assist you in developing an investing strategy to achieve it.

2. Identify Your Investment Strategy

Consider your time frame when determining how to invest your funds for your objective.

Short-term objectives (those reachable in a year or less), may be best suited to liquid assets such as cash, treasury bills, and money market accounts.

You may balance your portfolio between treasury notes and stocks for mid-term objectives that are three to 10 years away.

Finally, for long-term objectives that are more than 10 years in the future, you may take a more aggressive strategy by investing in stocks, mutual funds, and exchange-traded funds (ETFs), or consider 30 year bonds.

3. Start Small

People always ask how much money should they start to invest with? Or they will say "I don't have much money to invest." There is no magic number. Whatever you can afford to do outside of your other responsibilities is perfect. Whether it be $5 or $500, the point is just to get started. Starting small is advantageous as it limits the damage you may do while you are on the path to learning about investing. As your knowledge grows and you become more literate in investing, you can always adjust and invest more.

4. Look for Support

Finding the advice and assistance you need to achieve your financial objectives has never been simpler, which can make it more dangerous. Numerous social media sites provide detailed financial advice on investments and other issues. Always look for support from trustworthy sources. Many sources will try to steer you into investments that benefit them. Find like-minded individuals like yourself and work together to build wealth. Building wealth is a team sport believe it or not. Building your investment knowledge can be assisted by working together with other investors who are trying to achieve the same goals. The wealthy work together for support, however the middle class and poor do not. It is easier to build wealth with others who are trying to build wealth in a similar fashion.

Connecting with like-minded investors can be beneficial for various reasons:

1. Shared Interests: *It allows you to connect with people who share your interests in investing, making conversations more engaging and enjoyable.*

2. Validation: *When you discuss your ideas or beliefs about investing with like-minded individuals, you're likely to receive validation and support, which can boost your confidence.*

3. Learning Opportunities: *Like-minded investors can provide valuable insights, knowledge, and perspectives that align with your interests, helping you to learn and grow. They may also provide a different perspective to something you may not have considered, and vice versa.*

4. Networking: *Building relationships with investors who share your interests can lead to networking opportunities, which can be advantageous to your investment goals.*

5. Collaboration: *Collaboration with like-minded investors can lead to creative ideas on investing.*

6. Motivation and Inspiration: *Being around investors who share your goals and ambitions can be motivating and inspiring, pushing you to achieve more.*

7. Reduced Stress: *It can be comforting to know that you're not alone on your lifelong journey with investing, reducing feelings of isolation and stress.*

8. Community: *Joining like-minded investors can provide a sense of belonging and support, enhancing your overall well-being.* **This is why I created The Community Outreach Investment Network(C.O.I.N.)**

Connecting with like-minded investors can enhance your success in a variety of ways.

CHAPTER 3:
BASIC INVESTMENT KNOWLEDGE

Quiz No: 3

Serial No	Question	Answer
1.	The asset traded in the stock market is A. Currency B. Crude Oil C. Precious Metal D. Stock	
2.	The act of purchasing assets (stocks, bonds, property) with expectation that they will increase in value over time. A. Withdrawing B. Depositing C. Time Value of Money D. Investing	

3.	The percentage rate that is used when calculating the interest (money) paid on a savings, money market, or investment account. A. Rule of 72 B. Interest rate C. Simple Interest D. Rate of Return	
4.	Stocks and bonds are examples of _____. A. Musical instruments B. Financial liabilities C. Financial assets D. All of the above	
5.	All of the following are factors to consider when investing **except:** A. Your gender B. Your age C. Your income D. Your risk tolerance	
6.	What are mutual funds? A. Depositories B. Contracts C. Investments D. Loans	
7.	Which is **not** the purpose of the money market account? A. Provide a place for keeping surplus funds for short periods of time B. Provide a risky investment for a higher return C. Provide a safe investment for your money D. Provide higher interest yield	

8.	Which of the following markets is the most popular? A. Stock Market B. Derivatives C. Commodities D. Cryptocurrency	
9.	All of the following will help you set realistic investing goals **except:** A. Starting small B. Borrowing money C. Looking for support D. Identifying a goal	
10.	The role of financial markets in the success and development of an economy is extremely important. A. True B. False	

Key

1. D

2. D

3. B

4. C

5. A

6. C

7. B

8. A

9. B

10. A

CHAPTER
FOUR

BUDGETING FOR YOUR INVESTMENTS

Chapter 4.1: Personal Finance

"If you buy things you do not need, soon you will have to sell things that you do need."- Warren Buffet

Personal finance is critical. You cannot invest to the fullest if you are spending money with absolutely no discipline.

Spending wisely is demonstrated by spending less than you earn. You may become a prudent spender by changing a few behaviors and creating financial goals.

You might find it useful to categorize your spending as needs, wants, savings, or debt reduction. Most people struggle identifying their needs vs their wants. Many things we think we need are really just wants. This is where the conflict begins in regards to spending. For example, do you need food? Do you need a cell-phone? Do you even know the definition of a need or a want? People have different opinions of what is a need and what is a want in their own personal lives. This is where the average person gets in trouble. Needs should always come before wants. Once you have fulfilled all of your needs, then you can start to incorporate your wants with any money left over. Would you consider investing a need or a want? That's only for you to decide.

Needs

A need is something you require to survive. It is something you literally need to live. Without it, you would die. It's that simple. These are the inescapable expenses that help keep you and your family safe, comfortable, and fed. They include your mortgage or rent, food buying, utilities, transportation, and minimum loan and borrowing payments. Food may be a need(of course it is, I know), but is eating out at a fancy restaurant every Saturday a need?

Wants

A want is something that you desire. It is not needed for your survival. These are all the items you buy that aren't necessary. They include eating out, going to the movies, buying new clothing, joining a gym, going on vacation, and purchasing concert tickets. Would you classify a car as a need or a want? If you classify a car as a need, do you need to own a Mercedes-Benz or a BMW? I cannot answer that for you.

Savings or Reducing Debts

Savings can be used for emergencies, short-term goals (such as a vacation), or long-term aspirations (such as retirement). Debts include any debt repayments you make each month, as well as any required minimum payment.

Understanding Personal Finance

Personal finance refers to how you manage your money, savings, and investments. It encompasses many aspects of your financial life, including:

- Budgeting
- Banking
- Insurance
- Mortgages
- Taxes
- Making smart financial decisions

Understanding personal finance is crucial for your future because it helps you make informed choices about your money and achieve your financial goals.

Five Areas of Personal Finance

1. **Income:** This is the money you earn from various sources, such as:
   - Part-time jobs
   - Allowances
   - Gifts

2. **Spending:** How you use your money for different purposes:
   - Buying food
   - Purchasing clothes
   - Paying for entertainment

3. **Saving:** Setting money aside for future use:
   - Emergency fund(At least 3 months of your salary)
   - Saving for a big purchase (e.g., a car or college tuition)

4. **Investing:** Growing your money over time:
   - Stocks
   - Bonds
   - Mutual funds

5. **Protection:** Safeguarding your finances:
   - Insurance (health, auto, property)

Why Personal Finance Matters

Understanding and managing your personal finances is important because it:

1. Helps you meet financial goals (e.g., buying a car, paying for college)

2. Avoids excessive debt that can burden you for years

3. Prepares you for unexpected expenses (like car repairs or medical bills)

4. Secures your financial future (retirement planning)

   Example: If you want to buy a car when you turn 18, understanding personal finance can help you create a savings plan to reach that goal.

Understanding Insurance

Insurance is a financial safety net that helps protect individuals and businesses from unexpected financial losses. Think of it like a protective shield that guards you against potential financial hardships.

How Insurance Works

- You pay a small, regular amount called a premium
- The insurance company promises to cover larger potential losses
- Risk is spread across many policyholders
- Provides financial security and peace of mind

Types of Insurance

1. **Vehicle Insurance**
   - Protects against financial losses from car accidents
   - Covers damage to your vehicle
   - Provides liability protection if you harm others

2. **Health Insurance**
   - Covers medical expenses
   - Helps pay for doctor visits, medications, and treatments
   - Reduces out-of-pocket healthcare costs

3. **Life Insurance**
   - Provides financial support to your family if/when you pass away
   - Helps cover funeral expenses
   - Offers financial stability for dependents

Two Main Types of Life Insurance

Term Life Insurance

- Covers you for a specific time period (like 10, 20, or 30 years)
- Much cheaper and more affordable
- Good for temporary financial protection
- No money back if you outlive the policy

Whole Life Insurance

- Covers you for your entire life
- More expensive
- Includes a savings/investment component
- Builds cash value over time
- Can be borrowed against
- The younger you take out the policy, the cheaper it is

Key Differences

Feature	Term Life	Whole Life
Cost	Low	High
Coverage Period	Limited	Lifetime
Cash Value	No	Yes
Flexibility	Less	More

When to Consider Each Type

Term Life is Best For:

- Young families
- People with specific financial obligations
- Those on a tight budget
- Temporary financial protection

Whole Life is Best For:

- People with long-term financial planning needs
- High-income individuals
- Parents of children with special needs
- Small business owners

4. **Property Insurance**

- Protects your home and personal belongings
- Covers damage from fires, theft, natural disasters
- Helps rebuild or replace lost property

Real-World Example

Imagine Sarah, a 17-year-old student:

- She buys car insurance for $100 per month
- If she gets into an accident causing $5,000 in damages
- Her insurance covers most of the repair costs
- She only pays a small deductible (like $500)

How Insurance Pricing Works

Insurance companies determine premiums based on:

- Location
- Age
- Credit history
- Occupation
- Risk assessment

Insurance is an important aspect of personal finance. You must make sure to budget for it, and spend wisely on it as well before you begin investing.

Managing Debt Wisely

Debt is money that you owe to someone else, like a bank or a credit card company. When you borrow money, you promise to pay it back, usually with some extra money called interest. Borrowing money to purchase things is also known as **financing.**

At some point in life, virtually everyone will finance or borrow money for things they can't afford to pay cash for. However, not all things that are financed are good to go into debt for. Below are two different lists of things that may be ok to finance(responsibly), and things you should never finance no matter what.

Items that are ok to finance RESPONSIBLY:

Mortgage(primary residence or investment property)

Master's or a Doctorate degree

Small Business

Medical Surgery

Items you should never finance and should always pay cash for:

A car(buy a car you can afford)

Bachelor's degree(parents should be investing from birth for their children to pay for this in the future)

Furniture

Appliances

Weddings

Vacations

Boats

Luxury Items(handbags, expensive shoes)

Cosmetic Surgery

*This is just a suggestion. If you ever finance an item, make sure to pay off your debts as soon as possible. Remember, when you finance an item, you will have to pay interest on the money that you borrowed.

Two Smart Ways to Pay Off Debt

1. **Debt Avalanche Method**

How It Works:

List all your debts

- Pay minimum amounts on all debts
- Put extra money toward the debt with the HIGHEST interest rate
- Save the most money in the long run

Example:

- Imagine you have:
- Credit card debt: $10,000 at 18.99% interest
- Car loan: $9,000 at 3% interest
- Student loan: $15,000 at 4.50% interest

With the avalanche method, you'd focus on paying off the credit card first because it has the highest interest rate.

2. **Debt Snowball Method**

How It Works:

- List all your debts from smallest to largest
- Pay minimum amounts on all debts

- Put extra money toward the SMALLEST debt first
- Feel motivated by quickly paying off small debts

Example:

Using the same debts as before, you'd start by paying off the car loan first because it's the smallest amount.

Which Method is Better?

Debt Avalanche

- Saves more money overall
- Takes longer to see progress
- Good for math-loving people

Debt Snowball

- Helps you feel motivated
- Might cost more in interest
- Good for people who need quick wins

While you may not have much debt now, it's important to understand how to manage it:

1. Avoid spending more than you earn
2. Understand good debt (e.g., student loans for education) vs. bad debt (e.g., high-interest credit card debt for unnecessary purchases)

PAY OFF ALL DEBTS AS SOON AS POSSIBLE WHICH WILL ALLOW YOU TO INVEST!!!

Understanding Credit

What is Credit?

Credit is like a special promise where someone lets you borrow money or get something now, with the agreement that you'll pay it back later. However, nobody is that nice. When they loan you the money, you must pay that money back(the principal), with added money or a cost for borrowing the money(interest). The amount extra you have to pay back on top of the principal that you borrowed is based on an interest rate which is reflected as a percentage. The higher the percentage, the more expensive it is for you to borrow the money. You must also pay attention to the Annual Percentage Rate(APR) which is slightly different from the interest rate.

The interest rate and APR are different. Interest rate is the cost you pay to a lender for borrowing their money. APR is the interest rate AND the fees associated with the loan.

The 5 C's of Credit: Your Financial Report Card

1. **Character**: How responsible you are with money

Just like getting good grades in school, this shows how trustworthy you are at paying back money

Your "credit score" is like a grade that shows how well you handle money

2. **Capacity**: How much money you can borrow

This looks at how much money you make and can afford to pay back

3. **Capital**: The money and things you already own

Savings, investments, and other assets that could help you pay back money if needed

4. **Collateral**: Things you can use to secure a loan

Like how you might trade something valuable to borrow something else

5. **Conditions:** The agreement attached to the loan such as the interest rate, and the type of loan and tlme associated with the loan

Types of Credit

Revolving Credit

- Like a credit card
- You can borrow money repeatedly
- As you pay back money, you can borrow again

Installment Credit

- **Fixed number of payments**
- **Examples:**

    *   Car loans

    *   Home mortgages

    *   Personal loans

Understanding Credit Cards

What is a Credit Card?

A credit card is like a special card that lets you borrow money to buy things. Imagine having a tiny loan in your pocket that you can use to purchase items at stores or online. However, you need to return the money you've borrowed, and pay extra on top of that which is called **interest!**

Key Things to Know

- It's a thin plastic or metal card from a bank

- You can buy things now and pay later

- You must pay back the money you spend

- Different from a debit card, which uses your own money

- If you don't pay off the borrowed money before the due date, you must pay interest

- Credit scores range between 300-850; The highest scores are considered prime.

How Credit Cards Work

- You get a special limit on how much money you can borrow

- Each month, you get a bill showing what you've spent

- If you pay the full amount, you won't owe interest or extra money

- If you only pay part of the bill, you'll have to pay extra (called interest)

- Credit cards have some of the highest interest rates

Types of Credit Cards for Beginners

1. **Secured Credit Cards**

    - Requires a small deposit of your own money

    - Great for kids or teens starting to learn about credit

- Helps build good credit history

2. **Student Credit Cards**

- Designed for young people learning about money
- Usually have lower credit limits
- Often come with educational resources

The Golden Rules of Credit Cards

- Always ask a parent or guardian for help
- Never spend more money than you have
- Pay your bill on time
- Keep track of what you spend
- Protect your card information
- Limit what you can spend on a credit card to a small percentage of what is in your checking out if you decide to use one
- The interest or APR(Annual Percentage Rate) you have to pay on the borrowed money is variable, and extremely high
- **DON'T USE A CREDIT CARD IF YOU ARE NOT DISCIPLINED**

Buying a Car. The Real Cost of Car Ownership

Cars are more than just a way to get around they're a significant financial decision that can impact your long-term financial health. **The money you put into a car cannot be put into investing!! Knowing this will help you make a better financial decision when you do purchase a vehicle.**

Here are some things to remember to help you spend your money wisely when buying a car.

Car Depreciation: The Value Drain

What is Depreciation?

- A new car loses 63% of its value in just 5 years
- The moment you drive a new car off the lot, it loses 10% of its value
- Imagine buying an ice cream that melts instantly that's how quickly cars lose value!

3. **The Financial Challenges of New Cars**

The Triple Threat:

1. Borrowing money (paying interest)
2. Ongoing maintenance costs
3. Rapid value loss

Smart Car Buying Rules

Rule#1: Age Matters

- Buying a used car will cost less than buying a new car
- You will avoid the steepest depreciation period
- Save thousands of dollars instantly

Rule #2: Cash is King

- Save money to buy a car in cash
- Avoid paying interest on the depreciation
- Think of it like this: Paying interest on a car is like "gaining weight while exercising"

Rule #3: Know Your Financial Limits

- Only buy a car if you can comfortably save its monthly payment
- Example: Can't save $300/month? Don't take a $300 car payment

Long-Term Financial Impact

If you buy a used car for cash, you can invest your car payment savings:

This money could:

- *Help pay for college*
- *Start an emergency fund*
- *Begin investing for the future*

Tips for Young Buyers

- Research car values
- Consider total ownership costs

- Save money before buying

- Look for reliable, affordable models

- Avoid unnecessary upgrades

The 20/4/10 Rule of Car Buying

The 20/4/10 rule is a helpful guideline for buying a car that helps you make smart financial decisions. Let's break down what each number means:

- **20%**: Down payment on the car

- **4**: Maximum loan term in years

- **10%**: Maximum transportation costs compared to your monthly income

Down Payment (20% minimum)

- When you buy a car, putting 20% down of the purchase price helps you:

- Create instant equity(ownership) in your car

- Get better loan terms

- Reduce the total amount you'll pay in interest

Loan Term (4 Years max)

- Choosing a shorter loan term means:

- Less total interest paid

- Lower interest rates

- Paying off your car faster

Transportation Costs (10% max)

- This part helps you budget by including:

- Monthly car payment

- Car insurance

- Fuel costs

- Maintenance expenses

Let's say you earn $3,000 per month:

- 10% of income = $300 for total transportation costs
- Loan term = 4 years or less
- Down payment = 20% of the car's total price

Tips for Following the Rule

1. Know your monthly budget
2. Calculate potential car costs
3. Save money for the down payment
4. Compare different car options
5. Consider all transportation expenses

The 20/4/10 rule is a guideline to help you spend money more wisely on a car, allowing you to have more money in your budget for investing.

Car Leasing

A car lease is like a long-term rental agreement for a vehicle. Instead of buying the car outright, you're paying for its value as it depreciates over time. Consider it borrowing a car for a set period, typically 2-4 years.

Key Takeaways

- Not owning the car
- Paying for the vehicle's value loss
- Temporary use of a vehicle

The Real Cost of Leasing

Monthly payments include:

1. Value loss per month
2. Manufacturer's profit
3. Interest charges (hidden cost)

Leasing is ALWAYS more expensive than buying

Effective interest rates(called the Money Factor) can reach around 14%

Hidden Costs to Watch Out For

Potential Extra Charges

Mileage penalties

- Wear and tear fees
- Additional service charges
- No ownership at the end of the lease

Leasing Tips For Young Buyers

Before Leasing, Consider:

1. Your financial situation
2. Driving habits
3. Long-term financial goals
4. Total cost of the lease

Questions to Ask Yourself

- Can I afford the monthly payments?
- Do I drive more or less than the lease mileage limit?
- Do I want to own the car eventually?

Lease vs. Buy: Pros and Cons

Leasing Pros

- Drive a newer car more frequently
- Lower monthly payments
- Less maintenance worry

Leasing Cons

- No ownership
- More expensive long-term
- Strict mileage and condition restrictions

Financial Strategy

- Always calculate the total lease cost
- Compare lease terms carefully

- Read the fine print
- Consider buying instead of leasing

Buying a Home

Many people consider buying a home an achievement. However, it is an expensive process. If you're not careful, you can spend too much money on a home, hindering your ability to invest. Ideally, if you want to be in a good place financially once you buy a home, your house payments(including mortgage, interest, taxes, insurance, and maintenance) should be no more than 25-30% of your NET or take-home monthly pay. Your total debts, including your home, should be no more than 35-40% of your NET or take-home pay. If you follow these rules when you purchase a home, then financially, you should be able to save and invest comfortably for your future.

Things to consider when buying a home:

- Check your credit score
- Aim for the highest credit score possible
- A good credit score helps you get better loan terms
- Evaluate your income stability
- Set long-term financial goals
- Calculate affordable monthly payments
- Have you factored in the cost of renovations to the home that you are buying?
- Can you afford the endless and increasing maintenance that comes with owning a home?
- **Understand PITI:**
- Principal (loan amount)
- Interest (loan cost)
- Taxes
- Insurance

Aim for a 20% or higher down payment of the home's total value(any less, and you will pay **Private Mortgage Insurance or PMI)**, which will increase the monthly payment. You will have less money to invest.

- More down payment = lower monthly costs
- Savings tip: Start setting aside money early
- Most mortgage terms on a home are 15 or 30 years. You pay interest over that time.

Mortgage Types Explained

1. Conventional Loans
   - Standard bank loans
   - Typically requires good credit
2. FHA Loans
   - Government-backed
   - Lower credit score requirements
   - Smaller down payment options
3. VA Loans
   - For military veterans
   - Often no down payment required

*It may be in your best interest to pay off your home as soon as possible. Mortgage interest on a home is front loaded, meaning you pay most of the interest upfront. If you can make extra payments to your mortgage principal early on whether yearly or monthly, you will pay less in interest. Owning a home is way more expensive than the cost of buying the home. You want your amortization(gradual reduction of your debts through repayments) to occur faster by making extra payments to the principal that you owe on the mortgage.

Understanding Taxes

Taxes are financial contributions that individuals and businesses pay to the government.

Key Public Services Supported by Taxes:

- Schools and education
- Roads and infrastructure
- Social Security

- Medicare
- National defense
- Emergency services

Why Do Taxes Matter?

- Taxes are crucial because they:
- Pool community resources
- Support essential government services
- Help develop local and national infrastructure
- Ensure social programs continue to operate

Types of Taxes

1. **Income Taxes**
   - Taxes paid on money earned from:
     * Wages and salaries
     * Certain Investment profits
     * Business earnings

2. **Payroll Taxes**
   - Automatically deducted from paychecks
   - Funds Social Security and Medicare

3. **Sales Taxes**
   - An additional percentage is added to retail purchases
   - Varies by state

The Progressive Tax System

- People with higher incomes pay a higher percentage in taxes
- Not all income is taxed at the same rate(called a Marginal Tax Rate)
- Divided into different tax brackets based on income level

Tax Planning Strategies

1. Start tracking income early
2. Learn about potential deductions
3. Save financial documents
4. Understand your tax bracket
5. Consider future financial implications

Avoiding Tax Trouble

Legal vs. Illegal Tax Practices

- Tax Evasion (Illegal):
  * Not reporting income
  * Falsifying financial documents
- Tax Avoidance (Legal):
  * Claiming legitimate deductions(through owning a business for example)
  * Minimizing taxable income through legal methods(such as investments)

Student Loans

It is important that parents begin investing as soon as their children are born in preparation for the possibility that their child goes to college. Remember, time is your greatest resource. If your investments aren't enough, or you have no investments at all and you want to go to college, then you may need to take out student loans. If you are paying back student loans, that is less money you will have each month to invest. Student loans can generate generational debt, instead of generational wealth.

What Are Student Loans?

A student loan is money borrowed to help students pay for college or university expenses. These loans can cover:

- Tuition
- Textbooks and school supplies
- Living expenses

- Other education-related costs

Key Things to Know About Student Loans

Types of Loans

1. Federal Student Loans
   - Issued by the government
   - Lower interest rates
   - More flexible repayment options
   - Some loans have subsidized interest

2. Private Student Loans
   - Issued by banks or private lenders
   - Higher interest rates
   - Require credit checks
   - Less flexible repayment terms

3. Direct Subsidized Loans
   - What makes them special: The government pays the interest while you're in school
   - Eligibility: Based on financial need

4. Direct Unsubsidized Loans
   - What makes them different: You are responsible for ALL interest
   - Interest starts: From the moment the loan is disbursed
   - Not based on financial need

Important Loan Concepts

Grace Period

- Typically 6 months after:
  - Graduation
  - Leaving school
  - Dropping below half-time enrollment
- During this time, you don't have to make loan payments

Entrance Counseling

- Mandatory information session BEFORE receiving your first federal student loan
- Explains your rights and responsibilities as a borrower

Grants vs. Scholarships

- Grants:
  - Financial aid you don't have to repay
  - Usually based on financial need
- Scholarships:
  - Money awarded for academic or other achievements
  - Also, does not need to be repaid

Work-Study

- Part-time employment while in school
- Helps pay education expenses
- Provides work experience and income

Understanding Loan Costs

Net Price

- The actual amount you and your family will pay for education
- Calculated by:
  1. Taking total cost of attendance
  2. Subtracting grants and scholarships

Interest and Capitalization

- Interest: The cost of borrowing money
- Capitalization: When unpaid interest is added to your loan principal
- Result: You end up paying interest on your interest!

Loan Management Tips

Ways to Reduce Loan Needs

- Apply for scholarships

- Work part-time
- Consider work-study programs
- Attend a less expensive school
- Look for tuition reimbursement opportunities

Responsible Borrowing Strategies

- Only borrow what you absolutely need
- Understand the terms of your loan
- Have a plan for repayment
- Consider future job prospects

Potential Challenges

- Student loans can become a financial burden
- Excessive debt can impact future financial goals
- Some employers offer loan repayment assistance

Debt Reduction Strategies

- Pay off high-interest loans first
- Make extra principal payments when possible

1. **Know Your Total Debt**

Why It Matters:

- You need to understand exactly how much money you owe
- Most students have multiple loans from different sources
- Knowing your total debt helps you create a smart repayment plan

2. **Understand Loan Terms**

Important Things to Check:

- Interest rates for each loan
- Repayment rules
- Grace periods after graduation
- Different types of loans (federal vs. private)

3. **Explore Repayment Options**

Federal Student Loan Repayment Plans:

1. Graduated Repayment

- Payments start low and increase every two years
- Designed for people with entry-level salaries

2. Income-Based Plans

- Payments based on your income
- Can reduce monthly payments
- Some plans offer loan forgiveness after 20-25 years

4. **Debt Reduction Strategies**

The Debt Avalanche Method

- Pay off loans with highest interest rates first
- Example:
    * Loan A: 6% interest
    * Loan B: 5% interest
    * Loan C: 4% interest
- Focus extra payments on the 6% loan first

5. **Loan Forgiveness Options**

Who Might Qualify:

- Public service workers
- Teachers
- People with permanent disabilities
- In cases of school closure

What Happens If You Don't Pay?

Serious Consequences:

- Damaged credit score
- Wage garnishment
- Difficulty getting future loans

- Potential legal action

When taking out student loans, and paying them back, it is important to manage this debt wisely. It will be hard for you to invest while paying back student loans. Again, this is why investing early and utilizing time to your advantage is consistently stressed. Follow these rules to pay them off quicker:

Set up automatic payments (often gets you a small interest rate discount)

Pay extra on your principal when possible

Keep track of your loans

Don't ignore your loans if you're struggling

Chapter 4.2: Ways to Make a Plan to Spend Money

"Beware of little expenses; a small leak can sink a great ship."-
Benjamin Franklin

It's a good idea to keep these three areas in mind while making purchasing selections. If you realize that you are overspending in any
one category, this might be an indication that you need to change
your spending patterns.

Earning money is fantastic. It's a liberating sensation, but with tremendous power comes enormous responsibility. These suggestions
will assist you in spending money sensibly so that you do not begin
your adult life broke. Here are some ideas to help you spend wisely:

1. Create a Budget

To receive an accurate view of your financial condition, keep track of
your income and spending. For those of you who are undisciplined
in your spending, you may want to keep your receipts or a record
of your purchases in a journal as you make them. This way you can
visually see how much you are spending. Each month, go over your
bills and add them to your budget.

- Sort your purchases by category (food, clothing, entertainment, etc.). Categories with the largest monthly amounts (or
  shockingly high monthly amounts) may be ideal targets for
  saving money.

- Create a monthly (or weekly) limit for each category once
  you've been tracking your purchases for a time. Make sure
  your overall budget is less than your income for that time period, with some money left over for savings if feasible.

2. Plan Your Purchases In Advance

Making emotional purchases might cause your expenses to skyrocket. While you're relaxed and at home, make a list of things you need
to buy. STICK TO THE LIST. After you make this list, cut coupons to
save money. Have a plan for your spending. When you go to the
store to shop, it may indicate that you are looking just to spend money. When you go to the store to buy something, it may indicate you

know exactly what you need to spend your money on and you have a plan of action.

3. Avoid Impulse Purchases

While preparing ahead of time is a smart idea, buying anything on the spur of the moment is a bad one. Try not to shop when you are hungry, or upset for example. You may spend more.

4. Shop Alone

Your spouse, children, pals who like shopping, or even a friend whose preferences you admire might all inspire you to spend more money. Sometimes it is best to shop by yourself. Unless you are with someone who will hold you accountable for your bad spending habits. If you have someone like that in your life, then maybe you should shop with them.

5. Pay in Full and in Cash

Credit and debit cards enhance spending for two reasons: you have far more money to spend than you would otherwise, and because no visible money is passing hands, it does not register as a "genuine" transaction.

6. Don't Be Fooled By Marketing

Outside forces have a significant impact on how we spend our money. Keep an eye out for all of the reasons you're pulled to a product.

Don't buy something just because it is advertised well

Don't buy something just because it is on sale. You may not actually need it. Not buying it at all is always cheaper than buying it on sale.

Don't always buy something because the price is "low"

7. Wait for sales and discounts

If you know you'll need something but don't need it right away, wait until it goes on sale or attempt to get a coupon for it.

8. Conduct Research

Before making large purchases, look online or read consumer reviews to learn how to get the most bang for your dollar. Find the product that will last the longest and best satisfy your demands within your budget.

9. Take All The Costs Into Account

For many big ticket things, you'll find yourself spending far more than the advertised price. Before making a decision, read all of the fine print and tally the whole sum.

10. Only Purchase What You Actually Need

Again, figure out what you need vs what you want. Even when purchasing your wants, you may not need certain things. You may want a luxury car but do you need to purchase the extra trimmings that come with it?

Chapter 4.3: Understanding Budgeting and Its Importance

"A man who pays his bills on time is soon forgotten."- Oscar Wilde

If you want to keep track of your spending and meet your financial goals, you'll need a budget. A personal or household budget is a breakdown of your income and spending for a specific time period, usually one month.

A budget will show you how much money you plan to receive, as well as your mandatory costs (like rent and insurance) and discretionary spending (like entertainment or eating out). Instead of perceiving a budget as a roadblock, consider it a tool for achieving your financial goals.

What a Budget Does

A monthly budget is a written financial planning tool that assists you in determining how much money you will spend and save each month. You may keep track of your spending habits as well.

Keeping your financial home in order requires you to create a budget. Spending less in one area allows you to spend more in another, save for a major purchase, build an emergency fund, or invest your money.

Your budget will disclose where your money comes from, how much you have, and how much you spend each month.

If you pay your bills on time, creditors will not come chasing after you. If you are constantly late on payments, they will constantly harass you. Remember that.

Chapter 4.4: Steps to Make a Budget

"When prosperity comes, do not use all of it."- Confucius

To create a budget that works for you and allows you to live a comfortable and happy life, you must first assess what you are currently spending, what you can afford to spend, and what your objectives are.

1. Gather Your Financial Paperwork

Before you begin, gather all of your financial records. You need to be able to see all of your receipts and expenditures. One of the most important steps in the budgeting process is to calculate a monthly average. It is preferable to obtain as much information as possible.

2. Calculate Your Income

How much money do you make each month? If your income is in the form of a regular paycheck with taxes and other items deducted automatically, you may use the net income (or take-home pay) amount.

3. Create a List of Monthly Expenses

Make a list of all the expenses you expect to pay in a month. Examine your bank and credit card statements from the last three months to keep track of your spending.

4. Determine Fixed and Variable Expenses

Fixed costs are those that must be paid on a regular basis and for which you always pay the same approximate amount. Expenses like mortgage or rent payments and auto payments are fixed costs. Include any additional spending that is likely to be consistent from month to month.

If you anticipate saving a particular amount or paying off a defined amount of debt each month, include savings and debt repayment as fixed expenditures. Groceries, gas, entertainment, eating out, gifts, and so on are examples of variable costs that differ from month to month. If you're not sure how much you spend in each area, look at your credit card or bank bills from the past two or three months.

5. Total Your Monthly Income and Expenses

If your net income surpasses your costs, you're on the right route. This additional cash allows you to allocate money to other areas of your budget, such as retirement savings or investing. If your expenses surpass your income or you are breaking even, you are overpaying and should make some changes.

6. Make Adjustments to Expenses

Find areas in your spending that you may decrease if your spending is larger than your income. Consider strategies to save money, such as eating out less or canceling a subscription.

Lowering your spending may not be enough if your spending surpasses your income or if you have a lot of debt. You may need to lower fixed expenditures and increase income to balance your budget. You may also need to consider getting another source of income.

Chapter 4.5: Different Budgeting Strategies

"By failing to prepare, you are preparing to fail."- Benjamin Franklin

Here's a deeper look at a few fundamental budgeting principles that are popular.

1. 50/30/20 Budget

The 50/30/20 method is based on a hierarchy of needs/wants/savings and investments.. Determining which costs are requirements and which are desires can be difficult, but here are some examples for the average person:

50% Needs / Non-negotiable Essentials

Housing(Rent/Mortgage)

Groceries

Utilities

Debt Payments

30% Wants / Personal Expenses

Dining

Travel

Entertainment

20% Savings/Investments

Emergency Fund

Retirement Savings/Investments

Personal Investing

The 50/30/20 rule strives to provide you with a well-rounded lifestyle with the proper financial balance, including basic spending, unanticipated expenses, and even items you like while saving for your future.

2. Zero-Based Budget

Zero-Based Budgeting is when your income minus your expenses equals zero. In other words, you're striving toward a zero-waste situation, with none of your income going unaccounted for. This forces all of your dollars to serve a purpose.

3. Envelope Budget

This Envelope Budget splits up actual cash and places it in separate envelopes designated for the majority of your monthly costs. Having cash on hand offers a hands-on experience every time you spend money. Because the money in each envelope needs to last for the full month, you can't replenish it once it is gone.

4. Values-Based Budget

After covering your basic financial needs, such as food, housing, utilities, transportation, and all of your debt payments and savings, values-based budgeting allows you to spend any money left over on an item that aligns with things that you value most, such as eating out or investing.

5. Pay Yourself First Budget

The Pay Yourself First Budget is simple. When you get paid, you put money away towards your savings/investments before you pay anyone else like your credit card company or your mortgage. Meaning, you pay yourself first.

As with any budget, you begin by calculating your monthly net income. Instead of stating your monthly costs or separating your income into categories or percentages, establish your monthly savings/investing objectives, each with a cash amount. Then, reduce your entire savings/investing amount from your monthly net income. Whatever is left over you use for your expenses, and enjoyment of life. If you deduct your savings/investments from your budget first, you will be forced to operate financially on what is left over.

6. 70/30 Budget

The 70/30 budget states that you should live off of 70% of your TAKE HOME or net pay per month. So if you take home 6,000 after taxes and other withholdings from your paycheck, you only live off of $4,200 a month. The other 30% is to pay down any debt 1st, then save and invest.

Chapter 4.6: Using Budgeting and Tips for Your Budgeting

"The time to repair the roof is when the sun is shining."- John F. Kennedy

How To Use Your Budget

You must monitor and continue to track your spending in each area after you have set up your budget, ideally every day of the month.

Keeping track of your spending throughout the month will help you avoid overspending and detect unneeded or problematic spending trends. If you are an extremely undisciplined person financially, recording your costs until the end of the month might not be enough. You may have to record your spending daily.

Your budget's objective should be to maintain your monthly spending to less than your net income.

Review and Tweak Your Budget

Situations change. Our priorities change when we switch employment, move, or have children. Make it a point to sit down with your budget every few months and make sure it's still working for your current goals.

More Budgeting Tips

After you've constructed a basic budget, you may customize it to fit your own financial situation and objectives.

- If you work on commission, actively save to help you get through market downturns.

- If you only get paid once a month and have cash flow difficulties, divide your payment into weeks and keep the money you planned to spend over the next few weeks in a separate account until you need it.

- Use a credit card only if you are confident that you will be able to pay it off at the end of the month. You'll be charged interest on top of the purchase price if you don't.

- Make regular modifications to your budget if you discover that you have overestimated or underestimated your spending. Keep note of large expenses that happen just once or twice a year, such as insurance payments..

- Take the time to increase your financial literacy and make your money work harder for you by learning additional financial skills.

Chapter 4.7: Downloadable Budget Templates

Keeping track of your monthly costs in a budget template or app might help you manage your money more effectively.

Here are some budget spreadsheets or apps you may choose to use: **Source: nerdwallet.com**

The Federal Trade Commission's budget worksheet

NerdWallet's budget worksheet

Microsoft Office budget templates

Google Drive budget spreadsheets

Free Budgeting Applications
YNAB

Goodbudget

EveryDollar

Empower Personal Wealth

Pocketguard

Honeydue

Fudget

*There are many others. Choose the one that suits you best.

CHAPTER 4:
BUDGETING FOR YOUR INVESTMENTS

Quiz No: 4

Serial No	Question	Answer
1.	What are the three main categories to categorize your spending? A. Needs, Wants, Investing B. Essentials, Desires, Savings C. Needs, Wants, Savings or Debt Reduction D. Essential Expenses, Non-essential Expenses, Investments	
2.	Which of the following is not a tip for spending money wisely? A. Avoid impulse purchases B. Shop alone C. Pay in full and in cash D. Always go for the lowest-priced item in a category	
3.	What is the purpose of creating a budget? A. To limit your spending B. To track your income and expenses C. To restrict your financial goals D. To avoid spending money	

4.	What is the first step in creating a budget? A. Determine fixed and variable expenses B. Calculate your income C. Gather your financial paperwork D. Create a list of monthly expenses	
5.	Which budgeting strategy involves allocating 50% of your income to needs, 30% to wants, and 20% to savings? A. 50/30/20 Budget B. Zero-Based Budget C. Envelope Budget D. Pay Yourself First Budget	
6.	Which budgeting strategy aims to bring your monthly income down to zero by assigning every dollar a purpose? A. 50/30/20 Budget B. Zero-Based Budget C. Envelope Budget D. Values-Based Budget	
7.	What does the "pay yourself first" budgeting technique prioritize? A. Saving money B. Paying bills and expenses C. Spending money on wants D. Donating to charity	
8.	How often should you track your expenses when using a budget if you are undisciplined financially? A. Once a year B. Once a month C. Once a week D. Once a day	

9.	What is one benefit of using budgeting applications?	
	A. They make budgeting fun	
	B. They help maximize spending and saving decisions	
	C. They eliminate the need for budgeting	
	D. They offer free financial advice	
10.	You should only use a credit card:	
	A. When you are trying to build interest	
	B. When you can pay it off immediately before the end of the month	
	C. When you don't enjoy using cash	
	D. When you want to track your spending	

Key

1. C

2. D

3. B

4. C

5. A

6. B

7. A

8. D

9. B

10. B

CHAPTER
FIVE

STOCK MARKET
INVESTING

Chapter 5.1: Introduction to The Stock Market

"Investment philosophy is the clear understanding that by owning shares of stocks you own businesses, not pieces of paper"- Warren Buffet

The stock market refers to a diverse range of items as well as a variety of exchanges where equities(stocks) are purchased and traded. In general, the stock market is a collection of companies who offer publicly traded shares that may be purchased on an exchange by anybody. Stocks are listed by their ticker symbol(a series of letters assigned to a stock for the purpose of trading). For example, Coca-Cola's ticker symbol is *KO.*

Stocks provide shareholders with ownership in a publicly traded company. It's a legitimate investment in the company, and if you owned 100% of the stock, you would have complete influence over how it runs. Even if you don't own all of the shares, owning a significant number of them allows you to influence how the firm functions.

Many companies issue stock or shares(pieces of the company) for sale in order to raise money. When you purchase shares in a company, you are now a shareholder, and you own pieces of the company. Thousands of companies issue stock in their company. You can search for these companies in a variety of ways online using the ticker symbol, or simply by searching for the company. There are many companies that operate privately, and are not publicly traded in the stock market.

If you look at owning a stock as owning a piece of a business rather than just a stock, it may help you emotionally when investing. Stock prices rise and fall daily, sometimes dramatically. However, the fundamentals of the actual business do not change on a daily basis. If you believe you are buying a piece of a business(which you are), the daily movements of the stock price won't matter as much to you. If you own a piece of a great business, in the end that is all that matters. Long Term the business will succeed and the day to day fluctuations will matter less. This will help your emotional temperament. Yes you are buying stock in a business, but you are buying ownership in a company. If it is a great company from your analysis, you should do great in the market, and you will have better control over your emotions.

How The Stock Market Works

A stock exchange is basically a marketplace in which investors and brokers may exchange stocks for cash or vice versa. Anyone interested in purchasing shares can go there and purchase whatever is available from the stockholders.

As a result, the stock market permits investors to speculate on the future of a company. Finally, the price at which investors are willing to purchase and sell a corporation determines its worth. The stock market is always changing.

While stock prices change on a daily basis based on how many shares are demanded or provided, the market evaluates a company over time based on its financial performance and future prospects. A company's stock will almost surely rise if its sales and profits grow, whereas a company's stock will almost certainly fall if its sales and profits decline. However, in the short run, a stock's performance is mostly determined by market supply and demand.

The fundamental idea is that stock prices are influenced by investors' expectations of how the company's operations will perform in the future. As a result, the market is looking ahead. In general, the stock market is safe for the long term, however it can be unsafe or volatile in the short term.

When investing, know the difference between fundamental and technical analysis:

Technical analysis analyzes data from short periods, using things like charts(yearly, monthly, daily). It is usually used for short term investing and day trading.

Fundamental analysis analyzes the underlying aspects of the company(the financials) and is usually associated with long term investing.

Technical and fundamental analysis can apply to many types of investments.

Technical Analysis and Indicators in the Stock Market

Technical Indicators

Technical indicators are special tools that help people understand how stocks and other investments might move in the future. They look at things like the price of a stock and how many people are buying or selling it.

Types of Technical Indicators

There are two main types:

1. *Overlays: These are drawn right on top of the stock price chart.*

2. *Oscillators: These are usually drawn above or below the stock price chart.*

Examples of Technical Indicators

Here are some common technical indicators:

- *Moving Averages: This shows the average price of a stock over a certain time.*

- *Relative Strength Index (RSI): This tells us if a stock might be going up or down soon.*

- *MACD: This compares two different moving averages to spot trends.*

How People Use Technical Indicators

Traders (people who buy and sell stocks) use these indicators to help them decide:

- *When to buy a stock*

- *When to sell a stock*

- *If a stock's price might go up or down*

Why Technical Indicators Are Important

Technical indicators can be helpful because:

1. *They use math to look at past information about stocks.*

2. *They can work for many different types of investments, not just stocks.*

3. *They can help people make decisions about buying and selling.*

Below are some common Technical Indicators investors and traders use.

Moving Average Indicator

A moving average is a way to look at how stock prices change over time. It helps make the ups and downs of prices smoother and easier to understand.

Types of Moving Averages

There are two main types:

1. Simple Moving Average (SMA)
2. Exponential Moving Average (EMA)

Simple Moving Average

An SMA adds up a bunch of prices and divides by how many there are. For example, if we look at 5 days of prices:

Day 1: $10

Day 2: $12

Day 3: $11

Day 4: $13

Day 5: $14

We would add those up (10 + 12 + 11 + 13 + 14 = 60) and divide by 5.

The 5-day SMA would be $12.

Exponential Moving Average

An EMA is trickier. It prioritizes the newest prices, which means it can show changes faster than an SMA.

Why Use Moving Averages?

Moving averages help people who study stocks to:

1. See if a stock's price is going up or down overall
2. Decide if it might be a good time to buy or sell

Example

Let's say we're looking at the price of apples:

Week 1: $1.00

Week 2: $1.10

Week 3: $1.05

Week 4: $1.15

The 4-week SMA would be:

(1.00 + 1.10 + 1.05 + 1.15) ÷ 4 = $1.075

This tells us that, on average, apples cost about $1.08 over the past month.

Moving averages don't predict the future. They just help us understand what prices have been doing lately.

Crossover Indicator

A crossover is when two lines meet and cross each other on a stock chart.

Traders use crossovers to help them make decisions about buying or selling. Crossovers can give hints about what might happen next with the price.

Types of Crossovers

Moving Average Crossover

This is one of the most common types. It uses something called "moving averages". Imagine two lines on a chart:

- A short-term line (moves quickly)
- A long-term line (moves slowly)

When these lines cross, it can mean something important is happening!

The Golden Cross

The Golden Cross is a special type of moving average crossover. It happens when:

- The short-term line goes above the long-term line
- This usually means prices in the market might go up

The Death Cross

A death cross is the opposite of a golden cross. It's a sad sign that the market might go down for a while. Here's how it happens:

- The market was going up.
- Then, the short-term average price starts going down faster than the long-term average price.
- Finally, the short-term line crosses below the long-term line. This is the death cross!

When we see a death cross, some people might think about selling their stocks.

Stochastic Crossover

This type helps traders know if something is being bought or sold too much.

- If it goes above 80, it might be bought too much
- If it goes below 20, it might be sold too much

Important Things to Remember

1. Crossovers can help, but they're not always right
2. It's good to use crossovers with other tools
3. Surprises in the market can change things quickly

Crossovers are like clues for traders. They help guess what might happen next, but they're not magic! Traders still need to be careful when using them.

Bollinger Bands Indicator

Bollinger Bands are three lines that appear on a chart showing a stock's price over time:

1. The middle line is the average price over the last 20 days.
2. The top line is above the middle line.
3. The bottom line is below the middle line.

These lines move up and down as the stock price changes.

What do Bollinger Bands tell us?

Bollinger Bands helps us understand two important things:

1. How much the price is changing (called volatility)
2. If the price might be too high or too low

Volatility

When the top and bottom lines are far apart, the price changes a lot. When they're close together, the price isn't changing much.

Price levels

When the price touches the top line, some traders think it might be too high and could go down soon. They think it might be too low when it touches the bottom line and could go up soon.

Examples

Let's imagine we're looking at the price of apples:

1. The Bollinger Bands would be close together if the price stays between $1 and $2 for a long time.
2. If the price suddenly jumps to $3, the top band would stretch, making the bands wider.
3. If the price drops to $0.50, it might touch the bottom band, suggesting it could go up soon.

Oscillators Indicator

Imagine a line that goes up and down between two points. This line is the oscillator. When it gets close to the top, it means the stock might be too expensive. When it gets close to the bottom, it might be too cheap.

Think of a playground swing. When you swing high, you can't go much higher. You're ready to go up again when you're at the bottom. Oscillators work like that.

Oscillators are most helpful when a stock's price isn't going up or down. It's like when you're walking on a flat road you're not going up or down a hill.

How to Read an Oscillator

Oscillators usually have numbers from 0 to 100. Here's what they mean:

- The stock might be too expensive if the number is above 70 or 80.
- The stock might be too cheap if the number is below 20 or 30.

Example:

Imagine a toy costs $10 usually. If the price goes up to $18, it might be too expensive. If it goes down to $3, it might be too cheap. Oscillators help us see this for stocks

Moving Average Convergence Divergence(MACD) Indicator:

How MACD Works

MACD uses two lines on a chart:

1. The MACD line
2. The signal line

When these lines cross each other, it can mean something important is happening with the stock price.

When the MACD line goes above the signal line:

This might mean the price is going up. It could be a good time to buy the stock.

When the MACD line goes below the signal line:

This might mean the price is going down. It could be time to think about selling the stock.

Examples of Using MACD

Let's pretend we're looking at the price of ice cream cones:

1. If the MACD shows the lines crossing upwards, it might mean ice cream cone prices are going up. It could be getting warmer outside!
2. If the MACD shows the lines crossing downwards, ice cream cone prices will decrease. Maybe winter is coming!

Relative Strength Index (RSI) Indicator

RSI looks at how fast and how much a stock's price is going up or down.

- It gives a number between 0 and 100.
- If the number is above 70, the stock price might be too high.
- If the number is below 30, the stock price may be too low.

Price Rate of Change (ROC) Indicator

The ROC compares a stock's current price to its price a specific time ago and shows this as a percentage.

For example, if an apple cost $1 last week and now costs $1.10, the ROC would be 10%. This means the price went up by 10% in a week. If a toy car cost $10 last week and now costs $9, the ROC would be -10%. This shows prices are going down. If notebooks cost $5 last year and still cost $5 now, the ROC would be 0%. This shows prices aren't changing.

What Does the ROC Tell Us?

The ROC can tell us a few essential things:

1. If prices are going up or down
2. How fast prices are changing
3. If a price trend might be about to change

Money Flow Index (MFI) Indicator

The MFI is like a thermometer for stocks. It goes from 0 to 100:

- When it's above 80, the stock might get too expensive (we call this "overbought").
- When it's below 20, it might mean the stock is getting too cheap (we call this "oversold").

The MFI is unique because it looks at two things:

1. The price of the stock
2. How many shares are being traded (we call this "volume")

This makes it different from other tools that only look at price.

Here are some ways investors use MFI:

1. **Spotting Changes**: If the MFI starts going down when the stock price is still going up, it might mean the price will start going down soon.

2. **Finding Good Times to Buy or Sell**:

   - If the MFI goes below 20 and then starts going up, it might be a good time to buy.

   - If the MFI goes above 80 and then starts going down, it might be a good time to sell.

3. **Confirming Trends**: If a stock's price is going up and the MFI is also going up, it helps confirm that the stock is doing well.

Let's say we're watching a stock called "Burger Guys":

- The stock price has been increasing for a while and is now $50.

- But we notice the MFI has dropped from 85 to 70.

- This might be a sign that although the price is still high, fewer people are buying the stock.

- It could mean the price might start going down soon.

Divergence Indicator

Divergence is when the price of a stock is going in a different direction than what other signs are showing.

There are two main types of divergence:

1. Positive Divergence
2. Negative Divergence

Positive Divergence

This is when the price is decreasing, but other signs show it might go up soon.

Negative Divergence

This is when the price is going up, but other signs show it might go down soon. It's like when you're starting to feel tired even though you're still playing you know you'll probably need a rest soon!

Traders use divergence to help them guess what might happen next with prices. It's like a clue that helps them decide about buying or selling.

Let's imagine we're looking at the price of ice cream:

1. The price of ice cream is decreasing, but more and more people are lining up to buy it. This could be a positive divergence the price might go up soon!

2. The price of ice cream is going up, but fewer people are buying it. This could be negative divergence the price might go down soon!

Divergence doesn't always mean the price will change right away. Sometimes it takes a long time. Also, not every price change has divergence before it happens. That's why traders also use other tools, not just divergence.

Technical Analysis: Advantages and Disadvantages

Advantages of Technical Analysis

1. **Spotting Trends**

Technical analysis helps traders see if a stock price is going up, down, or staying the same. This is called a trend. For example:

- When more people buy a stock, the price usually increases. This is an uptrend.
- When more people sell a stock, the price usually decreases. This is a downtrend.

2. **Using Helpful Tools**

There are special tools in technical analysis that help traders. These tools look at things like how fast a stock price is changing. They can give signals about when to buy or sell a stock.

3. **Finding Good Times to Buy and Sell**

Technical analysis helps traders decide when it's a good time to buy or sell stocks. It does this by looking at things like:

- Support levels (where the price stops falling)
- Resistance levels (where the price stops rising)

4. Understanding How People Feel

Technical analysis can show how people feel about a stock. For example:

- If a stock price goes up very fast, it might mean people are too excited, and the price might go down soon.
- If a stock price goes down very fast, it might mean people are too scared, and the price might go up soon.

Disadvantages of Technical Analysis

1. Doesn't Look at Everything

Technical analysis only looks at prices and charts. It doesn't look at other important things about a company, like how much money it's making.

2. Can Be Confusing

Different people might look at the same chart and see different things. This can be confusing and might lead to mistakes.

3. Sometimes Late

Technical analysis tools sometimes show changes after they've already started happening. Traders might miss some of the best times to buy or sell.

4. Can Give Wrong Signals

Sometimes, technical analysis tools give wrong signals. A chart might show it's time to buy, but then the price goes down instead of up.

5. Based on Old Information

Technical analysis uses information from the past. But just because something happened before doesn't mean it will happen again.

Remember, technical analysis can be helpful, but it's not perfect. It's just one way to look at the stock market.

Fundamental Analysis and Indicators in the Stock Market

There are two main types of fundamentals:

1. *Qualitative fundamentals*
2. *Quantitative fundamentals*

Qualitative Fundamentals

Qualitative fundamentals are things we can describe but not easily measure with numbers. They're like the "quality" of something. Here are some examples:

Business Model

This is how a company makes money. For example, a lemonade stand's business model sells lemonade to thirsty people on hot days.

Competitive Advantage

This is what makes a company unique or better than others. For example, if your lemonade stand has the best secret recipe in town, that's your competitive advantage!

Management Team

These are the people who run the company. Good leaders can help a company succeed, just as a good coach helps a sports team win.

Brand Name

This is how well people know and like a company's products. For example, many people know and love McDonalds, so it has a strong brand name.

Quantitative Fundamentals

Quantitative fundamentals are things we can measure with numbers. They often come from financial statements, which are like report cards for businesses. Here are some examples:

Revenue

This is how much money a company makes from selling its products or services.

Profit

This is how much money is left after paying all the costs of running the business.

Financial Ratios

These unique math formulas help us understand how well a company is doing. For example:

Profit margin: Shows how much of the money made turns into profit

Debt-to-equity ratio: Shows how much the company owes compared to what it owns

Why are Fundamentals Important?

Understanding qualitative and quantitative fundamentals helps people choose which companies to invest in or do business with. It's like checking a car's interior and exterior before buying it—you want to ensure everything looks good!

Remember, both types of fundamentals are essential. A company might have great numbers (quantitative) but bad leadership (qualitative), or vice versa. The best companies usually do well in both areas!

Fundamental Analysis: Advantages and Disadvantages

Fundamental analysis is a way to study companies and decide if they're suitable investments.

Advantages of Fundamental Analysis

1. **Lots of Information**
   - You get to learn a lot about a company
   - You can look at things like how much money the company makes and spends
   - You can also learn about what's happening in the world that might affect the company

2. **Understanding the Company**
   - You can figure out if a company might grow in the future
   - It helps you know if your investments are good ones

3. **Good for Long-Term Investing**
   - If you want to invest for a long time, this method is great
   - It helps you find companies that will do well over many years

4. **Knowing a Company's Value**

   - You can figure out if a company's stock costs too much or too little

   - This helps you decide if it's a good time to buy

5. **Understanding Risks**

   - You learn about things that could hurt the company

   - This helps you be careful with your money

Disadvantages of Fundamental Analysis

1. **Takes a Lot of Work**

   - You have to look at lots of information

   - It can take a long time to do

2. **People Might Think Differently**

   - Different people might look at the same information and think different things

   - This can be confusing

3. **Can't Predict Everything**

   - Even if you do a lot of research, you can't know everything that will happen

   - Surprises can still affect companies

4. **Doesn't Work for Everything**

   - This method is suitable for stocks but not for things like gold or digital money

5. **Not Good for Quick Investments**

   - If you want to buy and sell quickly, this method isn't beneficial

   - It's better for people who want to invest for a long time

Remember, fundamental analysis can be beneficial, but it's not perfect. It's essential to understand the good and not-so-good parts of using this method when considering investments.

Fundamental analysis and metrics will be discussed more in the last chapter.

Stock Market Capitalization to GDP Ratio

The Stock Market Capitalization-to-GDP Ratio is a way to compare how much all stocks in a country are worth to how much money the country makes in a year.

Stock Market Capitalization is the total value of all the companies in the stock market over a specific period, usually a year.

Gross Domestic Product, or GDP for short, is a way to measure how much a country produces and how well its economy is doing.

GDP measures the total value of all goods and services a country makes in a year. This includes things like:

- *Products made in factories*
- *Food grown on farms*
- *Services like haircuts or doctor visits*
- *Things the government provides, like schools and roads*

GDP tries to add up the value of everything a country produces.

GDP helps us understand:

- *How big a country's economy is*
- *If the economy is growing or shrinking*
- *How one country's economy compares to others*

How Do We Calculate the Stock Market Capitalization to GDP Ratio?

We use this simple math:

(Value of All Stocks ÷ Country's Yearly Income) × 100

The answer we get is a percentage.

What Does the Percentage Mean?

* *If it's between 50% and 75%, the stock market might be a good deal.*

* *If it's between 75% and 90%, the stock market is priced just right.*

* *If it's between 90% and 115%, the stock market might be expensive.*

If it's over 100%, many people think the stock market is too expensive.

Why is it Called the Buffett Indicator?

Warren Buffett said this was the best way to see if the stock market was overvalued or undervalued. That's why some people call it the Buffett Indicator.

Let's say all stocks in a country are worth $100 billion, and the country makes $80 billion in a year. We would do this math:

($100 billion ÷ $80 billion) × 100 = 125%

This means the stock market might be a bit too expensive right now.

This number can help people decide whether it's a good time to invest in the stock market. But remember, it's just one way to look at the stock market. There are many other things to consider, too!

Chapter 5.2: History of the Stock Market

"We deceive ourselves when we believe that past stock market return patterns provide the bounds by which we can predict the future."- John Bogle

The Invention of the Stock Market

The idea of exchanging goods may be traced back to the earliest civilizations. Early businesses banded together to send ships across the sea to adjacent countries. Trading organizations or individuals have carried out these transactions for thousands of years. All civilizations have engaged in trade with other civilizations. This helped boost their economies. It provided jobs and sources of income for people.

Since the dawn of civilization, people have traded in different markets. The Silk Road between Europe and Asia allowed for massive trade. African Kingdoms traded much mineral wealth and commodities building vast and rich empires. Trading created markets of buyers and sellers.

The stock market operates in similar fashion. People around the world can trade in a variety of different assets allowing economies to function and wealth to grow. When you participate in the stock market, you are a buyer, a seller or both. The ultimate goal is to grow your wealth.

Stock Market Timeline

The following is a timeline of major events in the history of the stock market:

- **Late 1400s**: Antwerp, in modern-day Belgium, becomes a global trade center. Merchants buy products with the hope that prices will rise and they will benefit. Bond trading occurs as well.

- **1611:** The first modern stock exchange was founded in Amsterdam. The Dutch East India Firm was the first publicly traded corporation, and for many years it was the only company with trading activity on the market.

- **Late 1700s:** A small group of businesses formed the Buttonwood Tree Agreement. The men met every day to buy and sell stocks and bonds, which led to the establishment of the New York Stock Exchange.

- **1790:** The Philadelphia Stock Exchange is founded, contributing to the development of the financial sectors of the United States as well as the country's westward expansion.

- **1896:** Dow Jones Industrial Average (DJIA) is established. It started with 12 constituents, the vast majority of which were industrial firms.

- **1923:** Henry Barnum Poor started Poor's Publishing, which published the inaugural edition of the S&P 500. It began tracking 90 stocks in 1926.

- **1929:** Following the decade-long "Roaring 20s," when speculators put leveraged bets on the stock market, prices fell in the United States.

- **1941:** Standard & Poor's is founded by the merger of Poor's Publishing and Standard Statistics.

- **1971:** The National Association of Securities Dealers Automated Quotations, or NASDAQ, is another US stock exchange where trading begins.

- **1987:** Corporate takeovers boosted the market's rise until October 19, when a drop in the market was dubbed "Black Monday."

- **2000/2001:** The Dot Com bubble burst. In the late 1990s investors were putting money into technology companies, many of them that were unprofitable internet companies that ended with .com. It created a massive investing bubble that eventually burst in 2001. Many internet companies went out of business and many investors lost a lot of money.

- **2008:** Following the housing boom of the early 2000's and housing crisis, as well as the banking sector's expansion of mortgage-backed securities, the stock market declined.

- **2020:** The stock market had a wild ride during the year 2020. The Covid-19 pandemic was gripping the world and the stock market dropped more than 20% from its highs in February into late March. By the summer and going into the year 2021 the market had more than recovered. The rebound was mostly attributed to the actions of the Federal Reserve Bank with their monetary stimulus actions(pumping money into the markets and the economy).

Chapter 5.3: Understanding Income, Value, and Growth Stocks

"I'd rather have a $10 million business making 15% than a $100 million business making 5%."- Warren Buffet

"Growth and value are always joined at the hip."- Warren Buffet

Investors often acquire stocks for one of two reasons: they hope the price will grow and enable them to sell the stock at a profit, or they want to receive dividends as investment income. There are other reasons as well but these are just the basics. Certain stocks may meet both goals to some degree, but most stocks fall into one of three categories: growth, income, or value.

Growth Stocks

Growth stocks, as the term indicates, are those that have significant potential for growth in the near future. Growth stocks may be expanding faster than the overall stock markets at the moment, and they often commit the majority of their existing income to future growth. Growth stocks exist in every sector of the market, although they are more frequent in some sectors, such as technology, alternative energy, and biotechnology. They are usually not as established as other companies and can be a riskier investment, however, the potential for growth may allow for a better return. The fundamentals of a growth stock may not be as stable as an established company; however, they can still be a great investment if you can purchase them at the right price.

The majority of growth stocks are younger firms with unique goods that are projected to have a significant influence on the market in the future, but there are some exceptions. Some growth firms are simply well-run businesses with solid business strategies that have capitalized on product demand. Growth stocks may give significant returns on investments, but many of them are smaller, less reliable enterprises that may also face significant price drops. Growth stocks typically do not pay dividends(cash payouts for being a shareholder in the company) as they reinvest the cash to grow the company. If you are looking for steady income, growth stocks may not be for you. However, if you are looking for appreciation, growth stocks may be your play.

Examples of popular growth stocks currently:

Amazon(AMZN), Alphabet(GOOGL), Tesla(TSLA), Apple(AAPL),

Value Stocks

Value stocks typically produce long-term rewards. A value stock trades at a lower price than it should based on its fundamentals. This means that when you analyze the company, the company is in great financial standing however the price for whatever reason does not reflect this. Value stocks are great companies that are trading on a discount. If a fully loaded brand new car with high rankings was selling for 30% off the sticker price for a period of time, you might be getting a great value if you purchase it at that time. Value stocks might have high dividend payout ratios or low financial ratios like price-to-book or price-earnings. The stock price may have also fallen with the rest of the stock market at a particular time. Simply put, value stocks are great companies selling at a discount.

There are many reasons why a company's price may be trading lower than its value, from a drop in the stock market, to short term negative news, or it is just simply undervalued by buyers. Smart investors understand that now may be a good opportunity to purchase the company since the public may ultimately realize the price is too low and demand may rise forcing the stock price to rise and your return to rise as well.

Of course, the definition of a fair value for a certain stock is completely subjective and depends on the investor's philosophy and point of view. Because they are often those of bigger, more established firms, value stocks are seen to be less risky than growth stocks. Their prices, however, may not necessarily return to their earlier greater levels as projected.

Examples of a popular value stocks currently:

Johnson and Johnson(JNJ), Pfizer(PFE), Proctor and Gamble(PG), Coca-Cola(KO)

Income Stocks

Investors want income stocks to supplement their fixed-income portfolios since their dividend returns often outperform those of guaranteed assets such as bonds or CDs.

Income stocks are classified into two kinds. Some income paying stocks have typically maintained relatively steady prices while paying competitive dividends. Preferred stocks are a kind of hybrid security that acts more like bonds than stocks.

Examples of a popular income stocks currently:

> *Realty Income Corporation(O), Verizon(VZ), The Clorox Company(CLX), IBM(IBM)*

How to Find Stocks in These Categories

There is no one correct technique to find certain sorts of stocks. Those seeking growth may look for growing firms on investment websites or message boards, then conduct their own research on them. Many analysts also write blogs and newsletters that promote companies in all three categories. A simple search online in reality may be all you need.

The first thing you should follow are stock market indexes to monitor how the market as a whole is performing. A stock market index measures the performance of a group of stocks or companies. The 3 most popular indexes that are followed currently are:

Dow Jones Industrial Average Index

S&P 500 Index

Nasdaq Composite Index

Why Are Indexes Important?

Indexes help us in many ways:

1. *They show if the stock market is going up or down*
2. *People can use them to compare how well their investments are doing*
3. *Some people try to copy indexes when they invest*

Types of Indexes

There are many kinds of indexes. Some look at:

- *The whole stock market*
- *Just small companies*
- *Only technology companies*
- *Bonds instead of stocks*

Index Investing

Some people like to invest in funds that copy indexes. This is called "indexing". It's a way to invest without having to pick individual stocks.

For example, you can buy a fund that tries to do as well as the S&P 500 index. This way, you're investing in 500 companies all at once.

An index is like a big basket with many different items to show how well a part of the market is doing. It gives us a number that tells us how well a group of things in the market are doing overall.

Index Divisors: Making Stock Market Indices Easy to Track

What is an Index Divisor?

An index divisor is a unique number used to make stock market indices easier to understand and follow. When experts create a new index to track the stock market, they use this divisor to turn a big, complicated number into something simpler. These are the numbers you see associated with each Index.

Why Do We Need Index Divisors?

Imagine trying to keep track of a number like 246,876.54 every day. That would be hard. Instead, using an index divisor, we can turn that big number into something more manageable, like 100 or 1000. This makes it much simpler for everyone to see if the stock market is going up or down.

How Index Divisors Work

Let's break it down with an example:

1. First, experts add up the prices of all stocks in the index.

2. This total might be a large number.

3. They then choose a divisor or a specific number and divide it by the total price of the index to create a manageable number.

4. This is the number that you see associated with each index.

Types of Indices

There are two main types of stock market indices:

1. **Price-weighted index**: This type adds up the price of one share of each company in the index.

2. **Market capitalization-weighted index**: This type multiplies each company's share price by the number of shares they have, then adds these numbers together.

   Both types use divisors to make their final numbers easier to track.

The Dow Divisor: A Real-World Example

The Dow Jones Industrial Average (DJIA) is a famous stock market index that uses a divisor. Here's how it works:

1. Add up the prices of all 30 stocks in the DJIA.

2. Divide this sum by the Dow Divisor.

3. The result is the DJIA's current value.

Index divisors help us:

1. *Easily track stock market changes*

2. *Compare today's market to the past*

3. *Understand how individual stocks affect the whole market*

4. *When looking at an index, it is more important to track the gains and losses of the index than the actual number over a period of time.*

*There are many indexes that track the performance of stocks not only in the United States but around the world such as the FTSE 100 for the United Kingdom and the Nikkei 225 for Japan. Here are a few others....

The Wilshire 5000 Index

The Wilshire 5000 is a vast list of stocks. It includes almost all the stocks you can buy in the United States.

Even though it's called the Wilshire 5000, it doesn't always have precisely 5000 stocks. Sometimes, it has more, sometimes less. It tries to include all the stocks it can.

The Wilshire 5000 gives us a good idea of the performance of all American stocks. It's like taking the temperature of the whole U.S. stock market!

The Russell 3000 Index

The Russell 3000 is an extensive list of American companies. It includes the 3,000 largest companies in the United States, which covers almost all (about 96%) of the companies that people can invest in on the U.S. stock market.

- *It started on January 1, 1984*
- *It's updated once a year in June*
- *It includes companies from many different areas, like technology, healthcare, and finance*

The Russell 3000 helps people understand how well American companies are doing overall. It's like a report card for the U.S. stock market!

The Russell 2000 Index

The Russell 2000 is a list of 2000 smaller companies' stocks.

The Russell 2000 helps us see how smaller companies are doing. Sometimes, smaller companies grow faster than big ones, so people like to watch this index.

The Russell 1000 Index

The Russell 1000 Index lists 1,000 big companies in the United States. It's like a report card that shows how well these companies are doing. Investors use this list to help them make decisions.

- It includes the top 1,000 most prominent companies in America

- These companies make up about 93% of all the money in the U.S. stock market

- The list is updated every year in June

Here are some of the big companies you might know that are on the Russell 1000 Index:

5. *Microsoft (they make computer software and video games)*

6. *Apple (they make iPhones and iPads)*

7. *Amazon (where you can buy lots of things online)*

8. *Google (where you search for information on the internet)*

The Russell 1000 Index helps people understand how well big companies in America are doing. When these companies do well, it often means the economy is doing well, too. It's like taking the temperature of the business world!

A stock index is a way to measure how a group of stocks is performing. It's like taking the temperature of the stock market. Stock indexes look at many different stocks and combine their prices into one number. This number goes up when the stocks are doing well and down when they're not doing so well.

Example:

Imagine you have a fruit basket with five apples, three oranges, and two bananas. If you wanted to know how your "fruit index" was doing, you might:

1. Check the price of each fruit

2. Add up all the prices

3. Divide by the total number of fruits

This would give you an average price for your fruit basket. Stock indexes work similarly but with stocks instead of fruit!

Stock indexes help people understand the economy's performance. They also allow investors to compare their investments' performance to the overall market.

Chapter 5.4: Dow Jones & Company

Who founded the Dow Jones?

Charles Dow, Edwards Jones, and Charles Bergstresser founded Jones and Company. They went on to find The Wall Street Journal in 1889, which remains one of the world's most influential financial publications today.

Charles Dow was well-known for his ability to convey difficult financial information to the general public. He said that investors needed a simple indicator to tell whether the stock market was rising or declining.

What Is Dow Jones?

Dow Jones & Company, not the persons, is the firm founded in 1882 by Charles Dow, Edward Jones, and Charles Bergstresser.

The Dow Jones Industrial Average (DJIA)

The Dow Jones Industrial Average is the second-oldest market index in the United States, after only the Dow Jones Transportation Average (DJTA). The DJIA was designed to serve as an indicator of the overall health of the US economy. The DJIA, sometimes known as "the Dow," is one of the most highly followed stock market indices in the world. While the Dow has a varied range of companies, all are blue-chip organizations with consistently strong profitability.

The index included just 12 businesses when it originally appeared in 1896. The majority of these companies were in the industrial sector, such as railroads, cotton, gas, sugar, tobacco, and oil.

Early on, the performance of the Dow was linked to the health of the American Economy. This strengthened the connection between the Dow's performance and the overall economy. Even now, many investors assume that a high Dow implies a healthy economy (while a weak-performing Dow indicates a slowing economy). There are currently 30 blue chip companies(companies with great reputations) in the Dow Jones Index, and stocks are weighted by their share price. The higher the share price, the higher the weight or impact in the index.

Chapter 5.5: The S&P 500

The Standard & Poor's 500 Index, sometimes known as the S&P 500 Index, is a market capitalization-weighted index of 500 of the biggest publicly traded companies in the United States. The S&P 500 index is widely regarded as one of the most accurate predictors of the performance of large American stocks, and of the stock market as a whole.

S&P 500 Weighting Formula and Calculation

Because the S&P 500 is a capitalization-weighted index, companies with the highest market capitalizations receive a higher percentage allocation. Market Cap simply is the total value of the company. The market capitalization or market cap is basically the price you would have to pay in cash to purchase all the shares of the company. If a company has a market cap of $1 trillion, that means it would cost you $1 trillion dollars to purchase all of its shares.

*Company Weighting in S & P = Company market cap /
Total of all market caps*

The market capitalization of a company is calculated by multiplying the current stock price by the number of outstanding shares. The total market capitalization of the S&P 500, as well as individual business market capitalizations, are frequently provided on financial websites. This helps you as an investor save time from doing a lot of math.

S&P 500 Index Construction

The S&P only considers free-floating shares (shares that may be exchanged by the general public) when calculating market cap. To account for new shares, the S&P updates each company's market capitalization.

When the price of a stock rises or falls, we can evaluate if it will have an impact on the larger index. A company with a 10% weighting, for example, will have a greater effect on the index's value than a company with a 2% weighting.

The S&P 500 is one of the most impactful American indexes since it represents the largest publicly traded companies in the United

States. The S&P 500 index generally focuses on the largest publicly traded companies in the U.S. It is also a float-weighted index (a type of capitalization weighting), which means that the market capitalizations of companies are modified by the number of shares available for public trading.

Chapter 5.6: The Nasdaq

History of the Nasdaq Composite

The term "Nasdaq" is used to refer to the Nasdaq Composite, an index of over 3,000 companies. Nasdaq-listed equities include some of the world's most powerful technology and biotech businesses, including Apple, Alphabet (Google), Microsoft, Meta (formerly Facebook), Amazon, and Intel. Like the S&P 500, the Nasdaq composite is also market cap weighted. Currently technology is almost half of the index by weighting. However, the healthcare industry has the most companies represented.

The Nasdaq 100 Index, which was launched in 1985 only tracks the largest 100 companies that trade on the Nasdaq exchange.

Nasdaq stands for National Association of Securities Dealers Automated Quotations(Nasdaq) and was established in 1971.

The Nasdaq Trading Platform

The Nasdaq is also a global electronic exchange for the purchase and sale of stocks. The Nasdaq's electronic trading platform has become the industry standard for markets globally due to the rapid growth of technology. Since it is an electronic exchange, the Nasdaq does not have a physical trading floor.

Since it is an electronic trading platform, many of the world's greatest technology companies were drawn to the Nasdaq. As the Nasdaq gained prominence in the 1980s and 1990s, it became associated with the technology sector of the stock market

The rise and fall of the Nasdaq Composite—a separate index from the Nasdaq trading platform—exemplifies the late 1990s technology and dot-com boom and recession. The index topped 1,000 for the first time in July 1995, according to the Corporate Finance Institute, and then surged in the years that followed, culminating at over 5,000 in March 2000. During the subsequent market crash, it dropped by more than 80% by October 2002(this would have been a great time to buy into the Nasdaq; margin of safety).

In April 2000, the index fell to 3,227 before reaching a low of 1,108.49 in October 2002. The index slowly recovered after the catastrophe until the global financial crisis hit in 2007/2008(this was another great buying opportunity in the Nasdaq).

Chapter 5.7: Learn How To Start Trading

"The biggest risk of all is not taking one."- Mellody Hobson

Once you have started gaining a basic understanding of the stock market, you may want to start participating in the stock market. Buying and selling stocks is investing that is also known as trading.

1. **Open An Investment Account**

Open a stock brokerage account with a reputable online stock brokerage. Learn how to use your account interface and make use of the free trading instruments and research available only to customers. Vanguard, Schwab, Fidelity, Robinhood, and E-Trade are popular among new investors. Choose the one that works best for you.

2. **A Market Crash Course in Reading**

There is a multitude of information available on investing, much of it for free. Research anything market-related that may be of interest to you. However keep in mind that many things you read may be biased or may try to pull you in one direction or another. Consider all information, not just one before you make decisions about investing.

3. **Learn to Analyze**

Fundamental analysis(analyzing the basics of the company such as revenue, profit, cash flow) may provide a more direct path to profit since it examines growth curves and revenue streams, but technical analysis(those who trade daily using charts) live and die by daily market activity.

4. **Practice Trading**

Before you actually purchase stocks, you can practice with free virtual stock market simulators. This is known as paper trading, or virtual trading. This is a great way to get accustomed to investing in the stock market without the risk of losing money. You can google one or download an app by simply searching for a stock market simulator. Here are some Stock Market simulators according to ***wallstreetzen.com.***

eToro

Thinkorswim

Tradestation

NinjaTrader

Marketwatch

PilotTrading

Howthemarketworks.com

5. Other Methods for Learning and Practicing Trading

Experience is the best teacher. Being that you are new to investing however, you won't have much experience. Classes, whether online or in-person, may be helpful. Private tutoring on the stock market and investing is an option also. Seminars led by an active investor can be very helpful as they will allow you to ask questions directly to someone and interact with an actual person.

Since you are new to buying and selling stocks in a brokerage account, it is important to understand the different types of orders you can make in your account when buying or selling shares.

A market order- simply buys (or sells) shares immediately at the current price. It is the easiest trade to make.

A limit order- buys or sells shares at a certain price that you choose, but it is not guaranteed the order will trade if the limit is set too high or low. If you set a limit order to buy a stock at $5, the purchase will buy shares only at $5 or less.

Stop orders- a type of market order, are triggered when a stock moves above or below a certain level. They can lock in your profit or limit your losses.

Good 'Til Canceled (GTC)- This is an order that you can place that lasts until it is completed or until you cancel it. Your brokerage firm may limit how long you can keep a GTC open in your account.

Day orders- Orders that will only be filled by the end of the trading day. If not filled, you will have to replace the order the next trading day.

There are other orders as well, but they are for more experienced investors. You can learn more about those once you have a better understanding of buying and selling stocks. The orders above are pretty simple

Once you are ready to begin the process of purchasing stocks, it is important that you have a basic understanding of reading stock tables, which will give you basic information on the stock that you may purchase.

How to Read A Stock Table

1. Ticker Symbol: *A short abbreviation for the company's name and is used to identify the stock. For example, "AAPL" represents Apple Inc.*

2. Company Name: *The name of the company whose stock is listed.*

3. Last Price/Close Price: *The most recent price at which the stock was traded.*

4. Change: *The difference between the last price and the previous day's closing price. A positive number indicates a price increase, while a negative number indicates a decrease.*

5. % Change: *The percentage change in the stock's price compared to the previous day's closing price.*

6. Volume: *The number of shares traded during a trading day.*

7. Open: *The price at which the stock opened for trading on the current day.*

8. High: *The highest price the stock reached during the current trading day.*

9. Low: *The lowest price the stock reached during the current trading day.*

10. 52-Week High/Low: *The highest and lowest prices the stock has reached over the past 52 weeks.*

11. Market Cap: *The total market value of the company's outstanding shares of stock. It's calculated by multiplying the current stock price by the total number of outstanding shares.*

12. P/E Ratio (Price-to-Earnings Ratio): *This ratio reflects the price of the stock relative to the company's earnings per share (EPS) over the last 12 months. It's a measure of how much investors are willing to pay for each dollar of earnings.*

13. Dividend: *A dividend is when a public company decides to pay a portion of its profits to stockholders. It is expressed as a dollar amount.*

14. Dividend Yield: *If the company pays dividends to shareholders, this percentage indicates the annual dividend payment as a percentage of the stock's current price. Be careful investing in stocks, mutual funds or etfs with high dividend yields. Just because the yield is high does not mean it is a good investment. The return on the asset could be very low and a lot of high yielding assets are extremely risky. Always do your research and use your brokerage account to compare stocks and funds that pay dividends. There are plenty of resources available to do the proper research.*

15. EPS (Earnings Per Share): *The company's earnings divided by the total number of outstanding shares. It represents the portion of earnings allocated to each share of stock.*

16. Beta: *A measure of the stock's volatility compared to the overall market. A beta above 1 indicates greater volatility, while a beta below 1 suggests lower volatility.*

17. 52-Week Range: *The range of prices the stock has traded at over the past 52 weeks.*

These are the most common elements you'll find in a stock table.

CHAPTER 5:
STOCK MARKET INVESTING

Quiz No: 5

Serial No	Question	Answer
1.	Why would a company need to issue stock? A. To increase its customer base. B. To raise money. C. To stop the government from regulating it. D. To show customers that it's successful.	
2.	A professional that makes stock trades for their investor: A. Dividend B. Asset C. Stockbroker D. Stockholder	
3.	Owning a share of a company also means you own... A. Bond B. Stock C. Interest D. I.O.U.	

4.	The S&P 500, Nasdaq, and the Dow are all examples of market _____ which track stocks. A. indexes B. supers C. prices D. networks	
5.	What is the stock market? A. A type of farmers market where people buy and sell food. B. A special type of grocery store that sells stocks. C. A place where shares of businesses are bought and sold. D. A type of bank that gives out loans to new businesses.	
6.	The Dow Jones Industrial Average currently tracks the performance of how many companies? A. 500 B. 30 C. 2 D. 5	
7.	The name for a part of a business that is bought and sold on the stock market is: A. Part B. Marker C. Stocker D. Share	

8.	The Nasdaq composite has grown popular because it's commonly accepted as an indicator of popular _____ stocks in a digital age. A. agricultural B. technology C. industrial D. auto	
9.	How can you make money in the stock market? A. Buy low and sell high B. Earn dividends C. All of the above	
10.	The Stock Market allows people to have a _____ in attempting to make money in our capitalist system. A. no risk B. healthy risk C. huge risk D. bank loan	

Key

1. B

2. C

3. B

4. A

5. C

6. B

7. D

8. B

9. C

10. B

CHAPTER
SIX

OTHER TYPES OF INVESTMENTS

Chapter 6.1: Bonds

"Never depend on a single income. Make investments to create a second source."- Warren Buffet

A bond is a fixed-income product that reflects a loan from an investor to a borrower (typically corporate or government). Consider it as an I.O.U. between the lender and borrower which includes the loan information and payments. Companies, municipalities, states, and governments use bonds to finance projects and operations. Bondholders are the debtholders or creditors of the issuer.

Bond specifics typically contain the end date when the loan's principal is scheduled to be paid(maturity date) to the bond owner as well as the terms for interest payments made by the borrower.

Bonds are often used to borrow money for governments (at all levels) and businesses. Governments must build roads, schools, dams, and other infrastructure. The unexpected cost of war may also create a situation where governments need to issue bonds.

Companies will frequently borrow to grow the business. Companies can only borrow so much money from a bank, and may need more than just shareholders to raise capital so they may issue corporate bonds to borrow money from individual investors.

Bonds allow individual investors to act as lenders. Bond markets allow lenders to sell bonds to other investors or purchase bonds from other people.

How Bonds Work

Bonds are extremely popular for investors, alongside stocks (equities) and cash equivalents. They are popular because they can provide a fixed rate of income, with very little risk. Overtime, stocks outperform bonds as an investment, however many investors like to have a mix of the two. When the stock market is performing poorly, or interest rates in America rise, bonds become a better option as an investment for many people. Also, people with tremendous wealth may invest primarily in bonds as they do not want to risk their wealth in the stock market which can be volatile. They would rather buy bonds which are much safer and can provide a steady stream of passive income with little worry.

When a company or a government needs to raise funds, it may offer bonds to investors directly. The borrower (issuer) issues a bond that specifies the loan conditions, interest payments, and the time frame for repaying the lent cash (bond principal) (maturity date). The interest payment (the coupon) is the return that bondholders get for lending cash to the issuer. The coupon rate is the interest rate that affects the payment.

The face value of the bond is what the borrower will get when the bond matures(when the bond issuer must repay the original bond value to the bondholder aka the lender).

After they are issued, most bonds can be sold to other investors by the originating bondholder. A bond investor is not required to retain a bond until its maturity date(the date you get your money back). Bonds are also commonly repurchased by the borrower if interest rates fall or if the borrower's credit improves and it may issue new bonds at a cheaper cost. The interest received on a typical bond is subject to federal income taxes.

Categories of Bonds

There are different categories of bonds. These are the most popular types:

Corporate Bonds- *Corporations may issue bonds rather than get a loan from the bank because the interest rate on the bond may be cheaper*

Municipal Bonds- *A bond that is issued by a local government, city or the state to fund local projects such as building roads or schools. In many cases the interest received is tax exempt from federal and state/local taxes.*

Government Bonds/Treasury Bonds- *Bonds issued by the United States Treasury. There are 3 main categories:*

T BillsT Bills have a maturity date of one year or less(minimum purchase of $100)

Treasury NotesTreasury notes have a maturity date of 2,3,5,7 or 10 years(minimum purchase of $100)

Treasury BondsTreasury Bonds have a maturity date of 20 or 30 years(minimum purchase of $100)

Where To Buy Bonds

Stocks are traded on a centralized market, which means that all deals are routed to a single exchange and are purchased and sold at the same price. Bonds, unlike stocks, are not openly traded on an exchange. Bonds, on the other hand, are traded over the counter, which means you may purchase them through brokers and you may purchase through your brokerage account. You may, however, purchase US Treasury bonds directly from the government(treasurydirect.gov). You must create an account to purchase from the government website. Investors purchase bonds at auctions where they bid on the bond they would like to purchase. There are two types of bid. A non-competitive bid is where an investor agrees to accept the rate and yield of the bond that is determined at the auction. If you purchase bonds directly from the treasurydircet.gov website, you must bid non-competitively. To bid competitively, you must do this through your brokerage account. A competitive bid is where you as the investor specify the rate and yield that you will accept to purchase a specific bond. The auction date for the bond, and the issue date of the bond(the day you will receive it) are different dates. If you purchase bonds through treasurydirect.gov, the bonds will be deposited into your treasury direct account. If you purchase through your brokerage, the brokerage will get the bonds for you and deposit it into your brokerage account. This information and more can be found on the treasurydirect.gov website.

*Bonds and notes pay interest every 6 months

*T Bills are sold at a discount to par value(face value). When they mature, you get the full value

*Treasury Inflation-Protected Securities(TIPS) are treasury bonds where the principal goes up or down based on inflation. The interest rate is fixed, but the amount of interest you receive every 6 months may vary.

*I Series bonds protect you from inflation as you get a rate that changes twice a year, which sets the interest rate for the next 6 months.

*Bond yields are expressed as an annual percentage.

When investing in any bond, check the ratings of the issuer of the bond. Some bonds are rated by agencies such as Moody's, Standard and Poor's and Fitch. The strongest ratings are rated AAA. As a bond rating goes down in grade, the risk of investing in that bond increases. The lowest rated bonds pay higher interest to entice investors, however you may not get your money back. Low rated bonds are known as Junk Bonds.

You can also purchase a bond fund through your brokerage which can make your life easier such as ILTB(iShares), BND, BSV and BNDX(Vanguard). There are several others. You can locate them by doing a search online or through your brokerage. They provide more diversification however the returns may be lower than purchasing an actual bond yourself.

You can find tons more information on treasurydirect.gov. Do your research

Many people consider treasury bonds to be a no risk investment because the likelihood of the U.S. government collapsing or not paying back the loan is non-existent. However all investments do carry a level of risk. The risk of bonds is the opportunity cost. If you put cash into a US treasury and get a 5% yield for example, you could be for going a chance at a 10% yield somewhere else. Yes the 5% is guaranteed and lower risk than the investment yielding 10%, but the risk is the possible 5% difference you could have made. That is the risk. Also remember, if interest rates fall, the value of your bond increases. If interest rates rise, the value of your bond decreases.

Chapter 6.2: Real Estate

"The best investment on earth is earth."- Louis Glickman

The term "real estate" refers to the land as well as any permanent buildings, such as a house, or improvements related to the property, whether natural or man-made.

Real estate is a type of property. Personal property, such as automobiles, boats, jewels, furniture, and farm equipment, is not permanently tied to the land.

Real estate includes the land as well as any permanent man-made additions, such as houses and other structures. An improvement is defined as any additions or alterations to the land that impact the property's value.

Types of Real Estate

Residential- *A property used for residency/living purposes on a singular scale such as a single family home, townhouse or condominium*

Commercial- *Hotels, office buildings, large apartment complexes, shopping malls*

Industrial- *Properties used for industry such as a factory, or for manufacturing, or storage*

Land- *Agricultural land, or land that is simply undeveloped or not being used*

Special Purpose- *Parks, Schools, Churches, Theaters*

When investing in real estate there are also different class types. There are A, B, C and D classes. The class type is determined by the age of the property, its location, the type of tenant it will attract, condition and crime statistics of the area for example. When looking to purchase a rental property, it is good to know which class the potential property falls into:

Class A Real Estate: Newer properties(10 years or younger) that are in great condition and in fantastic/high desirable neighborhoods. They will generate high rent as well. A con of Class A real estate is they are extremely expensive to purchase, and due to the high rent may cut out many potential renters which could increase vacancy rates.

Class B Real Estate: Properties that are over 10 years old(10-40 years old) that are in good neighborhoods. They will be attractive to many potential renters. They are in very good condition and may require minor rehab. They are easier to purchase than Class A real estate. A con of Class B Real Estate is it may need more repairs than Class A and the property may not appreciate in value as much either.

Class C Real Estate: Properties that are older than both class A and B, and are generally smaller and in less desirable neighborhoods. The condition of the home may not be great and may require a lot of rehab(however this may increase the value of the property overtime). You may be able to purchase the property at a discounted price. Many real estate investors prefer Class C properties because they are cheaper to purchase and with rehab, they can add value quickly. Adding value to a property through rehab can be looked at as **sweatquity(increasing value in a property through sweat and labor).** Also, you may get help from local jurisdictions if you purchase these properties as rentals due to the fact that you will be providing affordable housing in the area which is always needed. A con of Class C properties is that the tenants may be less stable than in Class A or B. Also, you may have to deal with crime in the area which could hurt the chances of appreciation.

Class D Real Estate: Extremely old properties that are in need of full repair that are located in high crime and violent areas. These homes tend to be dilapidated. In fact, they may not even be up to code at the time of purchase. The rents will be extremely low. However they can be very cheap to purchase. Also, if you purchase a Class D property now in a high crime area, the area could change dramatically in the next 10-20 years. Buying the property cheap now and renovating it, will give you tremendous returns if the neighborhood is cleaned up in the future. Some real estate investors are attracted to this. However, nobody can accurately predict the future in investing consistently. Class D properties tend to have the highest cap rates(more on cap rate in a bit).

When looking for rental properties, there are other factors you may want to consider:

Are popular businesses(like a Starbucks or a Target) moving into the area or are already in the area? If they are, they may have done their research on the area and know something you don't

Is it close to a school?

Is it close to shopping and entertainment? Are restaurants in the area?

What is the neighborhood like at night?

If you are looking at a specific area to possibly purchase a rental property, make sure to do your research on the area. You may want an area with a high percentage of renters in relation to homeowners. You may also want to see the average income in the area, and possible businesses as well as other data. You can visit websites such as data.census.gov to gather information and data on the area you are interested in. You can also do searches online on the specific zip codes you are interested in as well. Always do your research.

Examples of Real Estate

Below are the most popular types of real estate investments for the average individual investor like yourself.

Single Family- *A free standing house built for a single family or an individual person. This is one of the easier and best forms of real estate to purchase*

Multi-Family- *A property that can hold multiple tenants*

Apartment- *A property in a multi-unit complex or building*

Townhouse- *A house with 2 or levels that is attached to a similar house by a shared wall*

Condominium(Condo)- *A property with separate units owned by individual people*

Mobile Home- *A moveable dwelling unit built on a chassis designed without a permanent foundation*

How to Invest in Real Estate

Rental properties, and house flipping(not suggested for beginners) are some of the most prevalent methods to invest in real estate.

Indirect real estate investing is done through a Real Estate Investment Trust (REIT), which is a company that owns a portfolio of income-producing real estate. REITs are categorized according to how their shares are acquired and sold, such as publicly-traded REITs, and private REITs.

The most common way to invest in a REIT is to purchase publicly listed shares on an exchange(just like a stock). REITs are liquid(easy to sell and get cash) and transparent since their shares trade like any other security traded on an exchange, like stocks. REITs generate income through dividend payments and share appreciation. Aside from individual REITs, investors can invest in real estate mutual funds and exchange-traded funds (ETFs).

Pros and Cons of owning Real Estate

Owning Real Estate is a great way to build wealth. Owning Real Estate provides a more passive form of income than a job, but not as passive as investing in a dividend paying stock simply because you must deal with tenants, repairs, insurance and other things. There are pros and cons to real estate, just like anything else.

Pros to owning Real Estate

When you think of the positives to owning a rental property, always remember the acronym **IDEAL** which stands for *Income, Depreciation, Equity, Appreciation and Leverage.*

Income- A rental property can provide you with income and cash flow.

Depreciation- The process of deducting the cost of buying and improving a rental property over time(wear and tear) that can be used for the purpose of taxes.

Equity- When the tenant pays rent, and you pay back the loan to the bank, you are building equity in the property with the money paid for rent by the tenant along with a rise in appreciation.

Appreciation- As you pay down the debt on the property using the proceeds from the rent, the rental property over time should increase in value adding to your wealth.

Leverage- You can use other people's money(the bank for example) to purchase the asset that can put cash flow in your pocket. This way, all of your own money isn't tied up in the deal.

Cons to owning Real Estate

Tenants

You must deal with someone living in your property. They may damage the property, and you are responsible legally to handle any repairs. They may contact you for the slightest reason and there is a chance they may not pay the rent. In certain states it may take a while to remove them. While they are not paying rent, you will still owe the bank money monthly on the mortgage. You must screen all tenants. A way to provide a buffer between you and the tenant is to hire a property manager, however you must pay them a percentage of the gross rent.

Over-Leverage

When you use the bank's money to purchase a rental property, you must pay back the mortgage. In many cases, landlords over leverage a property and do not give themselves enough margin of safety(I keep mentioning this for a reason). If you over leverage a property, and the tenant doesn't pay rent for 6 months, you must cover the cost. Not to mention if there is major damage to the property, you must cover this AND still pay back the bank.

Real Estate investing requires a lot of money

Even though you can leverage your investment in real estate, you still need money to make money. You will need a down payment, plus closing costs and money for repairs and to update the rental property. You also must pay property tax, insurance, mortgage payments and property maintenance.

Real Estate investing takes a lot of time

In the beginning, you will need to spend a lot of time learning and managing your real estate investment. You can hire a property manager to cut down on the time, however that will cost you and take away from your cash flow.

Real Estate investing is illiquid

Unlike stocks, real estate is not easily converted into cash when needed. If you are losing money on a real estate investment, you cannot just sell it in one day and cut your losses.

It can take months to sell a property and each month you will lose money in the process. This can be extremely stressful.

You may also have to drop the price of the property lower than its value to sell it faster.

In the chart below are 4 things to consider when analyzing a rental property:

• **INCOME**	• **CASH FLOW**
How much income is the property generating from Renting	Rental income minus expenses is the cash flow you will generate from owning the property
• **EXPENSES**	• **CASH ON CASH YIELD**
How much is the rental property costing you	What is the percentage yield on the investment yearly on the cash you used of your own money to invest in the property? What is your average yield on the property over time?

When analyzing any investment, great investors like Warren Buffet suggest that the analysis should be simple. If the investment is a great investment, it should generally be easy to see. The more complicated the analysis of the investment becomes in order to see its value, the less likely it is a good investment and the more likely you are to make a mistake in your analysis or fail to give yourself a level of margin of safety.

Let's look at another chart this time filling in the boxes to do a simple calculation of cash on cash return on a single family home that you are buying for $200,000:

Example(Rental Property cost-$200,000; Taxes-$1,800/yr; Property Manager-10% of gross monthly rent; Insurance- $1,200/

yr; Down Payment-$40,000(20% of the purchase price); Loan Amount- $160,000; Interest Rate- 5% FIXED(Never do an adjustable rate loan); Incidentals(Vacancy/Repairs)- $3,600/yr. (You may also want to consider getting a home warranty for your rental that covers things like appliances, leaks, plumbing etc. through a home warranty company. This can also be added as a monthly expense if you so choose. Some investors choose to get a home warranty, and others don't. It is up to you. If you plan to get one, then add that expense as well).

These are general assumptions to give you an idea. Of course there are many factors that determine these numbers. Also there may be other small expenses to consider such as a water or garbage pick up bill to factor in. This is just to give you a general idea of expenses. This is based on a 30 year fixed rate loan from a reputable lender or bank. Typically, in order to borrow money for an investment property, the requirements are much stricter than buying a property you plan to live in. Banks generally want at least 20% down, a high credit rating, and will go through all of your financials/assets thoroughly. You will want your debt to income ratio as low as possible. They will also usually charge you a 1% higher interest rate than the going rate for a personal home loan mortgage(called prime plus 1) because this is an investment property and carries a higher level of risk. Use an online mortgage calculator such as mortgagecalculator.org to plug in numbers to get an idea

• REVENUE	• CASH FLOW
RENTAL INCOME- $2000	$2,000-$1,710 = $290(A MONTH)
$2,000 A MONTH	$290 A MONTH X 12 = $3480 A YEAR

• EXPENSES	• CASH ON CASH YIELD
TAX= $150	DOWN PAYMENT- $40,000
INSURANCE-$100	CLOSING COSTS- $7,000
VACANCY-$100	REHAB- $3,000
REPAIRS-$200	$50,000 CASH INVESTED
PROPERTY MANAGEMENT-$200	**$3480 / $50,000 = 6.96%**
MORTGAGE-$860	
HOA(Homeowners Association)-$100	
*HOA fees are common in condos, townhomes and certain communities for maintenance and upkeep. If you purchase one of these homes, this will also be an expense.	
$1,710 A MONTH	

WHAT IS MY ANNUAL YIELD ON INVESTMENT?

$390(CASH FLOW) X 12(MONTHS) =$3,480

$3,480(YEARLY CASH FLOW) / $50,000(CASH INVESTED) =

6.96% YEARLY YIELD ON YOUR INVESTMENT.

IS THIS A HIGH ENOUGH YIELD FOR YOU TO INVEST IN THIS RENTAL PROPERTY? COULD YOU GET A HIGHER YIELD IN ANOTHER INVESTMENT? THAT IS UP TO YOU TO DECIDE.

Know the difference between a yield and a return:

Yield- The income the property generates over a year, shown as a percentage

Return- Money that is gained or lost averaged overtime in an investment in dollar amounts

Yield is important when analyzing rentals for income in a year

Return is important when analyzing a property for appreciation and income over time

*AS ALWAYS WITH ANY INVESTMENT, ANNUAL YIELDS AND RETURNS CAN ALWAYS CHANGE.

*Many real estate investors believe that if the interest rate on your mortgage is higher than the annual yield on your investment, you should not invest in that property. Again, do what is best for you.

* You may add 1% a year in appreciation to the return. Homes typically appreciate more than 1% a year but you may want to use a worse case scenario in your calculations. Any major repairs during the life of ownership of the property will cut into your return.

Keep in mind there are several other factors to consider when looking at a rental property, such as its location, if businesses are investing in the area, is it a high rent area, crime, etc. You will also of course want to have a home inspection done to the home. These are just basic things to look at when thinking about buying real estate

Criteria to Analyze a Rental Property

There are many ways to analyze Real Estate or a rental property. Single family homes are one of the easiest forms of real estate to invest in, and the following criteria are useful not only in analyzing a rental property, but also providing yourself with margin of safety. The criteria include:

Net Operating Income

Cap Rate

Cash on Cash Yield

Gross Rent Multiplier

1% Rule/2% Rule

Mortgage to Cash Flow Ratio

NET OPERATING INCOME(NOI)

Net operating income is the revenue generated by the property minus all the expenses **except** mortgage payments and interest. It includes all expenses to run or operate the property monthly, such as property management, property taxes, repairs, and any other expenses necessary to maintain the physical property. *NOI excludes* *mortgage principal payments, mortgage interest, and capital expenditures.*

Using the rental property from earlier, the revenue generated on the property yearly is $24,000($2,000 a month x 12). The yearly expenses, not including the mortgage, interest, and capital expenditures, are $10,200($850 a month x 12. The $860 mortgage is subtracted).

$24,000 - $10,200 = $13,800 a year in Net Operating Income(NOI)

Remember, NOI excludes: Mortgage principal payments, mortgage interest, and capital expenditures(upgrades you make to the property)

Net Operating Income vs. Net Income

Net Operating Income is revenue minus operating expenses (excludes mortgage payments, interest and capital expenditures)

Net Income is revenue minus ALL expenses

CAP RATE

Cap rate is short for Capitalization rate. It is the yield of a property over 1 year(the amount the investment earns over the course of a year, expressed as a percentage).

It is calculated using this formula: **Yearly Rent-Expenses(Net Operating Income)/Property value**

For example: If you purchase a property for $1,000,000, and the Net Operating Income a year is $100,000, then the cap rate is 10%

An easy way to look at Cap Rate is what is the yield on the property if you paid for it fully in cash including all costs such as renovations?(you will still have expenses, but no mortgage or interest payments).

Typically the higher the cap rate, the greater the risk, AND return. A high cap rate may indicate you are investing in a riskier area, or prices in the area are dropping

CASH ON CASH YIELD

Cash on cash yield simply measures the amount of cash flow you receive yearly in relation to the amount of cash you have invested in the deal

With the Cap Rate, the assumption is you paid all cash; In cash on cash however, you put a down payment on the property, and borrowed the rest of the money to purchase. *Your down payment, closing costs, rehab, and any other money you used to purchase the property is the actual cash you have in the investment.*

It is calculated by taking your annual cash flow(rent-expenses) then dividing it by the amount of money you actually used to purchase the property.

Referring to the home on the previous chart for $200,000 as an example, the annual cash flow was $4,680. The actual cash invested in the property(down payment, rehab, and closing costs) was $50,000.

$3,480/$50,000= 6.96% cash on cash return.

The higher the cash on cash yield, the more margin of safety you generally will have, and typically the better the investment, as a rule of thumb

GROSS RENT MULTIPLIER(GRM)

The Gross Rent Multiplier is simply the purchase price of a real estate investment vs the annual gross rent of the property(before expenses)

To calculate, you take the purchase price of the property, and divide it by the gross rental income.

Using the chart from the previous page, the purchase price of the property was $200,000. The gross rent annually($2000 per month x 12) is $24,000 a year

$200,000/$24,000 = 8.3 Gross Rent Multiplier.

*To interpret this number, the Gross Rent Multiplier tells you how many years it would take you to fully pay off this property with no money down just using the gross rental income. In this instance, it

186 | INVESTING Is the Best Thing

would take you approximately 8.3 years to pay $200,000 for the property just using the gross annual rent with no expenses.*

Typically, the lower the Gross Rent Multiplier, the better the investment and the higher the margin of safety. It means paying off the property generally should be easier the lower the number. It can be used to compare two different homes.

The GRM can also be used to compare different rental markets. If you were comparing similar style homes in 2 different cities, you may want to compare the GRM of both. The city with the lower GRM may be a better investment, but make sure to do your research.

1% RULE/2% RULE

The 1% Rule is simply a relation of the monthly rent received vs the purchase price of the rental property. The closer to 1% or above, generally the better, and the higher margin of safety.

It is calculated by taking the purchase price of the property, and dividing it by the monthly rent

If you buy a property for $100,000, and the rent you can receive monthly is $1000, then this would satisfy the 1% rule.

Using the previous chart, the home purchase price was $200,000, and the rent was $2000 a month. One percent would be $2,000 so rent of $2,000 gives a good margin of safety on the property.

Remember this is just a rule to help you analyze a property. Just because the property does or does not meet this rule does not mean you should or should not buy the property. Due your due diligence.

*There is also the 2% rule, which works exactly like the 1% rule only with 2%. So for example, if you purchase a rental property for $200,000, the monthly rent should at least be $4,000 a month. Of course this would give you a higher margin of safety, but many investors say this is much less likely to happen when investing in real estate. Again, these are just basic rules and you must do what is best for you.

*Additionally, there is the 50% rule which says you should expect to spend at least 50% of your gross rental income on expenses like

the mortgage, interest, taxes, insurance, and maintenance. This is just a rule of thumb. Of course, you should expect it to be more.

MORTGAGE TO CASH FLOW RATIO

The mortgage to cash flow ratio simply tells you how close your monthly cash flow is to paying off the mortgage monthly.

Simply take the monthly mortgage and divide it by the monthly cash flow.

Using the previous chart, the monthly mortgage was $860.

The monthly cash flow was $290 a month.

$860 / $290 = 2.96- This signals that the mortgage is about 2.96 times the monthly cash flow.

*Simply, the lower the number, the better. If you have a monthly mortgage of $1000, and your monthly cash flow is $100:

$1000 / $100 = 10- The mortgage is 10 times the monthly cash flow

Which property do you think provides a higher MARGIN OF SAFETY?

These metrics are just general metrics to introduce you to investing in real estate. Please do your due diligence. If you analyze a property, and it meets the requirements you desire for all 5 metrics, it may still be a bad investment. If it only meets 2 of the 5 metrics, it does not mean it is a bad investment. Continue to learn about real estate as you grasp the basics.

Somethings to consider:

*ALWAYS have cash set aside for repairs and capital expenditures to your property. Capital expenditures are to replace things like the carpet or cabinets when tenants move in and out of your property. Things will go wrong that will require cash. The more cash you have set aside, the higher the margin of safety

*You always have the option to pay for a rental in full cash. This is the safest way to purchase real estate. The good part of paying cash is you don't owe any bank any money and it cash flows well. The bad part is, you are tying up all of your money in that one property, AND it will take a long time to save up enough money to purchase the property. Some investors suggest paying all cash. Others say never pay all cash and use someone else's money. I am not here to tell you what to do. Do what is best for you.

*Your cash flow and rental income should only be used to go back into the rental you own either for repairs, or capital expenditures and improvements OR to go towards another asset like another rental property for example. You shouldn't use your cash flow for the enjoyment of life if you have debt on the property. Once the property is paid off in full, then you may use the cash flow for whatever you see fit, but until then, it is highly suggested that the rental income you receive is put aside for your current rental or a future rental.

*You are required to file taxes on your rental income. Many people forget this. It would be wise to put about 20% of your rental income away for tax purposes, however it does not mean you will actually have to pay it. When owning a rental property you will have many tax deductions that you will be able to apply.

Rental Income includes:

Rents

> *Fees associated with rent*
>
> *Security deposits*
>
> *Advance rent payments(1st and last month's rent)*
>
> *Lease termination payments*

Rental Property Tax Deductions includes:

Property management expenses

> *Maintenance costs*
>
> *Property taxes*
>
> *Advertising(trying to find a tenant)*
>
> *Insurance*
>
> *Homeowners Association fees(HOA fees)*
>
> *Travel expenses associated with your rental property*

Don't forget property depreciation(which also helps raise your total return on your investment)

There may be others as well. In the end, you may not owe any money in taxes on your rental property, but it would be wise to set aside some of your rental income for tax purposes. It cannot be stressed enough to hire an accountant or tax professional who specializes in real estate tax. They will be able to help you the most.

You can introduce a young child to real estate investing early. If you buy your child a doll house with Barbies for example, explain to the child that it is not a doll house but a rental property. Your child owns a doll house or rental property and the barbies are the tenants. On the 1st of each month, give the child $1 in rent from the Barbies. You are the property manager. This can help introduce a young child to the idea of cash flow. If part of the dollhouse breaks, take $.25 away for repairs. As the child sees the influx of cash monthly without doing a major chore for it, it should excite them. Explain to them as they get more money for not doing much, the next best thing is to buy another doll house acquiring more assets to add to their wealth. You then proceed to give them $1 for each "rental property". If you have a house full of doll houses, sure you may run out of space, but it signals your child is getting the concept. These are ways to creatively teach your young child how to build wealth over time.

RENTAL TERMS TO KNOW: Familiarize yourself with these terms if you are interested in purchasing a rental property:

Cash Flow- *The amount of money you keep each month after ALL expenses have been paid.*

1031 Exchange- *Selling a property and buying another one of equal or greater value which allows you to delay taxes on any capital gains on the property.*

Capital Expenditures- *Money spent on a property for improvements or renovations.*

HOA Fees- *Homeowners Association Fees that are paid for the maintenance or upkeep in a community(for example, a condo association).*

Appreciation- *An increase in the value of the property.*

Fixed Rate Mortgage- *A mortgage with an interest rate that is locked in for the duration of the loan.* ***NEVER TAKE AN ADJUSTABLE RATE MORTGAGE.***

Equity- *The difference between the value of the property and what you owe(when the property appreciates, and you pay down the loan, you gain more equity).*

Turnkey Property- *A property that is ready to live in immediately with little to no renovations.*

Capital Gains Tax- *A tax on the appreciation of a property when it is sold.*

Debt to Equity Ratio- *A ratio of how much of the property you own if you took out a loan from the bank. To calculate, the formula is: Mortgage loan balance/Equity = Debt-to-equity ratio.*

If you purchase a house for $200,000 and make a down payment of $40,000, you have $160,000 in debt and $40,000 in equity. $160,000/$40,000= ***4.*** *This means for every $1 you own in the property, you owe the bank $4. You can calculate this on your own or find a debt to equity calculator online to do it for you. The lower the ratio, the better.*

Escrow- *Something of value held by a separate party during a real estate transaction.*

Closing Costs- *Fees paid at the completion of a real estate transaction(usually about 2-5% of the loan amount or purchase price of the property you are buying).*

Internal Rate of Return(IRR)- *A long term measurement of the return of your property based on cash flow and equity.*

Inspection Contingency- *Allows the buyer to have an inspection of the property before buying. It is highly recommended to have a home inspection before agreeing to purchase a property.*

FSBO- *For Sale By Owner- A property sold straight from the buyer with no real estate agents involved.*

Formal Dining Room(FDR)- *Signals that a property has a dining room.*

Comparative Market Analysis(CMA)- Shows the activity of the real estate market in a specific area over a specific period of time.

P.I.T.I- Principal, Interest, Taxes, Insurance. The main expenses of owning a rental property. Your principal and interest payment won't increase. However, as an investor, you should always expect your property taxes and insurance costs to rise over time, especially if your home appreciates in value. **If your taxes and insurance Increase, but you have to decrease your rents for any reason this will hurt your return. Factor this in when analyzing your investment property. Remember, you always want to invest with a level of Margin of Safety!**

Fair Market Value(FMV)- A fair or reasonable price to pay for a property.

Loan To Value(LTV)- A percentage that measures debt to the value of the property. Take the amount owed divided by the property value.

The higher the percentage, the more likely you are to be over-leveraged.

Rent To Own(RTO)- A rental lease agreement with the option to purchase the property at a specified date. You rent the property, pay a certain amount of rent with a portion of that payment going towards renting, and the other portion going towards the purchase of the property.

Gross Rental Income(GRI)- All of the money collected monthly associated with renting the property out to a tenant.

HVAC System- Stands for Heating, Ventilating, and Air Conditioning systems.

Foreclosure- When a borrower fails to pay back the mortgage, and the lender(bank for example) takes back the house and looks to resell it. Many real estate investors look for foreclosed properties.

Short Sale- A short sale is when the seller of a property makes an agreement with their lender to sell the property for less than they owe. Being that the seller is in financial distress, an investor may get a good deal when buying the property.

ALWAYS REMEMBER

*Real estate investing takes time to learn. It is not as easy as this presentation makes it look. You should talk to successful real estate investors and learn as much as you can.

*Location of the property is extremely important. You want to buy a property in an area where people will want to live. Also, cities and states have different tenant/landlord laws. In some areas, it can be easy to remove a tenant who isn't paying rent in under 3 months. In other areas, it could take almost a year. Check the rental laws in the area you are looking for.

*Never assume what the rent will be. Do research. Check online using websites like zillow.com to get an idea of the rent in an area, and lowball it. Base your assumptions on the worst case scenario, this way if it is still a good investment, it will be a great investment in an actual scenario. You can also ask a reputable property manager. They should know the going rent for property types in certain areas. Typically, property managers charge 8-10% of the monthly rent, and make investing in real estate easier. However you must vet them well. Go over the contract thoroughly and ask plenty of questions.

*Price is important also(margin of safety). When it comes to investing in anything, you want to get the best price possible to maximize your investment returns.

*Never invest by yourself. You need a team of people to guide you. Your team should include at the very least: an accountant, a real estate lawyer, contractor/property management and a great real estate agent. You should be able to trust these people and should go to them with any questions you may have.

*A real estate agent will make it easier to find a property to look for and will help guide you. You can also do your own homework as well using websites such as mls, realtor.com, zillow.com etc.

*Banks aren't your only options for loans. There are other lenders, many of them private investors or companies who you may work with.

Hard money loana loan secured by real property. usually a loan that is given when a conventional bank loan is not an option.

Hard money loans raise money much quicker than through a bank, however the cost is much higher and it carries more risk. The loan must be paid back much quicker than with a conventional bank loan. also the interest rates are generally much higher. For new investors, this can be extremely risky.

*When looking to apply for a loan, keep your debt to income ratio as low as possible(DTI)

Debt to income ratio in simple terms compares how much money you owe to how much money you make

DTI ratio is calculated taking your monthly debts and dividing it by your gross monthly income

The lower the percentage, the better.

*A suggestion for a higher margin of safety would be to take your monthly debts and divide them by your net monthly income to calculate your DTI. Your net monthly income is what you actually take home. I may have a gross salary of a million dollars a year, but in the end if I only take home $100,000 a year that's all that really matters.

*Single family homes aren't your only option. You can buy a multi-family home. You can live in one unit, and rent the other. If you do that, you may be able to put down less than a 20% down payment since you will be living there. Also, multi-family homes may give better income streams. However, they are more expensive to purchase.

*Make sure you do your due diligence if you decide to pick a property manager. Look up their reviews online. Here are some questions you may want to ask before making a hire:

What are their qualifications?

What are the services they provide?

What percentage of the gross rent do they receive for their services?(8-10% is a normal range)

How many properties do they manage?

Will they go to court to represent you for any legal proceedings?

Do they understand local tenant/landlord laws?

How many times a year do they inspect the property?

When repairs are needed, will they be there to make sure things go as planned, and do they charge extra for this?

How do they find tenants? How long will it take to fill vacancies?

What is the minimal credit score they look for when looking for a tenant? Do they complete a criminal background check?

What is the process if you want to move on from their management services?

Who keeps any late fees associated with the collection of late rent?

How do you pay for repairs done on the property(money kept in an account, or taken directly from the next month's rental income?)

Do they prepare the necessary tax documents you will need at the end of the year?(1099 forms)

How do you receive your rental income, and by what date?

How long does it take to remove a tenant who is not paying rent?

*Read books on real estate investing. Listen to real estate podcasts. Go to real estate seminars or webinars. Talk to successful real estate investors. Learn the game as much as you can. ALWAYS DO YOUR OWN RESEARCH.

*Many real estate investors form a Limited Liability Company(LLC) and transfer ownership of their rental properties to the LLC. A Limited Liability Company is a business structure that provides protection for its owners from personal liability. You can create one by yourself, with a partner or with a group. Creating an LLC will have different requirements depending on the state with which you file. Ideally, you will want to create the LLC BEFORE you purchase the rental property. Once you purchase the property, you can transfer ownership from you personally to your LLC through what is called a Quitclaim Deed. You will have to notify your lender and insurance company of your intention to do this. Your real estate lawyer will be able to help you with all of this so please follow their guidance. It is also suggested that you open a

business account for your LLC and any financial dealings associated with your rental or LLC be done through this business account. This can help you with any potential tax write-offs. Keep receipts of all transactions associated with your LLC. The wealthy keep their business and personal transactions separate. You should as well. Benefits of owning your property in an LLC include:

1. Limited Liability Protection: *One of the main advantages of using an LLC is that it offers limited liability protection. This means that the personal assets of the LLC's owners (members) are generally protected from the liabilities and debts of the LLC. In the context of real estate, this protection can shield your personal assets from potential lawsuits related to the property.*

2. Separation of Assets: *Setting up an LLC allows you to keep your personal assets separate from your real estate investments. This separation can help protect your personal wealth in case of legal issues related to the property.*

3. Flexibility in Ownership: *An LLC can have multiple members, and ownership can be structured according to your preferences. This flexibility is especially useful for real estate investments involving multiple investors or partners.*

4. Tax Flexibility: *Depending on the structure you choose, an LLC can offer tax advantages. It can be taxed as a pass-through entity, where the profits and losses are passed on to the members and reported on their individual tax returns.*

5. Ease of Management: *Operating an LLC is generally less complex than other business structures, such as corporations. It involves fewer formalities and administrative requirements.*

6. State-Specific Laws: *LLC regulations vary by state, so it's important to understand the specific rules and requirements in your state when forming and operating an LLC.*

Consult with legal professionals before setting up an LLC for real estate ownership. An LLC may not be right for everyone so do your due diligence.

If you truly want to understand the importance of margin of safety when investing in real estate, just look at the impact of the Covid 19 pandemic in 2020 on landlords. Due to the economic disruptions and changes in rental demand caused by lockdowns,

job losses, and financial uncertainties, many real estate investors lost big in their investments as they did not factor in a level of margin of safety. Here are some ways in which landlords were affected:

1. **Rent Payment Challenges:** Many tenants faced financial difficulties due to job losses or reduced incomes, leading to challenges in paying rent on time. Landlords had to navigate negotiations, implement flexible payment plans, or face potential rental income reductions.

2. **Vacancy Rates:** Some landlords experienced increased vacancy rates as tenants relocated. This put pressure on rental income and made it harder to find new tenants.

3. **Legal and Regulatory Changes:** In response to the pandemic, some cities and states enacted temporary eviction moratoriums to protect tenants from being evicted due to non-payment of rent. This created legal problems and financial strains for landlords who still had to make mortgage payments to the banks.

4. **Maintenance and Repairs:** Lockdowns and health concerns made it challenging to conduct routine maintenance and repairs. Landlords had to balance ensuring tenant safety with keeping properties in good condition.

5. **Remote Management:** Social distancing measures made it harder for landlords to conduct in-person property visits, inspections, and tenant interactions, necessitating remote management solutions.

6. **Financial Strain:** Some landlords faced financial strain if they depended on rental income for their livelihood and experienced rent payment delays or reductions.

7. **Property Value Changes:** In certain markets, property values and rental rates fluctuated due to changing demand dynamics, impacting potential returns on investment properties.

8. **Adapting Lease Terms:** Landlords had to adapt lease terms to accommodate changing circumstances. These changes in lease terms hurt many landlords financially.

9. **Uncertain Market Conditions:** Uncertainty about the duration and severity of the pandemic made it challenging for landlords

to make long-term decisions about property investments and management strategies.

The Covid 19 pandemic was an unforeseen event that NOBODY could have seen or predicted. As an investor, you cannot predict the future. Nor should you try to. However you can prepare for the unforeseen. Those real estate investors who invested with high levels of margin of safety certainly had a rough time during the Covid 19 pandemic, however their investments were still solid. Those who did not, lost out on their investment in many cases. We do not know when the storms will come, but we can make sure our investments are built to withstand them. The Covid 19 pandemic is just an example of why margin of safety is so important with investing.

BRRRR Method in Real Estate Investing

The BRRRR method is a strategy used by real estate investors to grow their property portfolios. BRRRR stands for:

- Buy
- Rehab
- Rent
- Refinance
- Repeat

This method helps investors buy properties, fix them up, rent them out, and then use the increased value to buy more properties.

How Does the BRRRR Method Work?

1. **Buy**

The first step is to find a property that needs some work but has potential. This could be:

- A fixer-upper house
- A foreclosed property
- A house in a good location that needs updating

2. **Rehab**

After buying the property, you fix it up. This might include:

- Painting the walls

- Putting in new floors
- Updating the kitchen or bathrooms
- Fixing any major problems

The goal is to make the property nicer and more valuable.

3. **Rent**

Once the property looks good, you find tenants to live there and pay rent. As the landlord, you:

- Find good tenants
- Make sure they sign a lease
- Collect rent each month

4. **Refinance**

After the property is fixed up and rented out, it's usually worth more money. You can then get a new loan (refinance) based on this higher value. This lets you:

- Get some of your original investment back
- Possibly have extra money to invest in another property

5. **Repeat**

With the money from refinancing, you can start the process over with a new property!

Pros and Cons of the BRRRR Method

Pros:

1. Can help build wealth over time
2. Creates a source of regular income from rent
3. Allows you to improve properties and neighborhoods

Cons:

1. Requires a lot of money to start
2. Can be hard to find the right properties
3. There's always a risk the property might not increase in value
4. Being a landlord takes a lot of time and work

Example:

Let's say you buy a house for $100,000 that needs work. You spend $30,000 fixing it up. Now it's worth $150,000 and you can rent it out for $1,200 a month. When you refinance, you might be able to get most of your $130,000 back to use on another property, while still owning this one that gives you rent money each month.

Remember, real estate investing can be risky and complicated. It's important to learn a lot about it and possibly talk to experts before trying strategies like the BRRRR method.

Real Estate Crowdfunding

Real estate crowdfunding is a new way for many people to invest in buildings and land together. It's like if you and your friends put your money together to buy a car to share. But instead of a car, it's a building or piece of land.

How Does It Work?

1. A company finds a building or land they want to buy
2. They ask many people to give a little bit of money each
3. When they have enough money, they buy the building or land
4. If the building makes money (like from people paying rent), everyone who gave money gets a small share

Why Do People Like It?

*   You don't need a lot of money to join in
*   You can be part of buying big buildings even if you're not rich
*   It's a way to make your money grow over time

What Are Some Risks?

*   Sometimes, the building might not make as much money as people hoped
*   You can't get your money back right away if you need it
*   There are rules about who can invest and how much

Example

Let's say there's a big apartment building that costs $1,000,000. Instead of one person buying it, 1,000 people might each give $1,000. Then, they all own a tiny part of the building together.

More and more people are getting interested in real estate crowdfunding. In the future, it might be a common way for people to invest their money and help build new buildings in their cities.

Flipping Houses

What is House Flipping?

House flipping is when someone buys a house, fixes it, and sells it quickly to make money. It's like giving a home a makeover and then finding it a new family!

Important Things to Remember

1. **You Need Money**

Fixing up houses can cost a lot. You need money to:

- Buy the house
- Pay for materials to fix it
- Pay workers if you can't do all the work yourself

2. **It Takes Time**

Flipping a house isn't quick. You might spend:

- Weeks or months looking for the right house
- More time fixing it up
- Even more time trying to sell it

3. **You Need Skills**

If you know how to do things like:

- Paint walls
- Fix leaky pipes
- Put in new floors

Then you can save money by doing the work yourself. If not, you'll have to pay others to do it.

4. You Need to Know a Lot

To flip houses well, you should understand:

- Which houses are good to buy
- What fixes will make the house sell for more
- How much things cost
- What buyers want in a house

5. You Need to Be Patient

Flipping houses takes time. You can't rush it, or you might make mistakes. Sometimes, you might not make as much money as you hoped.

Pros and Cons of Flipping Houses

Flipping houses means buying, fixing, and selling them quickly for a profit. Let's look at some good and bad things about flipping houses.

Good Things (Pros)

1. You can make money faster

When you flip a house, you can often sell it and get your money back in about 6 months. This is much quicker than waiting years for a home to go up in value.

2. It can be safer than other investments

The housing market usually doesn't change as quickly as other investments like stocks. This makes flipping houses safer if you know what you're doing.

Not-So-Good Things (Cons)

1. It can cost a lot of money

Flipping houses can be expensive. You need money to:

- Buy the house
- Fix it up
- Pay taxes
- Pay for utilities while you own it

Sometimes, it's hard to have enough money for everything you need to do.

2. **You might have to pay more taxes**

If you sell a house less than a year after buying it, you might have to pay more taxes on the money you make than if you purchased a property and rented it out. This is because the government wants people to own houses for extended periods.

Did you know that, on average, it takes about 6 months to flip a house? Remember, flipping houses can be fun and rewarding but also a lot of work. Learning as much as possible before trying it yourself is essential.

Landlord-Friendly States in the United States*(Source- RealWealth. com)*

What Makes a State Landlord-Friendly?

Landlord-friendly states usually have:

1. Easy eviction process
2. No rent control
3. Low property taxes

Top 5 Most Landlord-Friendly States currently

1. North Carolina
    - No rent control
    - Can charge up to 1.5 times monthly rent for security deposit
    - Quick eviction process (about 45 days)
2. Texas
    - Fast eviction process (3-day notice for missed rent)
    - No rent control
    - No limits on security deposits
3. Florida
    - Quick evictions (2-3 weeks)
    - No rent control

- Low property taxes

4. Alabama

- Lowest property taxes in the U.S.
- No rent control
- Simple 7-day notice for evictions

5. Montana

- No rent control
- No caps on late fees
- Quick eviction process (3-day notice)

Top 5 Least Landlord-Friendly States currently

1. New York

- Strict rent control
- Long eviction process (3 months to a year)
- New laws make evictions very difficult

2. California

- Statewide rent control
- Many rules for evictions
- Strict safety requirements for landlords

3. Hawaii

- Strict rules for property maintenance
- Limits on security deposits
- Long notice periods for rent increases

4. Illinois

- New rules about rent payments
- Strict rules about security deposits
- Short time to make repairs

5. Oregon

- Rent control for older properties
- Rules about helping tenants move
- Strict laws about keeping properties safe

States with High Eviction Rates

1. Virginia
2. Delaware
3. Indiana
4. Texas
5. South Carolina

Remember, being landlord-friendly isn't the only thing to consider when buying property. It's also essential to look at other things, like how many people want to live there and the local rules. Along with landlord-friendly states, make sure to monitor landlord-friendly towns and cities as well.

Chapter 6.3: Options Trading

"Amateurs think about how much money they can make. Professionals think about how much money they could lose."-
Jack Schwager

Options are contracts that provide the owner the right, but not the duty, to purchase or sell a certain quantity of an underlying asset at a specified price at or before the contract expires. One options contract represents 100 shares of a particular stock. Options, like other asset types, may be acquired via brokerage investing accounts.

Options can improve a person's portfolio. They do this through increased revenue, protection, and even leverage. Options can be used as an effective hedge against a declining stock market to prevent downside losses.

Options can also provide regular income. They are frequently used for speculative purposes, such as betting on the direction of a stock. This makes them risky, and as a new investor it is not advised you start investing with options until you can grasp what you are doing.

Before placing a deal, the investor should be informed of the dangers associated with options trading. Options trading typically is not recommended for people new to investing.

Call and Put Options

Option contracts are a derivative security. A derivative is an investment product whose price is connected to the price of something else. When you buy an options contract, you are given the right, but not the obligation, to buy or sell an underlying asset at a specified price on or before a certain date.

A call option grants the holder the right to purchase a stock, whereas a put option grants the holder the right to sell a stock.

How Options Work

With an options contract, you are essentially betting on the future of particular stock. Nobody can predict the future of the stock market with certain accuracy. Options can act as a hedge in your portfolio against certain movements in the market(taking an opposite position against a stock you own for protection). Options can also provide you with steady income. Some compare it to gambling, while others do not. It can produce rewards but you must understand there are risks involved. The main reason an investor will participate in options trading is for income, hedging in their portfolio and to create extra flexibility.

The shorter the period until expiration of the options contract, the less valuable an option will be. This is because the likelihood of a price movement in the underlying stock decreases as we get closer to expiration. If you buy an out-of-the-money one-month option and the stock does not move, the option loses value with each passing day. Because time is a factor in option pricing, a one-month option will be less valuable than a three-month option. This is because having more time improves the likelihood of a price shift in your favor, and vice versa. An option expiring in a year will cost more than the same option expiring in one month.

Buying & Selling Calls and Puts

You have four possibilities when it comes to options:

Buy Calls(long)

Sell Calls(short)

Buy Puts(long)

Sell Puts(short)

Purchasing shares results in a long position. Purchasing a call option allows you to take a long position in the underlying stock. Shorting stock results in a short position. Selling a naked or uncovered option puts you in the position of being short on the underlying stock.

Shorting a stock is when you sell shares of a stock at a price, without owning it. You borrow the shares at the particular price and sell them immediately at that price. You want the stock to go down in price, this way you can buy it at the lower price, give back the borrowed shares, and you keep the difference making a profit. This is easy to do through your brokerage as they will facilitate this.

Remember this formula for shorting a stock: Borrow, Sell, Buy, Replace.

Shorting stocks can be highly profitable, but is EXTREMELY risky, as your losses can be incredible. This is not recommended for new investors.

Purchasing a put option allows you to take a short position in the underlying stock. When you sell a naked put, you may take a long position in the underlying stock. It is critical to distinguish between these four possibilities.

Option holders are those who buy options, and option writers are people who sell options. The key contrast between holders and authors is as follows:

1. Call and put holders (buyers) are not required to buy or sell. They have the option. This restricts the risk of option buyers to the premium they paid to purchase the contract, making their losses limited.

2. However, call and put writers (sellers) are required to purchase or sell if the option expires in the money (more on that below). This means that a seller may be obligated to fulfill a purchase or sale commitment. It also suggests that option sellers are exposed to additional, and in some circumstances limitless, risks. This means that option writers might lose far more than the cost of the option premium they received.

Key Options Terms:

Strike price- The price that that the underlying stock of the options contract can be purchased or sold(the time that you can exercise your right or option to purchase or sell the stock)

Expiration- When the options contract expires

Premium- How much the option costs

In The Money- The point above or below the strike price where the buyer of the options contract is making money

Out Of The Money- The point where the options buyer will not make money from exercising the option

Holder- The buyer of an options contract

Writer- The seller of an options contract

Bid Price- The highest price a buyer will pay for an options contract

Ask Price- The price a seller is willing to accept for an options contract. The difference between the bid/ask price is called the spread

Four Key Option Greeks

Option Greeks are mathematical tools that help traders understand how different factors affect an option's price. They're like warning signs for financial investments.

1. **Delta**
   - Measures how much an option's price changes when the underlying stock price moves
   - Ranges from -1.0 to +1.0
   - Example: A delta of 0.50 means the option's price will change 50 cents for every $1 change in stock price

2. **Gamma**
   - Shows how quickly delta changes as the stock price moves
   - Helps traders understand potential rapid price swings

3. **Theta**
   - Calculates how much value an option loses each day
   - Time decay accelerates as the expiration date approaches
   - Imagine an ice cube melting faster as it gets closer to room temperature

4. **Vega**
   - Measures how sensitive an option's price is to market volatility
   - Higher volatility means higher option prices
   - Longer-dated options are typically more sensitive to volatility changes

*Buying options is great if you don't have much money yet want to have access to a stock that is a bit expensive. You can purchase an options contract on the stock instead of purchasing the stock

outright. It also limits the potential losses for the buyer of an options contract.

*Writing or selling options is great because it can provide steady income to your portfolio. However it can be risky as your losses can mount depending on the performance of the stock if you are selling uncovered calls or puts.

*If you think the price of a stock will rise, you can either by a call option or sell a put option.

*If you think the price of a stock will fall, you can either buy a put option or sell a call option.

*A call option gives the holder the right to purchase the underlying asset at a set price before the contract expires. The call option gains value for the holder as the underlying asset increases in value.

*A put option gives the holder the right to sell the underlying asset at a set price. The put option gains value for the holder as the underlying asset decreases in value.

*A covered call is when the seller or writer of an options contract already owns the stock or asset they are selling.

*A protective put option is when you buy a put option against shares of a stock you already own. It is a way to create insurance in your portfolio. If the value of the shares you already own drop in price, the put options you own against the stock will rise in value creating a portfolio hedge.

*Naked/Uncovered options is when an options seller does not own the underlying stock that they are selling to meet their potential obligation. This is highly risky, and not suggested for new investors like you.

Chapter 6.4: Funds

"By periodically investing in an index fund, the know nothing investor can actually outperform most investment professionals."- Warren Buffet

A fund is a grouping of money put aside for a certain purpose. The fund is used for investments and is usually managed by a professional.

How Funds Work

Funds allow people and entities to put their resources together for various investment purposes. Investors can invest in various types of funds with the purpose of making money. Mutual funds pool money from many participants and invest it in a diverse portfolio of assets. Hedge funds invest the money of high-net-worth individuals. Governments invest money to pay for certain costs, such as a pension fund for employees.

Common Types of Funds

Some types of funds in the investment world are:

- **Mutual funds** are investment vehicles managed by professional managers that invest cash raised from individual investors in stocks, bonds, and/or other assets. Most mutual funds do not outperform the stock market over long periods of time and may charge high fees. Make sure to do your research. Mutual funds are only purchased at the end of the stock market trading day.

- **Money-market** funds are highly liquid mutual funds that invest in short-term interest-bearing assets such as Treasury bills to earn income for investors.

- **ETFs** are similar to mutual funds in that they are traded on public markets (similar to stocks). They can be bought and sold anytime during the day unlike mutual funds.

- **Hedge funds** are investment funds for high-net-worth individuals or organizations that use high-risk methods such as short selling, derivatives, and leverage to improve the return on investors' pooled capital.

- **Government bond** funds are designed for investors who want to invest in low-risk Treasury securities, such as Treasury bonds.

Index Funds

"Index funds" mirror or track the performance of a particular stock index, such as the Standard & Poor's 500 index. If you invest in an index fund that tracks the S&P 500, you'll be invested in all of the companies within that index. For most investors, and beginners like you, Index Funds are the easiest way to begin investing, and can help you build tremendous wealth if you consistently invest in them. Some examples of S&P 500 ETF Index funds that are popular are(*SPY, VOO, IVV, SPLG*). Of course, you can do a simple google search or do research in your brokerage account to find more, and compare different funds. You can also compare their performances against one another using your brokerage account.

Index Funds are recommended for most investors who do not have the time to actively research stocks and who want to diversify their investments for protection. Investors like Warren Buffet have stated that if you know what you are doing in picking stocks, it is better to invest in one great business than to spread your money around in multiple businesses through diversification. Since the average investor/beginner does not know how to analyze most companies, diversification is needed and index funds are fantastic for this reason(this is true for seasoned investors as well). You go as the market goes. If the point ever comes where you become adept at picking stocks, he would suggest getting out of index funds and investing in those particular stocks that you choose. Until then, you may want to start with index funds. According to Warren Buffet, 99% of people should diversify. If you really know what you are doing, you don't diversify. As a beginner, do you really know what you are doing?

How Index Funds Work

Index funds work by investing with a passive management strategy rather than an active management strategy. Active management is when an investment manager actively chooses when to buy or sell specific investments. Since there is someone doing the work of choosing these investments, the management fees for actively managed investments tend to be higher. Many mutual funds use active management strategies.

Passive management, on the other hand, is a strategy where a fund manager builds a portfolio of investments that reflect an existing market index. A market index is a collection of a group of stocks that reflects a particular part of the economy. For instance, the S&P 500 is a stock market index that measures the performance of about 500 companies in the U.S. Typically, the S&P 500's performance offers a picture of the health of the U.S. stock market and the economy.

An index fund will be made up of the same investments that make up the market index it tracks. This way, the performance of the index fund usually closely mirrors that of the index, and no hands-on management is necessary. Index Funds are great because they make investing as easy as possible without as much worry as other assets. You are betting on all of the companies in the index long term. In order to lose all of your money, all of those companies would have to go out of business. If that were to happen, don't worry about losing money because your money would be worthless anyway as that is a signal that something catastrophic is happening in the world. You can invest in index funds if you have a very low risk tolerance, and you want to enjoy life no matter what the market is doing. Index Fund investing is suggested for the average investor, especially those with a low risk tolerance.

How Much Do Index Funds Cost?

Index funds may be less expensive than other funds, but they can still incur some costs.

- **Investment minimum.** The minimum required to invest in a mutual fund can run as low as nothing or as high as a few thousand dollars. Once you've crossed that threshold, most funds allow investors to add money in smaller increments. There is generally no investment minimum in an ETF.

- **Account minimum.** This is different from the investment minimum. Although a brokerage's account minimum may be $0, that doesn't remove the investment minimum for a particular index fund.

- **Expense ratio.** This is one of the main costs of an index fund. Expense ratios are fees that are subtracted from each shareholder's returns as a percentage of their overall investment. You can find the expense ratio for the mutual fund/ETF in your brokerage account. The lower the expense ratio, typically the better.

- **Tax-cost ratio.** In addition to paying fees, owning the fund may trigger capital gains taxes if held outside tax-advantaged accounts, such as a 401(k) or an IRA. Like the expense ratio, these taxes can take a bite out of investment returns(this typically is related to mutual funds, not ETFs).

What index should I invest in?

Index funds track various indexes. For example, the S&P 500 is one of the best-known indexes because the 500 companies it tracks include large, well-known U.S.-based businesses representing a wide range of industries. But the S&P 500 isn't the only index. Here are some other options:

- **Nasdaq Composite:** Follows more than 3,000 equities listed on the Nasdaq stock exchange and is largely tech-focused.

- **Dow Jones Industrial Average:** Measures 30 blue-chip companies in the U.S. and covers all industries except for transportation and utilities.

- **Wilshire 5000:** Includes all of the publicly traded companies with headquarters in the United States; often called the "total stock market index."

- **FTSE Global All Cap:** Features a broad range of stocks across several market caps within the U.S. and across the globe; covers developed and emerging markets.

How To Invest In Index Funds

Investing in index funds is easy. Here's a quick rundown of how to do it:

1. **Have a goal for your index funds**

If you want your portfolio to simply match what the stock market is doing, then index fund investing is probably your play. Let's say that the S&P 500 has averaged an 11% return since its inception. This means that if you had consistently invested in an S&P 500 fund, you would have averaged around the same percentage. The expense ratio of the fund and dividends may alter this slightly but you get the idea. Would you be happy with this return for doing nothing but placing your money consistently in a fund without much research or headache? If so, index fund investing may be the way to go. Again, it is not guaranteed that you will get this percentage in the future as nobody can predict the future accurately. However, based on the track record, you may feel comfortable investing in index funds. Individual stocks may give you a better return, however there is more risk involved. Also to invest in an individual stock correctly, you should be doing heavy research into that stock before purchasing. If you're looking to let your money grow slowly over time, particularly if you're investing for retirement, or a child's college, index funds may be a great investment for your portfolio.

2. Research index funds

Once you know what index you want to track, it's time to look at the actual index funds you'll be investing in. When you're investigating an index fund, it's important to consider several factors. Here are some things to keep in mind:

- **Company size and capitalization**. Index funds can track small, medium-sized, or large companies (also known as small-, mid-, or large-cap indexes).

- **Geography.** There are funds that focus on stocks that trade on foreign exchanges or a combination of international exchanges.

- **Business sector or industry.** You can explore funds that focus on different sectors of the economy such as technology, or healthcare.

- **Asset type.** There are funds that track bonds, and commodities for example.

- **New Market opportunities.** These funds examine emerging markets or growing sectors for investment.

There are many choices to choose from but you may need to invest in only one. You may also invest in a broad stock market index to be properly diversified. A broad stock market index invests in the ENTIRE stock market. The VTI etf from Vanguard is an example.

3. Pick your index funds

Once you've decided which index you're interested in, it's time to choose which corresponding index fund to buy. Low costs are one of the biggest selling points of index funds. They're cheap to run because they're automated to follow the shifts in value in an index. However, don't assume that all index mutual funds are cheap.

Even though they're not actively managed by a team of well-paid analysts, they carry administrative costs. These costs are subtracted from each fund shareholder's returns as a percentage of their overall investment.

Two funds may have the same investment goal — like tracking the S&P 500 — yet have management costs that can vary wildly. Those fractions of a percentage point may seem like no big deal, but your long-term investment returns can take a massive hit from the smallest fees.

4. Decide where to buy your index funds

You can purchase an index fund directly from a mutual fund company or a brokerage. The same goes for exchange-traded funds (ETFs), which are like mutual funds that trade like stocks throughout the day (more on these below).

When you're choosing where to buy an index fund, consider:

- **Fund selection.** Which index funds are you interested in?

- **Convenience.** You may want to find a single provider who can accommodate all your needs. For example, if you're just going to invest in mutual funds (or even a mix of funds and stocks), a mutual fund company may be able to serve as your investment hub. But if you require sophisticated stock research and screening tools, a discount broker that also sells the index funds you want may be better.

- **Trading costs**. If the commission or transaction fee isn't waived, consider how much a broker or fund company charges to buy or sell the index fund. Mutual fund commissions are higher than stock trading ones.

- **Commission-free options.** Do they offer no-transaction-fee mutual funds or commission-free ETFs?

5. Buy index funds

In order to purchase shares of an index fund, you'll need to do so from an investment account. You can then open an investment account, such as a traditional brokerage account or a Roth IRA, through the brokerage. You can then buy the fund from that account.

When you go to purchase the fund, you may be able to select a fixed dollar amount to spend or choose a number of shares. The share price of the index fund, and your investing budget, will determine how much you're willing to spend. For instance, if you have $1,000 you'd like to invest in an index fund, and the fund you're looking at is selling for $100 a share, you'd be able to purchase 10 shares.

6. Keep an eye on your index funds

Index funds have become one of the most popular ways for Americans to invest because of their ease of use, instant diversity, and returns that typically beat actively managed accounts. But passive management doesn't mean you should completely ignore your index fund. Here are some things to think about over time:

- **Is the index fund doing its job?** Your index fund should mirror the performance of the underlying index. To check, look at the index fund's returns. In your brokerage account it should show the index fund's returns during several time periods, compared with the performance of the benchmark index. Don't panic if the returns aren't identical. Remember, those investment costs, even if minimal, affect results, as do taxes. However, red flags should wave if the fund's performance lags the index by a lot.

- **Is the index fund you want too expensive?** If the fees start stacking up over time, you may want to reevaluate your index fund.

- **Want to buy stocks instead?** If you want to be hands-on with your investments, you may want to explore stocks.

Chapter 6.5: Mutual Funds and ETF's (Exchange Traded

"Equity mutual funds are the perfect solution for people who want to own stocks without doing their own research."- Peter Lynch

Investors seeking diversity frequently turn to the world of funds. ETFs, index mutual funds, and actively managed mutual funds can give wide, diversified exposure to an asset class, region, or market niche without requiring the purchase of a large number of individual securities.

The difficulty comes in limiting your alternatives. Do you go with an ETF that tracks an index, such as the S&P 500 Index, or a low-cost index mutual fund? Or how about a mutual fund with excellent management?

The solution is determined by your objectives and requirements. Before you decide on the best blend for you, consider the advantages and disadvantages of each sort of investment.

Mutual Funds

Mutual funds are often purchased directly from investing firms rather than from other investors on an exchange. They have an expense ratio and maybe extra sales costs (or "loads").

Front Load Mutual Fund- An upfront sales charge investors pay when they buy fund shares.

Back Load Mutual Fund- a fee paid by investors when selling mutual fund shares, and it is expressed as a percentage of the value of the fund's shares.

No Load Mutual Fund- A fund that charges no sales fees either on the front end (when you buy fund shares) or back end (when you sell fund shares).

Open-End Mutual Fund

An open-end mutual fund is a type of investment that pools money from many investors to create a diverse portfolio of assets. These funds are called "open-end" because they can create an unlimited number of shares. This means new investors can always buy in, and existing investors can always sell their shares back to the fund.

Key Features:

- Can issue unlimited shares
- Priced daily based on Net Asset Value (NAV)
- Most mutual funds and ETFs are open-end funds
- Very common in retirement plans like 401(k)s

How Open-End Funds Work

1. Investors buy shares directly from the fund
2. The fund uses this money to invest in various securities
3. Shares are priced at the end of each trading day based on NAV
4. Investors can sell shares back to the fund at any time

Closed-End Mutual Fund

When a closed-end fund starts, it sells a set number of shares. This is called an Initial Public Offering (IPO); no new shares are created after this. Once the IPO is done, people can buy and sell these shares on stock exchanges, just like they do with company stocks. Unlike regular mutual funds that can always accept new money, closed-end funds work with the money they raised at the start.

To understand closed-end funds better, let's compare them to open-end funds:

1. **Open-End Funds:**
   - Can create new shares anytime
   - Accept new money from investors regularly
   - Examples: Most mutual funds and ETFs (Exchange-Traded Funds)

2. **Closed-End Funds:**
   - Have a fixed number of shares
   - Don't accept new money after the initial offering
   - Examples: Some municipal bond funds and global investment fund

Imagine a closed-end fund like a big jar of cookies. Once the jar is filled and sealed, no more cookies can be added. People can trade these cookies, but the total number of cookies stays the same!

Index mutual funds

Index mutual funds, like most ETFs, are considered passive investments since they replicate an index. They can also be an inexpensive method to invest, with many having yearly fees of less than 0.10 percent.

Here are a few instances where an index mutual fund may be preferable over an ETF:

- **You can invest in an index mutual fund with reduced yearly operating costs.** Don't assume that ETFs are always the cheapest alternative. You might be able to discover an index fund that is less expensive than a comparable ETF.

- **The ETF is not widely traded.** ETFs have a bid/ask spread, where the seller may ask you to purchase the ETF higher than the trading price. The higher the bid/ask spread, the more expensive to purchase. Mutual funds, on the other hand, have no bid-ask spreads.

- **Automatic Investments.** With a mutual fund, you can have a set amount of money at regular intervals allotted to keep purchasing shares of the mutual fund, making investing automatic with no work needed. You cannot do this with an ETF, as you will have to purchase shares each time you would like to buy.

The disadvantages of an index mutual fund are as follows:

- **It will never outperform the market.** Because index funds are linked to the performance of an index, they can never outperform a top-performing actively managed fund. They cannot provide the exciting short-term market-beating performance that an actively managed fund can(this isn't necessarily a bad thing, just a disadvantage).

- **You have no say over your holdings.** An index fund may not contain a firm or a group of companies that you like or feel will perform well. Companies that you dislike might be listed in an index. An index fund's specific holdings are beyond your control.

- **You have no safeguards in place.** While an index fund such as the S&P 500 has shown to be a pretty safe long-term investment, you remain at the whim of the market. When the market falls, so does your index fund.

Actively Managed Mutual Funds

An actively managed mutual fund's investments are chosen and managed by a portfolio manager (or managers), who are typically assisted by a team of research analysts.

Active investors construct a portfolio that represents their strategy and perspective. In difficult markets, for example, active managers might play defense by selling more speculative or risky assets and increasing their allocation to more conservative investments. Actively managed funds are often more expensive than ETFs or index funds, owing to management fees.

Consider investing in an actively managed mutual fund if you meet the following criteria:

- **You're looking for a fund that can outperform the market.** The major reason individuals invest in actively managed funds is the possibility that they may outperform their benchmarks (albeit most will not do so consistently). Active management with a specific strategy may also supplement index funds in a portfolio.

The following are some of the potential disadvantages of an actively managed mutual fund:

- **They may underperform the market.** There is the possibility that it will underperform the market.

- **They usually have higher fees.** Actively managed funds, as the name implies, are actively managed, and the managers will be paid a fee for any change they make to the fund.

- **They are less tax efficient in general.** Actively managed funds have a greater tax expense than index funds or ETFs because, when management sells stocks in the funds and acquires investments to try to outperform the market, capital gains are generated more frequently and are taxed. The greater the activity in a fund, the greater the accumulation of taxes.

ETFs (Exchange Traded Funds)

ETFs are funds that trade like stocks and are largely passive investments that strive to mirror the performance of a specific index or sector of the market(although actively managed ETFs are also available).

The cost ratios paid by passively managed funds are frequently lower than those charged by actively managed funds. Some passive ETFs charge less than 0.05 percent, while others charge nothing. That's a significant benefit over actively managed funds.

Passive ETFs are also tax efficient, in part because index following does not require frequent trading. Investing in ETFs used to include paying trading commissions every time ETF shares were purchased or sold, but listed ETFs now trade commission-free in many brokerages.

Consider purchasing an ETF if:

- **You trade actively.** Mutual funds do not enable intraday trading, stop orders, limit orders, or short selling, but ETFs do.

- **You want specific exposure to a certain industry or market.** ETFs that focus on certain sectors or commodities might provide exposure to specific market segments.

- **You want tax efficiency.** Passive ETFs and index mutual funds are both taxed less than actively managed mutual funds. ETFs, in general, can be more tax efficient than mutual funds.

Potential disadvantages of an ETF include:

- **Some have large bid/ask spreads.** A bid/ask spread is the amount that the ask price exceeds the bid price for an asset. It is the difference between the highest price a buyer is willing to pay, and the lowest price the seller is willing to sell. The seller will see the bid price, while the buyer pays the ask price. This difference, known as the bid/ask spread, is normally insignificant, but for specialized ETFs with little trading activity, the gap can be significant.

Stock Market sectors and ETFs

There are ETFs for almost anything from airlines, to entertainment, to semiconductors, to dividends. Generally, there are 11 Sectors associated with the stock market, and there are plenty of ETFs that allow you to invest in a specific sector of the stock market if you are attracted to that specific sector.

A stock market sector is a group of stocks that have many things in common and generally operate in the same industry.

Below are the major sectors of the stock market, and examples of ETFs that currently invest in those sectors:

Information Technology *(QQQ, VGT, XLK)*

Financials *(XLF, VFH, IYF)*

Health Care (*XLV, VHT, IBB***)**

Consumer Discretionary (*XLY, VCR, XRT***)**

Consumer Staples (*VDC, XLP, IYK***)**

Communication Services (*VOX, XLC, IXP***)**

Industrials (*XLI, VIS, IYJ***)**

Materials (*XLB, VAW, IYM***)**

Real Estate (*VNQ, XLRE, REET***)**

Energy (*XLE, VDE, ICLN***)**

Utilities (*XLU, VPU, FUTY***)**

*New ETFs are created every year, and there are ETFs for everything. Always do your research before buying an ETF. Things you may want to look at when researching ETFs include:

Total assets(how much money is invested and how many shares of assets are owned by the ETF)

Year to date return(YTD)- How is the ETF performing this year at the current moment

Average Volume- How many shares of the ETF are traded daily

*You may also want to check the historical performance of the ETF, and compare it to an index such as the S&P 500, or the stock market as a whole. If the ETF sector consistently underperforms the stock market, you may just want to invest in the broader market or an index instead, but that is totally up to you. You can always

compare ETFs in your brokerage account with a little research and on websites like etf.com.

Sector Cycling

Sector cycling is an investment strategy that some people use. Basically, you take a small lump sum of money and invest in the most beaten down sector in a given year towards the end of that calendar year.

Let's say at the end of this year, the technology sector was the best performing sector in the stock market, and the energy sector was the worst performing, and you had $2000 to put into an investment. Which sector would you invest that $2000 into at the end of the year?

The strategy states you should invest in the energy sector, since it is the sector beaten down the most. It will give you a higher margin of safety than the technology sector which is performing well. If you buy the technology sector on its rise, you may end up being the greater fool, as eventually the tech sector will pull back.

Cycles occur in investing yearly. A popular sector this year, will not necessarily be popular next year or the year after. Every year, if you take a small amount of money lump sum, and invest it in the worst performing sector that year, when it rebounds you will get a better return possibly than if you put that same money into a sector that is flying high. It may not happen the following year, but eventually according to the strategy, that sector will rebound giving you a better return. Many people are loyal to a particular stock or sector. Others are loyal to better returns.

Chapter 6.6: Cryptocurrencies

Cryptocurrency, sometimes abbreviated as crypto, is a sort of digital currency that is used as a medium of trade and is secured by something called cryptography which is supposed to protect it from being counterfeited. Cryptocurrencies are a type of digital money that exists on computers.

Cryptocurrencies operate on decentralized networks(unlike the money in your bank which is centralized). They use a technology called blockchain which records and sends information related to crypto transactions to a network of computers and is intended to be impossible to be hacked or manipulated.

Things you can Do with Cryptocurrencies

While some cryptocurrencies like Bitcoin have aspects of both money and investments, some people argue as to whether it is clearly one or the other.

As the name indicates, cryptocurrencies may be used to make purchases.

Types of Cryptocurrencies

Although the term "cryptocurrencies" refers to all types of cryptocurrencies or digital currencies, the term "coins" is occasionally used interchangeably.

1. **Coins:** Coins are any crypto that has its own blockchain technology such as Bitcoin

2. **Altcoins:** Despite the fact that they are coins, they are all regarded as alternatives to Bitcoin, the first cryptocurrency.

3. **Tokens:** Tokens are cryptocurrencies that do not have their own blockchain technology and must use another blockchain.

Cryptocurrency Exchanges

A cryptocurrency exchange is a website where you may buy and sell digital money. You may use exchanges to convert one cryptocurrency to another, or to purchase cryptocurrency with traditional currency, such as the US dollar. Exchanges display the current market value of the cryptocurrencies that they provide. You may also exchange cryptocurrencies for US dollars or other currencies to keep as cash in your account (for eventual trading back into crypto) or withdraw to your regular bank account.

Steps to Start Investing in Cryptocurrency

These are the procedures you must complete before you can start trading digital currencies.

Step 1: Select the Right Crypto Exchange

To purchase Bitcoin for example, first select a broker or cryptocurrency exchange.

Step 2: Create and Verify Your Account

Once you've chosen a cryptocurrency broker or exchange, you may open an account with them. Depending on the platform and the amount you plan to purchase, you may be required to validate your identity. This is a necessary step in preventing fraud.

Step 3: Deposit Cash to Invest

You must first check that you have funds in your account before you can purchase cryptocurrencies. You may fund your cryptocurrency account by linking your bank account, authorizing a wire transfer, or paying with a debit or credit card. You may have to wait a few days before you can utilize the money you deposit to buy cryptocurrencies, depending on the exchange or broker and your financing method.

Step 4: Place Your Cryptocurrency Order

After you've deposited funds into your account, you're ready to place your first order. There are several cryptocurrencies to select from.

Step 5: Store your Cryptocurrency

Cryptocurrency exchanges are vulnerable to theft or hacking since they are not insured by the Federal Deposit Insurance Corporation (FDIC) as of the year 2025. Things may change in the future. You may even lose your investment if you forget or lose your account's passcode.

Leave the crypto on the exchange. When you acquire Bitcoin for example, it is usually held in a cryptocurrency wallet linked to the exchange.

- **Hot wallets.** These are online cryptocurrency wallets that work on internet-connected devices including tablets, PCs, and phones. Hot wallets are handy, but because they are still linked to the internet, they are more vulnerable to theft.

- **Cold wallets.** Because they are not linked to the internet, cold crypto wallets are the safest way to store Bitcoin. They are external devices, such as a hard disk or a USB drive.

Step 6: Choose a Strategy

As with any investment, have a strategy for your crypto investments if you decide to invest in crypto. Investing in cryptocurrencies can be very risky, and the crypto market tends to be extremely volatile. Many cryptocurrencies have no actual use so if you do decide to invest in crypto, do your research. One of the many criticisms of investing in crypto is it doesn't actually generate income like a business or rental property may, so therefore what are you actually investing in. Again, if you choose to invest in crypto do your research.

In January 2024, the U.S. Securities and Exchange Commission approved applications for ETFs that track Bitcoin and other cryptocurrencies through financial institutions. This will be another way for people to invest in the crypto market.

Popular Cryptocurrencies

Below are cryptocurrencies that are highly popular.

1. **Bitcoin (BTC)**

Bitcoin was the first cryptocurrency. It was created in 2009 by someone using the name Satoshi Nakamoto. Bitcoin is like digital gold - people buy it hoping it will be worth more in the future.

2. **Ethereum (ETH)**

Ethereum is the second biggest cryptocurrency after Bitcoin. It's special because people can use it to create and run computer programs called "smart contracts".

3. Tether (USDT)

Tether is a type of cryptocurrency called a "stablecoin". That means its value is supposed to stay close to $1 all the time. People use Tether when they want to trade other cryptocurrencies.

4. BNB

BNB was created by a company called Binance. People use BNB to pay fees when they buy and sell cryptocurrencies on Binance's website.

5. Solana (SOL)

Solana is newer than Bitcoin and Ethereum. It can handle more transactions very quickly. People use Solana for things like digital art and online games.

6. USD Coin (USDC)

Like Tether, USD Coin is also a stablecoin that tries to keep its value close to $1. It's regulated, which means the government keeps an eye on it to make sure it follows rules.

7. XRP

XRP was created by a company called Ripple. It's meant to help banks and money transfer companies send money around the world faster and cheaper.

8. Dogecoin (DOGE)

Dogecoin started as a joke based on a popular internet meme of a Shiba Inu dog. But it became very popular and now some big companies accept it as payment.

9. Tron (TRX)

Tron was created to help people who make digital content (like videos or music) share their work and get paid for it directly.

10. Cardano (ADA)

Cardano was created by scientists and researchers. They did a lot of studies to try to make it better than other cryptocurrencies.

Remember, the value of cryptocurrencies can change a lot very quickly. It's important to be careful and learn more before thinking about buying any.

Quantum Computing and Cryptocurrencies

Quantum computing is a new type of super-fast computer. It uses special bits called qubits instead of regular computer bits. Qubits can be 0 and 1 at the same time, which lets quantum computers do many calculations at once.

Think of it like this: A regular computer can only look at one book at a time. But a quantum computer can look at all the books in a library at once!

How Quantum Computing Affects Cryptocurrencies

Cryptocurrencies like Bitcoin use special codes to keep people's money safe. Right now, regular computers can't break these codes. But quantum computers might be able to crack them very quickly.

This could be a big problem for cryptocurrencies according to some. If someone could break the codes, they might be able to steal people's digital money.

Protecting Cryptocurrencies

Scientists are working on ways to protect cryptocurrencies from quantum computers. They're creating new types of codes that even quantum computers can't break easily.

Some new cryptocurrencies are being made to be "quantum-resistant." This means they're designed to be safe even when quantum computers become more common.

What Can People Do?

If you have cryptocurrencies, here are some things you can do to keep them safer:

1. *Use special wallets that need more than one key to open*
2. *Keep your digital money offline when you're not using it*
3. *Make sure your wallet software is always up to date*
4. *Look for new "quantum-resistant" wallets if or when they become available*

Chapter 6.7: Intellectual Property

"The real source of wealth today is intelligence, applied intelligence."- Charles Handy

The phrase "intellectual property" refers to a broad category of intangible assets that are owned and legally protected for the owner. Intangible assets are those that a company or person owns but cannot be touched.

Intellectual property refers to the idea that creations of the mind should be owned and legally protected. This encourages people to come up with ideas and creations that will not only benefit themselves, but society as a whole.

Types of Intellectual Property

There are several intangibles that might be considered intellectual property. When looking to file for ownership over intellectual property, you can visit uspto.gov, and it may be useful to hire a lawyer to help you with your filing.

Patents

The United States Patent and Trademark Office(USPTO.gov) grants investors the legal right to patent inventions via the issuance of patents. The patent grants the creator exclusive ownership of the invention, which might be a design, procedure, improvement, or physical innovation such as a machine. Patents for designs are often held by technology and software businesses.

Copyrights

Copyrights protect the exclusive privilege of using, copying, or replicating a work's original creation by its authors or creators. Book authors and musicians hold copyright on their works. Copyright also specifies that the original authors may offer anybody permission to utilize the work via a license agreement.

Trademarks

A trademark is a recognized symbol, phrase, or emblem that identifies a product and legally distinguishes it from other items. When a corporation, business, or individual is granted exclusive ownership of a trademark, that mark may not be used by any other business in any way, shape, or form in regards to how the trademark is filed. Branding is often associated with a company's trademark. For instance, "Coca-Cola" is a registered trademark of The Coca-Cola Company (KO). When a symbol, phrase or emblem is a registered trademark, it usually has an **R** next to it signaling it is a registered trademark owned by a business or individual.

Franchises

A franchise is a license that a business, person, or party—referred to as the franchisee—purchases that allow them to utilize the name, trademark, intellectual information, and methods of another firm—the franchisor.

The shop or franchise is often operated by a small company owner or entrepreneur. Franchisees are granted permission to use the company's brand while offering and delivering goods and services to customers. In exchange, the franchisee pays the franchisor a start-up fee and annual license costs. McDonald's Corporation employs the franchise business model (MCD).

Trade Secrets

A trade secret is a business method, technique, or process that is not generally known to the public but provides an economic advantage to the business that employs it. Trade secrets must be actively safeguarded by the corporation.

Trade secrets may be anything from an idea to a specific method of production or even just a formula. Trade secrets are used in the development of a business model that distinguishes the company's services from its clients by creating a competitive edge.

Digital Assets

Digital assets are increasingly becoming recognized as intellectual property. This includes online digital material such as the creation of an online course.

Type of Intellectual Property		
IP	Protection	Duration (in the U.S)
Patents	Inventions, industrial designs, computer code	20 years

Trademarks	Unique identifiers for a business or its products or services (e.g., logos, brand names)	As long as the trademarked material remains active
Copyrights	Works of authorship, including books, poems, films, music, photographs, online content	70 years after the author dies

Reasons You Should Invest in Intellectual Property

Intellectual property (IP) is an excellent investment for companies of all sizes and in all industries. It may also be a great investment for an individual investor.

1. It is a valuable asset that grows with your business

Many individuals are surprised that intellectual property assets account for the majority of a company's market value. For organizations that rely heavily on brands or technology, intellectual property (IP) may account for almost all of the company's worth.

Unlike other investments, intellectual property does not have a fixed value and is not tied to a market. As your company expands and knowledge of your brands, goods, or services rises, so does the value of your intellectual property.

For those of you who are interested in starting your own business, legal protection for your ideas, trademarks, and designs should be included in your business plan from the start.

2. IP rights increase the value of your business in different ways

Investing in your patent portfolio gives you the right to prevent others from using your ideas and may also generate direct cash via licensing and sale of your patents.

A registered trademark preserves the value of your trademarks and may significantly boost the value of your company, particularly if you want to sell it or list it on a stock market. It is also an excellent tool for anti-counterfeiting efforts.

Competitors cannot just ride on your famous or consumer-preferred designs and must invest their own time and energy in creating alternatives.

3. **You can license, sell, or otherwise leverage your IP**

Your intellectual property assets may be utilized, such as via licensing agreements, to generate considerable profit.

IP, like any other asset, may be sold, and the price will be determined by a variety of criteria, including demand, development expenses, IP lifespan, and so on. This is especially beneficial for "surplus" IP that you no longer need, maybe owing to a change in company strategy, but for which there is still a market.

4. **It is cost-effective**

Trademarks are an important asset for every company. Trademark protection is also quite affordable, given that registered trademark protection lasts 10 years and may be renewed forever.

While acquiring patent protection is far more costly than other registered intellectual property, the benefit of having a valid and enforceable patent may be enormous. A valid patent may provide a significant financial or competitive advantage in a certain market for the term of the patent's life. A patent on a critical breakthrough or breakout technology may do wonders for your business.

5. **It can increase your business reputation and attract investors**

Unfortunately, intellectual property is not always valued as highly as it should be, and many businesses fail to protect their intellectual property. This might present significant issues in the future since most patent and trademark systems are first-to-file, and patents must be submitted before you sell or promote your innovations.

A business that invests in its ideas and brand early on is seen as being more committed to its business ventures. It also demonstrates faith in your technologies and/or brands. If you plan to invest in the creation of your own business, it is extremely important to protect your intellectual property.

The Trademark Registration Process

Step 1: Application and Review

- You submit an application to the United States Patent and Trademark Office (USPTO) using a trademark attorney. You can visit USPTO.gov and search the trademark database to see if the trademark is already registered

- An examining attorney carefully reviews your trademark application

Step 2: Publication

- If the application looks good, your trademark is published in the Trademark Official Gazette
- This is like a public announcement of your trademark

Step 3: Opposition Period

- For 30 days after publication, other businesses can:
    - Object to your trademark
    - File an opposition if they think it might harm their business
- If no one objects, your trademark moves to the next stage

Two Types of Trademark Applications

1. **Trademark Based on Current Use**

   - You're already using the trademark in business
   - If approved, you'll receive a registration certificate
   - You must file maintenance documents to keep the trademark active

2. **Trademark Based on Intent to Use**

   - You plan to use the trademark in the future
   - Receive a "Notice of Allowance"
   - You have 6 months to:
       - Start using the trademark
       - Submit a Statement of Use
       - Request a 6-month extension

Important Things to Remember

- Trademark registration isn't automatic
- You must prove your trademark is unique
- There are fees and specific legal requirements

- You can appeal if your trademark is initially rejected

The Patent Application Process

There are three main types of patents:

1. Utility Patents (for new machines, processes, or improvements)
2. Design Patents (for new and original designs of products)
3. Plant Patents (for newly discovered or created plant varieties)

1. **Prepare Your Invention Description**
   - Write down exactly what makes your invention special
   - Explain how it works
   - Describe what problem it solves

2. **Create Detailed Drawings**
   - Draw clear pictures of your invention
   - Show different views and essential details
   - Use black ink and clear lines

3. **File Your Application**
   - Choose between a provisional (temporary) or non-provisional (permanent) application
   - Pay the required filing fees
   - Submit your detailed description and drawings

4. **Wait for Review**
   - A patent examiner will carefully check your application
   - They'll look to make sure your invention is:
     * Completely new
     * Useful
     * Not obvious to other experts

5. **Respond to Questions**
   - The examiner might ask you to clarify things about your invention

- Be prepared to explain more details
- Make any necessary changes to your application

You will want to do a search to see if there is an application in the works for your particular patent and you will want to consult a patent attorney

Steps to Register a Copyright

A copyright attorney can complete this process for you

1. **Application Form**
   - Different forms for different types of creative works
   - Must be completely and correctly filled out
   - Can be submitted online or on paper

2. **Filing Fee**
   - Pay any associated filing and attorney fees
   - The fee is a Non-refundable payment

3. **Deposit Copy**
   - Send an actual copy of your creative work
   - The Copyright Office keeps this copy
   - Cannot be returned to you

Chapter 6.8: Commodities

"Commodities such as gold and silver have a world market that transcends national borders, politics, religions and race."-
Robert Kiyosaki

Commodities are physical products that are used by people that investors canC trade and invest in. Examples of commodities include:

Gold

Silver

Oil

Wheat

Grain

Many investors invest in commodities such as gold or silver as a hedge in their portfolios. Many times for example, an investor will purchase gold or silver to protect them against a drop in the value of currency. If the U.S. dollar loses value or the stock market drops, many times precious metals such as gold will increase in value.

Commodities are popular in what is known as **future contracts.** A commodity futures contract is an agreement between 2 parties to buy or sell a commodity at a future date at an agreed upon price on an agreed upon future date. If the value of the commodity goes above the agreed upon price by the agreed upon date, the buyer will make money. If the value of the commodity goes below the agreed upon price by the agreed upon date, the seller will make money. With a futures contract, you must buy or sell the commodity on the agreed upon date at the agreed upon price.

Commodity ETFs are popular for new investors as it simplifies the process of investing in commodities. Some current examples are *GLD(Spdr), IAU(iShares), SLV(iShares), PDBC(Invesco), FTGC(First Trust).* There are plenty others. Do your research.

Pros of investing in commodities:

Can be a great hedge against inflation

Can create diversification as part of your investment portfolio

Can create short term profits

Cons of investing in commodities

High volatility

Can create short term losses

Unpredictable events around the world can greatly impact the value of many commodities

Ways to Invest in Commodities

1. **Physical Ownership**
   - Buying actual items like gold bars
   - Requires safe storage
   - Works best with precious metals

2. **Futures Contracts**
   - An agreement to buy or sell a commodity at a future date
   - Like making a promise to trade something later
   - Mostly done through special trading accounts

3. **Company Stocks**
   - Buying shares in companies that produce commodities
   - Example: Investing in a mining company that digs for copper

4. **Investment Funds**
   - Special funds that collect money from many investors
   - Can focus on specific commodities
   - Easier and safer for beginners

5. **Collectible Items**
   - Some commodities, like special coins, can be collected
   - Value can increase over time
   - More about historical interest than pure investment

*Many famous investors do not invest in commodities such as gold. The reason is that generally, commodities by themselves do not generate income the way stocks, bonds, or real estate can. Its

value is based on speculation, not its ability to generate income. You can only make money from commodities generally if some-one is willing to purchase the commodity from you in the future at a higher price(Greater Fool Theory). However, there are many in-vestors who love commodities as an investment. There is no right or wrong answer. Investing in commodities is a personal choice. Do what is best for you.

CHAPTER 6
OTHER TYPES OF INVESTMENTS

Quiz No: 6

Serial No	Question	Answer
1.	Which of the following is NOT a form of intellectual property? A. Patent B. Mutual Fund C. Copyright D. Trademark	
2.	Which letter/letters next to a symbol or phrase indicates the symbol or phrase is owned and trademarked by a company or individual? A. TM B. T C. TR D. R	
3.	The letters in REIT stand for: A. Real Estate Investment Trust B. Registered Estate Initial Trade C. Reverse Equity Interest Transaction D. Rare Equities Investment Transactions	

4.	What is a Mutual fund? A. An investment that you put in your checking account B. Investment that you put in your swimming pool. C. An investment in which investors pool their money to buy stocks, bonds or other investments. D. Investment that you put in the ground.	
5.	ETF stands for: A. Exchange Traded Fund B. Extra Transaction Fee C. Entire Total Fund D. Equities Timed Transaction	
6.	All of the following are pros to investing in real estate except: A. Income B. Appreciation C. Equity D. Over-Leverage	
7.	Approximately how many major sectors are there associated with the stock market? A. 8 B. 9 C. 0 D. 11	

8.	The annual yield percentage on a property if you bought it all cash is the.... A. Cash on Cash yield B. Cap Rate C. Gross Rent Multiplier D. Mortgage to Cash Flow Ratio	
9.	A fixed-income product that reflects a loan from an investor to a borrower is known as a... A. Stock B. Bond C. Index Fund D. Mutual Fund	
10.	When an investor shorts a stock, that signals they want the stock to.... A. Go down B. Go up C. Break even D. Pay a dividend	

Key

1. B

2. D

3. A

4. C

5. A

6. D

7. D

8. B

9. B

10. A

CHAPTER
SEVEN

START
INVESTING

Chapter 7.1: Create an Investment Plan

"Successful investing takes time, discipline and patience. No matter how great the talent or effort, some things just take time. You can't produce a baby in one month by getting nine women pregnant."- Warren Buffet

"An investor without an objective is like a traveler without a destination."- Anonymous

As a beginner investor, the first and most crucial thing you'll need to do is decide your ideal asset mix of stocks, ETF's, mutual funds, bonds, etc. The overall mix of your investments is a personal choice.

Stock Allocation

There are several methods to invest in stocks. Whatever you choose, make sure you invest in stocks or mutual funds or ETFs that you understand.

U.S. vs. International

There are funds that solely invest in domestic stocks and funds that only invest in overseas stocks. Many investors invest in international stocks and funds because investing in companies overseas may provide better growth opportunities. A strategy that some investors employ Is investing in a mix of U.S. and international stocks or funds.

Large Cap, Mid Cap and Small Cap

Market capitalization indicates how large or small a company's size is. Market capitalization is calculated by multiplying the share price of the stock by the number of total shares outstanding. There are basically 3 categories when it comes to cap size.

LARGE CAP- *A company with a market capitalization value that is over $10 billion dollars*

MID CAP- *A company with a market capitalization value between $2 billion and $10 billion dollars*

SMALL CAP- *A company with a market capitalization value between $300 million and $2 billion*

Small cap stocks/funds generally do not have the stable track record of a large cap company however they can provide tremendous growth potential. Purchasing at the right price may produce tremendous long term returns. The problem is not all small cap companies will grow tremendously, so picking the right small cap stock can be tricky. Some examples of current small cap etfs are: *VB(Vanguard), RWK(Invesco), IVOO(Vanguard).* There are plenty others. Do your research.

Mid cap stocks/funds are in between. They are companies that have great growth potential in comparison to a large cap stock and may have more of a proven track record than a small cap stock. Some examples of current mid cap etfs are: *IJH(iShares), VO(Vanguard), MDY(Spdr).* There are plenty others. Do your research

Investing in large cap stocks/funds will allow you to invest in the world's largest corporations. These are safer options, but your returns may be lower. Small Cap funds will invest in small, growing businesses. They are riskier but can yield better profits in specific instances. Mid Cap lies somewhere in the middle. Some examples of current large cap etfs are: *SPY(Spdr), VOO(Vanguard), IVV(iShares)*

Many investors create a portfolio with a mix of all 3. That is a personal choice. Do what makes you comfortable. Compare the performance over time of small, mid and large cap funds over time. This may help you make your decision. Just remember past performance does not guarantee future performance

Emerging Markets

Emerging market stocks/funds invest in firms based in developing or emerging markets. These countries are neither underdeveloped nor completely developed. They are shifting away from industries such as agriculture and toward corporate firms and increasing the quality of life for its citizens.

They are more volatile and less established, but they may provide faster growth and larger returns than companies from more industrialized nations. This comes with greater risk, but the potential for higher reward. Remember it is wise to only invest in what you understand.

Bond Allocation

Bonds have generally provided lower returns over long periods of time but also reduced risk and maybe an important part of any investing strategy.

REITs

Aside from stocks and bonds, you may come across (or be interested in) certain other asset classes. REITs, or **Real Estate Investment Trusts**, are highly popular.

REIT funds are an excellent way to enter the real estate market without spending all of your money on actual property or taking on all of the risks of becoming a landlord.

REIT funds invest in corporations that invest in income-producing real estate. As a result, it is a diverse group of enterprises dealing in many types of real estate.

REITs must distribute 90% of their taxable income to the shareholder, so REITs may be a good option if you are looking for consistent passive income.

Chapter 7.2: Decide on Account Types

"Don't work for money; Make it work for you."- Robert Kiyosaki

Another important decision you must make is choosing the type of account/accounts you would like to have.

If you work in a career field you will most likely have access to a 401(k), 403(b), 457 or Thrift Savings Plan. Let's pretend it's a 401(k) for the sake of argument.

Consider your 401(k) contribution restrictions for this year.

This maximum is not affected by any form of employer match you get. There are several advantages to maxing out your 401(k), including the amount you save and the fact that you reduce your taxable income.

You may or may not want to max out your 401(k)

Then you may want to create an IRA. There is some dispute over whether Roth or Traditional is preferable, but it all comes down to personal opinion. Many argue the Roth should be your 1st option, but do what works best for you. If you are under the age of 50, you can contribute up to $7,000 to an IRA every year (after 50, you can contribute up to $8,000). This is as of the year 2025. This will change over time, so make sure you check with your accountant or simply on irs.gov, or with your brokerage custodial account over the following years. Some will argue that you should only contribute to your 401(k) up to the amount or percentage that your company will match and then contribute to a Roth IRA or a traditional brokerage account. This is because when you contribute to a 401(k), you do not control the access to the money, or how it is withdrawn and the tax implications. If you needed money to purchase a rental property for example, and the money is tied up in your 401(k), you do not have access to your own money without a huge penalty and heavy taxes. You do not have control over your own money. Also remember 401(k)'s are tax deferred, not tax free. Again, this is a personal choice. DO WHAT IS BEST FOR YOU!

If you've maxed out your 401(k), you may or may not want to max out your Roth or Traditional IRA.

After you've contributed to your 401(k) and IRA, you can consider taxable investments(such as a brokerage account with stocks, etfs, REIT's etc.) Again, these are just suggestions. DO WHAT IS BEST FOR YOU!

Chapter 7.3: Select your Investments

"Do something today that your future self will thank you for."-
Anonymous

Having a diverse portfolio of assets is encouraged, but do what works best for your investing strategy. With a 401(k), your selections will be somewhat limited, but the important items to look for are:

- **The expense ratio-** Is there a less expensive alternative?

- **The type of fund -** For example, you can invest in a Large Cap Growth (expanding firms) or a Large Cap Value (lower-cost, more stable stocks) while still falling into a Large Cap fund. Choose what is best for you.

- **The historical performance-** There is no scientific evidence that prior stock performance is a reliable predictor of future success. However, it can help you make a decision. Most investors go with the fund with the superior past performance.

You may make things easier and less stressful for yourself by investing in a Target Date Fund. A Target Date Fund allows you to select a fund that closely matches your intended retirement age/date. So, if you're 27 and expect to retire at 65, you may invest in a Target Date Fund for the year that you turn 65.

The fund will invest in assets that are suitable for this time horizon. For example, if you aim to retire in five years, your portfolio will be heavier on bonds, which are generally safer. However, if you're 30 or 40 years away, the fund would prioritize stocks, which are more volatile but give a higher return because you won't need the money for a long time.

A target date fund may be recommended to a novice investor who is just getting started. It's just easier and will give you more time to become used to investing. You may always alter your investment strategy later on.

Chapter 7.4: Monitor Your Investments

"If you're not interested in your own money, someone else will be."- Anonymous

Always keep track of your money. Even if you pick a target date fund, never "set it and forget it." Check up on your assets regularly.

It's simple to select a mutual fund or index fund and forget about it, but many new investors make this error. Keep an eye on your money while it is working for you.

Here's a list of reasons why it's important to monitor your investments and not ignore them:

Protect Against Losses

* *Markets change; ignoring your portfolio can lead to small losses turning into big ones.*

Adjust to Life Changes

* *Your goals, income, or risk tolerance might change over time.*

Rebalance Your Portfolio

* *Asset values drift; rebalancing keeps your investment mix aligned with your strategy.*

React to Market Trends

* *Staying informed helps you capitalize on opportunities or avoid risks.*

Ensure Performance Matches Expectations

* *You need to know if your investments deliver the expected returns.*

Manage Risks

* *Unmonitored portfolios might become too concentrated in one sector, asset, or region.*

Tax Optimization

* *Monitoring allows you to harvest losses, plan for capital gains, or adjust for tax efficiency.*

Stay Aligned with Financial Goals

- *If you don't check in, you might drift off course and not meet your retirement or savings targets.*

Respond to Economic or Regulatory Changes

- *New laws, interest rate changes, or global events can impact investments.*

Capture Dividends, Interest, and Other Income

- *Monitoring ensures you reinvest or correctly use the income generated by your assets.*

Keep Fees and Expenses in Check

- *Some investments increase cost over time, and ignoring them can eat into returns.*

Prevent Fraud or Mismanagement

- *Regular reviews are a key safeguard, especially if someone else is managing your money.*

Adapt to Technological Advances

- *New tools, platforms, and asset classes (such as ETFs and digital assets) could offer better options.*

Stay Educated and Informed

- *Following your investments helps you become a better, more confident investor.*

CHAPTER 7
START INVESTING

Quiz No: 7

Serial No	Question	Answer
1.	Emerging market funds invest in.... A. Well established markets B. Developing Markets C. Bond Markets D. Derivatives Markets	
2.	Market capitalization is calculated by multiplying the share price by A. Total shares outstanding B. Price to Earnings Ratio C. The Dividend D. Expense Ratio	
3.	Which of the following is a way to start investing? A. Purchase stocks on your own B. Pool money into a mutual fund managed by an advisor C. Purchase an index fund D. All of the above	

4.	REITs must distribute what percentage of their taxable income to the shareholder? A. 80% B. 90% C. 95% D. 100%	
5.	How do you make money from bonds? A. The company pays you part of their profit B. The company or government pays interest on the money borrowed C. If the price goes down and you sell it for a lower price, you make a profit D. You don't make money if interest rates go up	
6.	A mid-cap stock has a market cap between: A. $2 $10 billion B. $520 $ billion C. $10 $20 million D. $60 $80 million	
7.	A Target Date Fund allows you to select a fund that closely matches your: A. Retirement Age B. Capital Gains Rate C. Salary D. Tax Date	
8.	After you've maxed out your 401(k), you may want to: A. Take out loans against it B. Invest in an IRA C. Begin withdrawing from the account D. Stop investing	

9.	Large Cap funds will not invest in the world's largest corporations. A. True B. False	
10.	REIT funds invest in corporations that invest in income-producing real estate. A. True B. False	

Key

1. B

2. A

3. D

4. B

5. B

6. A

7. A

8. B

9. B

10. A

INVESTMENT STRATEGIES AND STOCK ANALYSIS

Chapter 8.1: Strategies for Long-Term Investing

"Investing is simple. Not easy."- Warren Buffet

A long-term investment strategy is the way to go if you want to develop a substantial retirement, save for your child's higher education, or fight inflation. How should this be done?

1. Know Your Financial Goals

Before you begin long-term investing, consider your overall financial goals. Unless you have a clear grasp and vision of your goals, you are unlikely to succeed in the rigors of long-term investment.

Play around with compound interest calculators online(investor. gov) and plug in different numbers to gauge different ideas on future returns. If for example you would like to have a minimum of $2 million dollars in your retirement account 30 years from now, figure out with the calculator how much you would have to invest monthly and at what average return you would need to get there.

2. Start Investing Early

Long-term investment involves discipline and patience and it is critical to begin early. An early start instills financial discipline and allows compounding to take effect. Compounding is crucial in the creation of wealth. This is why it is so important to start investing immediately for your children when they are born.

3. Invest in reputable products

Investing and gambling are two different things. Throwing your money at something with no research or knowledge to make quick money is gambling. You can do that in a casino. You may win, but you increase your chances of losing. Researching and giving yourself a level of margin of safety over a long period of time is investing. Decide what you want to do.

4. Invest in the stock market

Stocks can be volatile, particularly in the short term. They can however be lucrative and have the potential to outperform inflation in the long run. Panicking and quitting in response to short-term market swings can turn theoretical losses into actual losses(you only make or lose money when you sell. Until then, the numbers you see in your account are unrealized, and are simply just numbers). The stock market is one of the easiest ways to begin investing because it doesn't require much money or energy and you can get out quickly if you need to.

5. **Ignore Market Noises**

Markets are full of opinions and points of view that usually are useless. Everyone's an "expert" and shares their thoughts. Noise must be avoided when investing in the long run since they serve as a distraction and can derail your plans. Predicting the future of markets accurately on a regular basis is impossible. Even the experts are wrong a lot. Have a strong foundation and plan, and ride it through all the ups and downs.

6. **Diversify**

You may want to diversify your assets across asset types - including stocks, bonds, and gold, real estate - as well as within asset classes. You may want to spread your stock assets between large-cap, mid-cap, and small-cap funds, for example. Diversification stabilizes your portfolio and balances risk and return. BUT ONLY INVEST IN WHAT YOU ARE COMFORTABLE WITH! Don't invest in things you do not understand, or you do not feel comfortable with.

Chapter 8.2: Determine your Financial Goals

"When investing, it is not necessary to do extraordinary things to get extraordinary results."- Warren Buffet

Investing and trading are two unique strategies to profit from the financial markets. Both investors and traders want profits through market participation. In general, investors seek higher returns over a longer period of time by acquiring and holding. Traders, on the other hand, exploit rising and falling markets to enter and leave positions more quickly, resulting in smaller, more frequent profits. As a beginner, investing is highly suggested in relation to trading. Active trading should be for investors with more experience. Trading is considered a type of investing, and the two words in many cases are used interchangeably.

Investing

The purpose of investing is to accumulate and maintain a portfolio of stocks, stock baskets, mutual funds, bonds, real estate, intellectual property, commodities and other investment vehicles over time to grow and build your wealth. Investing is a long term action. It is centered on the basis of buy and hold investing.

Trading

Trading on the other hand is a short term action. When you buy and or sell a stock, you are trading. Active trading comprises more frequent transactions, such as buying and selling stocks, commodities, currencies, and other products on a regular basis. The aim in the event of a return is to outperform buy-and-hold assets. Active or daily trading is not recommended for new investors like yourself, however as you learn and grow as an investor you may decide to participate in this style of investing.

Examples of Trading Strategies(For more experienced investors)

- **Day trading.** The activity of attempting to profit by acquiring and selling an item on the same day is known as day trading. This can be very profitable. A con however is you must monitor your investments constantly during the day. If you don't you could lose big.

- **Swing trading.** Swing traders will hold an asset for a longer period of time in anticipation of a shift in the market. Because markets fluctuate, swing traders look for indicators that a shift is coming and time their trades accordingly. A con to this is trying to time the market, which is virtually impossible to do on a regular basis.

- **Position trading.** Position trading is more comparable to investing than trading. It is related to swing trading in that it involves a more in-depth examination of long-term patterns. For example, a position trader may hold a position for months before selling it.

- **Scalping.** Scalping is one of the most rapid trading strategies. Scalpers trade slight price movements for minor profits, but they make so many transactions that the minor profits (hopefully) add up. A con to scalping is you may have many minor profits that add up, but one loss could completely wipe them all away. As a new investor, it is encouraged not to do this.

Examples of long term investing strategies

It's always best to have a strategy in place when investing. While no single investing strategy is perfect, several have proven to be beneficial. Here are three options for your investment needs:

- **HODL:** This is the long-term strategy. HODL is an acronym for Hold on for Dear Life. Essentially, it means to purchase an asset(-like a stock or ETF) and keep it forever through all the ups and downs of the market.

- **Dollar Cost Averaging:** Dollar-cost averaging has been well-researched and proven to be efficient over time. It is really simple to put into action. Essentially, it means investing in a stock or ETF for example in little amounts over time regularly. You'll pay more for assets as the price rises, and less when the price is down. This strategy is good for limiting the impact of market volatility on your investment because it will average out over time. DCA is highly recommended as nobody can predict the market. It takes the guessing out. Deposit a set amount of money into your brokerage account weekly, bi weekly or monthly(it can be automatically deposited into your account from your checking account and on periodic intervals you can purchase more shares of the stock or ETF no matter what the market is doing. This is a simple way to increase shares of ownership, and create compounding in your portfolio. Again, highly recommended for long term investing

- **Buy On Red Days:** This simply means if you intend to purchase shares of a stock or ETF or you intend to dollar cost average, only buy on red days. Red days are the days when the market and/or your stocks/ETFs are down that day. Green signals they are up that day. Simply look at the stocks app on your phone, or on tv or online and if you see the market is down, that is a great day to buy. You want to buy shares as cheap as possible. The larger the drop in the market, the better the buying opportunity.

Chapter 8.3: Risk Tolerance

"It's much easier to stay out of trouble now than to get out of trouble later."- Warren Buffet

"Progress always involves risk; you can't steal second base and keep your foot on first."- Frederick Wilcox

The ability and readiness to absorb a loss in the value of your investments is referred to as risk tolerance. Consider how comfortable you will feel maintaining your assets if the stock market falls drastically when calculating your risk tolerance. Understanding your risk tolerance is essential for becoming a sensible investor. Certain financial instruments, such as stocks generally have a higher level of risk than others, such as government bonds. This is because there is no guarantee of profit when owning shares of a company. If a firm performs badly or loses popularity with investors, its stock price may decline – and you may lose money. With all this talk about risk tolerance, let's actually define the word risk.

According to *investor.gov*, **Risk is the degree of uncertainty and/or potential financial loss that is inherent in a financial decision.** To simplify it, risk can be looked at as the likelihood something bad can happen with your investment. Your decisions when investing will affect your level of risk and should be based on your risk tolerance. Keep in mind however, generally speaking, the higher the risk, the higher the reward

The simplest way to analyze risk in any investment is to compare the price of the asset to its true value. Price vs value will determine the risk you are taking. An asset viewed as extremely risky can have a very low risk for an investor if purchased at a price far below its true value. This is because the investor is giving themselves a tremendous margin of safety. However, an asset that is viewed as being very low risk can carry more risk than the asset viewed as extremely risky if purchased far above its true value. In this instance, the margin of safety is very low. An asset is an asset. Would you purchase a small unassuming rental property that may be challenging to rent worth $50,000 for $2,000 or a beautiful rental property that will rent easily in the same neighborhood worth $300,000 for $1 million dollars?

Your risk tolerance should be focused on the price you are getting the asset in relation to its true value. The price you pay is extremely important, and if you have a low risk tolerance it is even more important. Price in relation to value matters. It is simple. Buy assets at a price that is lower than its true value, and this generally will lower your risk.

Determine Your Risk Tolerance

Answering a few key questions can assist you in determining your risk tolerance:

- **What are your investment objectives?** Do you invest on a regular basis in order to grow the value of your portfolio? Or if you currently have a portfolio to your liking, do you want to safeguard it rather than grow it and live off the income it produces? Each will reflect a different amount of risk tolerance.

- **When do you need the money?** Again, you must always consider time when investing. The faster you need the money, the lower your risk tolerance should be. The money you'll need for a down payment on a house next year has a far shorter time horizon than the money you'll need for retirement, which may be several years away.

- **What would you do if your portfolio lost 50% this year?** Consider hypothetical obstacles and worst-case scenarios to determine your risk tolerance. Would you lose sleep if your investment lost 50% of its value? Or would you get excited, keep it invested and consider investing more money to take advantage of the lower cost? Remember, you only make or lose money when you sell a stock. Until then, it is just a number in an account.

Do you know the difference between a realized gain and an unrealized gain?

Realized gain- *Selling an asset that is at a higher price than what you purchased it for. You pay taxes on a realized gain. If the asset has been held for more than a year, you pay capital gains tax instead of income tax, which is generally lower. Holding it over a year is considered a long term investment.*

Unrealized gain- *An asset that has a higher price than what you purchased it for that HASN'T been sold yet. You pay no taxes on an unrealized gain, because you haven't profited from it yet.*

Realized loss- *Selling an asset that is at a lower price than what you purchased it for. You pay no taxes on a realized loss, AND in certain cases it can be used against a realized gain to offset paying taxes on the realized gain. If the asset is held for more than a year, it is considered a long term investment.*

Unrealized loss- *An asset that has a lower price than what you purchased it for that HASN'T been sold yet. You pay no taxes on an unrealized loss not only because you haven't sold it yet, but there is no income or profit to tax.*

*Remember, until you sell an asset at a higher price than you purchased it for, your investment is just a number in an account. This is why the government does not tax unrealized gains. People get overly excited when the figures in their account rise, and overly depressed when they drop. Until you actually sell the asset, the gain or loss is unrealized. You only make or lose money when you actually sell. Keep this in mind to check your emotions when investing. Don't get too high or low emotionally.

Chapter 8.4: Portfolio Diversification

*"The Noah rule states that predicting rain doesn't count:
building the ark does."- Warren Buffet*

Diversification is a strategy that involves spreading investments among numerous financial instruments, sectors, and other categories. It seeks to reduce losses by investing in many sectors that might react differently to the same occurrence.

Understanding Diversification in Investing

Assume your portfolio consists only of airline stocks. Any unfavorable news, such as an extended pilot strike that results in flight cancellations, will cause share values to plummet. This indicates that the value of your portfolio will decrease significantly. You may counteract this by purchasing a few railroad stocks, affecting only a small amount of your portfolio. There is a strong likelihood that railroad stock values will climb as passengers seek alternate forms of transportation. The railroad stocks could be a hedge against your airline stocks.

Let's look at the United States of America. There are many different agencies that protect our nation. You have the Army, Airforce, Navy, Marines, Navy SEALS, CIA, FBI, NSA, ATF, US Customs, Police Departments and countless more. They all have specific duties, and they in many cases work to support each other. However they all serve one purpose: The protection of our entire nation.

Diversification can work in a similar fashion. You can own stocks, ETF's, real estate, intellectual property, cryptocurrencies, mutual funds, private brokerage accounts, a 401(k), gold and so on. They all serve different functions in your investment portfolio but in the end, they all operate in helping you build wealth. When one asset is down, another can support you and vice versa.

Ways to Help Diversify Your Portfolio

Diversification is not a new idea. Here are suggestions that may help you with diversification:

1. Spread the Wealth

Stocks may be fantastic but you may not want to invest all of your money into a single stock or industry. Consider building your own fund by investing in a few companies that you know and trust, after doing your own research.

Stocks aren't the only thing to consider. Commodities, exchange-traded funds (ETFs), and real estate investment trusts are additional options (REITs).

2. Consider Index or Bond Funds

Consider including index funds to your portfolio. Investing in funds that replicate multiple indexes is another method to diversify your portfolio over time. You may further protect your portfolio from market volatility and unpredictability by including certain fixed-income products(like bonds).

3. Keep Building Your Portfolio

Regularly increase your investment if possible. If you have $10,000 to invest, you may want to use dollar-cost averaging. This method is used to offset the highs and lows caused by market volatility. The goal of this technique is to reduce your investment risk by investing the same amount of money over time.

Dollar-cost averaging is a method of investing money on a regular basis in a certain portfolio of assets. When using this method, you will purchase more shares when prices are low and fewer shares when prices are high.

You may invest the full $10,000 in one lump sum. Lump sum investing works best if you buy the asset on the lowest day of the year. Your return will be better than if you dollar cost average. The problem is, how do you predict the bottom of the market in a year? Lump sum investing works best when the market is on its way up. Dollar Cost Averaging works best when the market is on its way down. Again, nobody can accurately predict the course of the market.

4. Know When to Get Out

Buying and holding and dollar-cost averaging are both popular investment strategies. However, just because your assets are on autopilot does not mean you should ignore them.

Maintain your investments and be aware of any changes in general market circumstances. You'll want to know what's going on with the companies in which you've invested. You'll also be able to recognize when it's time to cut your losses, sell, and move on to your next investment by doing so. There are times where it is beneficial to take profit from an investment and move it into another. For certain assets you can use a buy and hold or dollar-cost average strategy. For other investments, you can set a limit on profit or losses where you will decide when to get out. All of your investments do not have to operate by the same exact rules or do the same exact thing.

5. **Own as many assets as you are comfortable with**

The world's wealthiest people own many assets that can potentially generate income. Do you? They own stocks, businesses, real estate and intellectual property among others. Many of them have written books. Have you ever considered writing a book? A book is an asset that can garner royalty income. How about creating an online course about something that you are well versed in? These are additional assets that you can own. You don't always have to look for high income generating assets. Some assets will earn more than others but when you put all of the assets together they will assist you in building your wealth. If there is an asset that can generate income for life, I want to own it. Owning one asset is too close to owning no assets. This is why I want to own MANY income producing assets. Do you have the same mindset? However, you should only own assets that you are comfortable with AND that you can manage within your investment portfolio. If you love stocks and have no interest in owning real estate, then DON'T buy a rental property. You may want to focus on investing in stocks, and owning one or two rental properties, not fifty of them. You may have interest in owning residential real estate and not commercial. If you love real estate, but have no interest in cryptocurrency, then you shouldn't invest in crypto if you don't understand it or have any interest in it. Owning many income producing assets does not mean you need to own ALL income producing assets. Invest in what you can manage. In the end, only invest in what you understand AND what you feel comfortable with investing in.

*Here why it is important to own as many assets as you are comfortable with owning. If you own one tree and it burns down, that will have a huge impact. However if you own a forest and one tree

burns down, you still have endless trees to support you. Makes sense? Just remember, only own a forest that you can manage. Too much forest can be stressful. If you try to invest in multiple assets that you cannot manage, it could lead to failure. Do what makes you comfortable in the end.

Diversification can be great for most individuals when buying stocks for example, however there can be drawbacks to it......

Diversification means putting your money into different types of investments. It's like not putting all your eggs in one basket. Many people think this is a good way to invest because it can help protect your money.

Diversification however may make very little sense for anyone that knows what they're doing and is willing to do deep research into any company they are buying. Remember, when buying a stock you are buying a piece of a company. How many companies can you possibly analyze and purchase is the question? The wealthiest people built their wealth focusing and creating one company, not 7 or 8*(think Jeff Bezos and Amazon, or Mark Zuckerberg and META/ Facebook, or Elon Musk and Tesla).*

This could mean spreading your money around isn't always the best idea. Sometimes it's better to focus on one or two stocks if you've done deep research, as this may give you a much better return than buying several stocks. Here's why.....

1. **It might lower your profits**: If you spread your money too much, you might not make as much money.

2. **Knowledge is important**: It may be better to really understand a few things you're investing in, rather than knowing a little about lots of things.

3. **It can cost more**: Buying and selling lots of different investments can cost more money.

4. **It might limit your strategy**: If you spread your money too much, you might not be able to focus on the best opportunities.

If you buy Company A, and pour all of your resources into that company, and it gets a 50% return, then you get a 50% return

If you diversify and buy Company A, B, C and D, and split your resources 25% for each one, and their returns respectively are 50%, 40%, 30% and 20%, then your total return is only 35%.

*You would have done better investing all of your money into Company A, had you done your research. Of course however, this is riskier.

When thinking about diversification, it can be argued that diversification should apply to diversification of sources of income, rather than diversification within a stock portfolio for example. Having multiple streams or sources of income is diversification as well, and maybe the BEST form of diversification.

As always, do what is best for you.

Chapter 8.5: Understanding the Balance Sheet

"If you can't read the scoreboard, you don't know the score. If you don't know the score, you can't tell the winners from the losers. - Warren Buffet

"I do not like debt and do not like to invest in companies that have too much debt, particularly long term debt. With long term debt, increases in interest rates can drastically affect company profits and make future cash flow less predictable."- Warren Buffet

When deciding which stocks to add to your portfolio, a strategy that is extremely important is analyzing the financial health of the company. The balance sheet of the company is a good way to start. A balance sheet is a financial document that indicates the real worth of a corporation or organization—its "book value." The balance sheet does this by identifying and counting all of a company's assets, liabilities, and owner's equity as of a certain date known as the reporting date.

A balance sheet is often presented quarterly or yearly. Every publicly traded company that issues shares of ownership by law must provide financial statements. A Form 10-k shows financial statements yearly. A Form 10-Q shows financial statements quarterly. To find a company's financial statements, simply google sec.gov/EDGAR and type in the company or its ticker symbol(the abbreviated letters that represent the company; Coca-Cola would be KO for example). You can also go directly to the company's website.

The Purpose of the Balance Sheet

A balance sheet is a snapshot of a company at a certain moment in time. It is a snapshot of a company's financial status, as defined by assets, liabilities, and equity. A balance sheet is intended to provide insight into whether a firm is successful or failing when it is evaluated.

A balance sheet will show what resources are available to a firm and what the company owns and owes. Potential investors may determine whether or not to invest in a company based on this information.

Remember that a balance sheet presents information as of a given date. A balance sheet is, by definition, based on prior data. While investors and stakeholders may use a balance sheet to forecast future performance, prior outcomes are no guarantee of future results.

The Balance Sheet Equation

A balance sheet's information is usually structured according to the following equation: **Assets = Liabilities + Owners' Equity.**

While this is the most popular method for balance sheets, it is not the only way to organize the data. Here are some additional equations you could come across:

Owners' Equity = Assets - Liabilities

Liabilities = Assets - Owners' Equity

A balance sheet must always be balanced. The assets must always equal the liabilities plus the owners' equity. Equity must always equal assets minus liabilities. Assets minus owner's equity must always equal liabilities.

If a balance sheet does not balance, the document was most likely created incorrectly. Mistakes are often caused by incomplete or missing data, wrongly recorded transactions, or equity miscalculations.

Here's a deeper look at what each of those value categories normally includes: assets, liabilities, and owner's equity.

1. Assets

An asset is everything that a firm has that has value. If needed, a company might turn an asset into cash via a process called liquidation. In a balance sheet, assets are normally counted as positives (+) and divided into two categories: current assets and noncurrent assets.

Current assets are often anything that a corporation hopes to turn into cash within a year, such as:

Cash and cash equivalents

Marketable Securities

Inventory

Supplies

Noncurrent assets are long-term investments that are unlikely to be turned into cash in the near future, such as:

Land

Property

Plant and equipment

Trademarks

Patents

Businesses invest in assets to grow their wealth. Like individual investors, corporations need assets that can help them generate income in order to be successful.

2. Liabilities

Liability is the opposite of an asset. A company's asset is something it owns that can make it money, but a liability is something it owes that takes money out. Liabilities are financial and legal obligations to pay a sum of money to a debtor, which is why they are usually accounted for as negatives (-) on a balance sheet.

Just as assets are classified as current or noncurrent, liabilities are classified as current or noncurrent.

Current obligations are often defined as any debt liability due within one year, which may include:

Short term debt

Accounts payable(money owed to suppliers)

Taxes

Dividends

Utility payments

Rent

Payroll Payments

Noncurrent liabilities are often defined as any long-term commitments or debts that are not due within one year, such as:

Leases

Deferred taxes

Pension payments

Lines of credit

Corporate bond payments

Bank loans

A liability may also entail a future duty to supply goods or services.

3. **Owners' Equity**

Owners' equity, also known as shareholders' equity, is commonly defined as whatever belongs to a company's shareholders after all obligations are deducted.

If you add up all of a company's resources (its assets) and deduct all of its obligations(its liabilities), the remaining amount is the owners' equity.

Owners' equity generally consists of two major components. The first is money, which is donated to the company as an investment in return for partial ownership (typically represented by shares). The second is profits that the corporation creates and keeps over time.

A Balance Sheet Example

Important information about the health of a company can be seen in a balance sheet. Take a look at the fictitious balance sheet below. Let's choose Company X stock. Below, we will look at some(not all) key hypothetical elements from Company X's balance sheet as an example. We will also analyze it over a 5 year period. Definitions of these elements and their meanings will be provided.

COMPANY X STOCK- BALANCE SHEET(*In Millions*)

When numbers are expressed in millions, simply take the number and multiply by 1,000,000. Many of the figures will be in the billions. If a company expresses the figures in thousands, you take the figure and multiply it by 1,000. This is done due to the fact that the figures can get high and this will make it easier for investors to read.

ITEM	2018	2019	2020	2021	2022
Cash & Cash Equivalents	$66,300	100,580	90,980	62,640	48,300
Total Current Assets	$131,340	162,820	143,710	134,840	135,410
Total Assets	$365,730	338,520	323,890	351,000	352,760
Short Term Debt	$11,960	5,980	6,430	7,450	11,520
Total Current Liabilities	$116,870	105,720	105,390	125,480	153,980
Long-Term Debt	$93,740	91,810	107,050	119,380	109,710
Total Liabilities	$258,580	248,030	258,550	287,910	302,080
Total Liabilities / Total Assets *This will not appear on a Form 10-K. You can calculate this yourself.	70.70%	73.27%	79.83%	82.03%	85.64%
Total Shareholders' Equity	$107,150	90,490	65,340	63,090	50,670
Liabilities & Shareholders' Equity	$365,730	338,520	323,890	351,000	352,760

Liabilities and Shareholders' equity should be exactly the same as Total Assets for the balance sheet to be balanced

Key takeaways from this balance sheet:

- Total liabilities has increased

- Shareholders equity(the amount owners of the company have invested in the business) has decreased

- Total Assets of the company has fluctuated

- Total liabilities/Total Assets percentage has increased(meaning a higher percentage of the companies assets are financed through loans or debt)

There are many questions to ask yourself after reviewing the balance sheet, such as why has shareholder equity gone down? Again, you must do your research.

Chapter 8.6: Understanding the Income Statement

"I try to buy stock in businesses that are so wonderful that an idiot can run them. Because sooner or later, one will."- Warren Buffet

An income statement is an important financial document needed to analyze a publicly traded company.

Income statements are known as profit and loss (P&L) statements. It will provide all income and expenses for a certain time period. Income statements are often distributed in the form of quarterly and yearly reports.

Purpose of An Income Statement

An income statement's goal is to demonstrate a company's financial success over time. It provides the success of a company's operations. The income statement contains all revenue and spending accounts for a certain time period.

Income statements can assist you in determining whether the business is profitable. Accountants, investors, and business owners study income statements on a regular basis to understand how well a company is doing in comparison to its planned performance, and they use that information to run the business.

Always keep in mind that income statements can be manipulated by businesses to some degree in a way that a balance sheet or a cash flow statement cannot. The income statement is heavily influenced by accounting measures however it is still important to analyze.

Elements of an Income Statement

While all financial data contributes to a picture of a company's financial health, an income statement is one of the most essential pieces of information that a company's leadership team and individual investors may evaluate since it contains a complete breakdown of revenue and spending throughout a reporting period. This includes the following:

Revenue/Total Revenue- Money earned by the company over a period of time

Total Cost of Revenue- *The total cost to produce the goods or services that is being sold(This includes Cost of goods sold which is just the direct cost to produce a good or service)*

Gross Profit- *Total Revenue minus Total Cost of Revenue*

Net Income- *Total Revenue minus ALL expenses*

Earnings Per Share(EPS)- *How much a company earns for each share of the company. Net income divided by outstanding shares*

Income Statement Analysis

To keep things as simple as possible, when analyzing the income statement of a company's financials, you typically would like to see an increase in the *Revenue, Gross Margin, Gross Profit, Net Income, and Earnings Per Share(EPS) over a 3-5 year period. This is a good sign; however it does not mean you should jump into buying the company. This is just a helpful gauge.*

Basic Shares outstanding you want to stay steady, not grow typically. Why? If a company keeps issuing more and more shares, it could mean they need more money and it also means that you will own a lower percentage of the company as a shareholder as more people buy into the company.

Income Statement Example

Below, we will look at some(not all) key hypothetical elements from Company X's income statement as an example. We will also analyze it over a 5 year period. Definitions of these elements and their meanings will be provided.

COMPANY X STOCK- INCOME STATEMENT/STATEMENT OF OPERATIONS(*In Millions except Earnings per share*)

When numbers are expressed in millions, simply take the number and multiply by 1,000,000. Many of the figures will be in the billions. If a company expresses the figures in thousands, you take the figure and multiply it by 1,000. This is done due to the fact that the figures can get high and this will make it easier for investors to read.

ITEM	2018	2019	2020	2021	2022
Total Revenue	$265,810	259,970	274,150	365,820	394,330
Total Cost of Revenue	$163,830	162,260	170,140	212,980	223,550
Gross Profit *(Total Revenue - Total Cost of Revenue)	$101,980	97,700	104,010	152,840	170,780
Net Income *Net Income is the bottom line on the income statement, and the top line on the cash flow statement	$59,530	55,260	57,410	94,680	99,800
EPS(Earnings Per Share)	$3	2.99	3.31	5.67	6.15
Basic Shares Outstanding	19.82	18.47	17.35	16.7	16.22

Key takeaways from this income statement:

- Total Revenue has increased
- Net Income has fluctuated but increased
- Earnings Per Share(EPS) has increased
- Basic Shares Outstanding has been steady

*Company X appears to be making money from sales, which you always want to see. Revenue and Net Income increases are always welcomed. They haven't issued more outstanding shares which could be why Company X has taken out more debt to raise money(Remember, 2 ways for a company to raise money are to issue more shares or take out debt). Again, do your research.

Chapter 8.7: Understanding the Cash Flow Statement

"Cash is to a business what oxygen is to an individual."- Warren Buffet

Cash flow is classified as cash flow from operating operations, cash flow from Investment activities, and cash flow from financing activities. It is the cash that flows in and out of a business. A cash flow statement's objective is to present a complete picture of what occurred to a company's cash over a set time known as the accounting period. It displays a company's capacity to function in the short and long term depending on how much cash flows in and out of the firm.

Typically, the cash flow statement has three main sections:

Operating Activities

Investing Activities

Financing Activities

Operating activities describe the cash flow created when a firm provides its regular products or services, which includes both income and costs. Investing operations include cash flow from the purchase or sale of assets, such as real estate or automobiles, as well as non-physical property, such as patents. The cash flow created through loan and equity financing is referred to as financing operations.

A company's cash from operations should ideally frequently surpass its net income because it generally shows that a company has more cash coming in than going out. Many investors value operating cash flow over net income.

How To Interpret A Cash Flow Statement

It could be argued that the cash flow statement is the most important document of all the financial statements because in the end cash is the bottom line. It shows how the company creates cash through the main sources of a business which are its operations, financing and investing. Cash flow statements may indicate if a company is in its early stages or is a mature business that is a cash cow.

Understanding the cash flow of a business will help you in evaluating the stock you are interested in purchasing. It will help you provide value to the company, and make a determination if the price you are paying is the right price. A company that is generating lots of cash, and is increasing its cash flow is most likely doing something right in its business. Even a new company that doesn't have a reputation just yet may be a good investment if it shows solid cash flow, and is trading at an undervalued price. Consistent growth in its cash flow may mean the company is poised to grow in the near future.

Cash flow is often shown as either positive (the company receives more cash than it spends) or negative (the company spends more cash than it receives).

Positive Cash Flow

Positive cash flow means that a corporation has more cash coming into the business than out of the business during a certain time period. This is a good position since having extra cash enables the firm to reinvest in itself and its shareholders, pay off debt and identify new methods to develop the company.

Negative Cash Flow

Negative cash flow shows that your cash loss exceeds your cash intake within a certain time period. A mismatch between spending and income may be causing negative cash flow.

Negative cash flow may also be created by a firm's choice to expand its operations and invest in future development. When a company has negative cash flow, it is important to gain an understanding of why, as the cash they are spending may be going to grow the company which could help the business make money in the future.

Net Income vs Cash Flow: What's the difference?

Cash Flow and Net Income are both extremely important metrics to a business. Many times it can be hard for people to understand the difference between the two.

Net Income

- *Revenue that is left over after all expenses are deducted*
- *Deals with the earnings of a company from its business after all expenses are paid*
- *Shows the actual profits of a company*

Cash Flow

- *The actual cash that flows in and out of a business*
- *Deals only with the cash available to a company when all is said and done*
- *Shows how much cash a company has*

When analyzing a company, you want the free cash flow higher than the net income

Cash Flow Statement Example

Below, we will look at some(not all) key hypothetical elements from Company X's cash flow statement as an example. We will also analyze it over a 5 year period. Definitions of these elements and their meanings will be provided.

When numbers are expressed in millions, simply take the number and multiply by 1,000,000. Many of the figures will be in the billions. If a company expresses the figures in thousands, you take the figure and multiply it by 1,000. This is done due to the fact that the figures can get high and this will make it easier for investors to read.

ITEM	2018	2019	2020	2021	2022
Net Cash from Operations/Cash generated from Operating Activities	$77,430	69,390	80,670	104,040	122,150

Property, Plant, Equipment Payments(Capital Expenditures) *Under the Investing activities portion of the cash flow statement*	$13,300	10,500	7,310	11,090	10,710
Net Investing Cash Flow/Net Cash Used In Investing	-$16,070	-45,900	-14,290	-14,550	-22,350
Net Financing Cash Flow/Net Cash Used In Financing	-27,880	-30,980	-36,820	-33,350	-31,750
Free Cash Flow *Does not appear on a cash flow statement. You can calculate this yourself* *Cash From Operations minus Capital Expenditures*	$64,130	58,890	73,360	92,950	111,440

Key takeaways from this cash flow statement:

- Net operating cash flow has increased
- Capital Expenditures has been fairly steady. Company X is trying to grow the business
- Free Cash Flow has increased

*Company X increasing its Free Cash Flow is a great sign. This may signal that Company X financially is in a good position to operate. It shows how much actual cash a company has to use. When it is all said and done, having cash and increasing the amount of cash you have increases a company's safety net. Think about it.

Would you feel more comfortable with $10,000 cash in the bank or $10,000,000 cash in the bank?

Free cash flow is an important metric to any company. Free cash flow is cash from operations minus capital expenditures. The company can allocate that cash to whatever they want. Simply, it's the cash they have left over. With free cash flow, a company can:

Pay down debt

Buy back shares

Make acquisitions

Pay a dividend

Reinvest back into the company

The cash flow statement is regarded by many as the most important financial statement. On an income statement, revenue, earnings and earnings per share can be manipulated to some degree. Revenue can be increased by a business by opening more stores. Earnings per share can increase if a company buys back its own shares. However cash flow cannot be manipulated. Free cash flow is arguably the most important metric to a company. You want to see free cash flow increasing every year. Also, you want free cash flow to be able to cover a company's total liabilities as much as possible. Take the long term debt or total liabilities of the company, and divide it by the current free cash flow. The number that you get tells you how many years it would take to pay off all the debt or total liabilities of the company with the current free cash flow figure. The lower the number, the better as this indicates the company is most likely in good financial standing.

If company Z has $50 billion dollars in total liabilities, and last year made $10 billion in free cash flow, the math would be:

$50 billion / $10 billion = 5; It would take company Z 5 years to pay off all of its total liabilities with last year's free cash flow.

If company D has $75 billion in total liabilities, and last year made $8 billion in free cash flow, the math would be

$75 billion / $8 billion = 9.3; It would take company D 9.3 years to pay off all of its total liabilities with last year's free cash flow

Which company appears healthier financially to you?

The statements shown are basic, just to introduce you to the financials. They are more complicated than what you see here, and this is just to help introduce you to the terms. To really get an understanding of the balance sheet, income statement and cash flow statement, please practice looking at the actual financial statements of a company, and practice reading them. It will take time.

Other Cash Flow Metrics

If you wanted to do an even deeper analysis using the cash flow statement, here are some ratios that may help you in analyzing the financial health of a company:

Cash Flow to Net Income Ratio

The cash flow to net income ratio calculates the ability of a business to generate cash from its operations. Investors generally want to see a ratio of 1.00 or higher. It is calculated by:

Cash Flow to Net Income Ratio = *Cash from operating activities / Net Income*

Using Company X in 2022 as an example: $122,150 / $99,800 = **1.22**

This ratio shows that for every $1.00 in net income, Company X generated $1.22 in cash.

Cash Flow Margin Ratio

The cash flow margin ratio calculates the ability of a business to generate cash from its sales revenue. The ratio is calculated by dividing the operating cash flow of the business by its revenue.

Cash Flow Margin Ratio = *Cash from operating activities / Revenue*

Using Company X from 2022 as an example: $122,150 / 394,330 = **30.9%**

This ratio shows that 30.9% of Company X's revenue/sales is converted into actual cash

Company X- Would you buy?

After analyzing Company X's financial statements, would you invest in this company?

It's a trick question. Let's say based on the financial statements you think Company X is a good company to invest in. What you have to figure out is if it is worth the price it is currently trading at. Company X may be overvalued at $100 a share, however at $35 a share it may be undervalued. Buying it at $35 a share may be a better investment than buying it at $100 a share. There are other metrics you must look at such as Price to Earnings ratio(P/E), Price to Sales Ratio(P/S), 52 Week Range, and others to help you determine if the price is currently a fair price. The average person who buys stocks never once looks at this information, which is why when economic storms hit, they lose money. A company can be a good company, but the price may be too expensive in relation to its value. You can search for a company's annual report which is fairly easy to read. You can find the annual report of a company by doing a search online, or possibly going to its website. You can also look at the Form 10-K of the stock/company, which is a detailed version of the annual report of the financial health of the company. The Form 10-K gives information on the company from the vision of the company, to the risks they may be undertaking as well as its financials. A Form 10-K is more difficult to understand but is still important for potential investors in a particular company. This would be the most accurate. Just go to SEC.gov/EDGAR and perform a search. Or you can go to the company website and you may find it there. A smart move also would be to compare Company X to one or two of its competitors to get an idea of how it is performing in relation to other companies in that industry.

*To check out the financial statements of a company(balance sheet, income statement and cash flow statement), search its Form 10-K. Then go to Item 8 which is Financial Statements and Supplementary Data. Financial Statements and Supplementary Data requires the company's audited financial statements. This includes the company's income statement (which is sometimes called the statement of earnings or the statement of operations), balance sheets, statement of cash flows and statement of stockholders' equity. The financial statements are accompanied by notes that explain the information presented in the financial statements.

Source- *https://www.sec.gov/files/reada10k.pdf*

A Form 10-K is one of the most boring things on earth to try and read. Unless you have a specific hobby in reading them, you probably will not enjoy it. However they are extremely important IF you plan to invest your hard earned money in a particular stock. Think about it. If you have to read a Form 10-K for EVERY stock you are interested in, you will naturally become pickier with the stocks you may choose to purchase. This could be a good thing for your investment strategy. If the company is worthwhile enough for you to read its Form 10-K, then that may be the one you should pick to invest in. And if you read the Form 10-K and you don't like what you see, you may have saved yourself a lot of money.

What to Analyze in a Company's Annual Report(Form 10-K)

An annual report is like a big book that tells us how a company did during the year. Knowing how to read it is crucial to understand how well a business is doing. Let's look at some of the main parts:

1. The CEO's Letter

The CEO is like the boss of the company. They write a letter at the beginning of the report. This letter tells us:

- How the company did that year
- Important things that happened
- What they think will happen next

It's like getting a note from the teacher about how the class is doing!

2. What the Company Does

This part tells us:

- What does the company sell, or what service they provide
- Who buys their products or uses their services
- What makes them special compared to other companies

For example, if it's a toy company, it might say it makes fun toys for kids aged 5-10 and that its toys are unique because they're made from recycled materials.

3. Money Matters

This is where we learn how much money the company made and spent. It's like looking at a piggy bank to see how much money went in and how much came out.

There are three main parts:

1. Income Statement: Shows how much money they made and spent

2. Balance Sheet: Shows what the company owns and owes

3. Cash Flow Statement: Shows how money moved in and out of the company

4. **Notes and Explanations**

Sometimes, there are extra notes that explain things in more detail. It's like when your teacher writes notes on your homework to help you understand better.

5. **The Auditor's Report**

An auditor is like a detective for money. They check to make sure all the numbers in the report are correct. Their report tells us if everything looks okay or if there might be problems.

6. **Corporate Governance**

Corporate governance is like the rules and practices that help a company run smoothly and fairly. It's about making sure the company does the right thing for its owners (called shareholders) and everyone else involved.

Reading an annual report takes practice. It's okay if you don't understand everything at first. The more you read, the better you'll understand how companies work!

To make things even easier for you, you should be able to view the fundamentals of the company you are interested in within your brokerage account if you click on the fundamentals tab for the stock you are researching. The balance sheet, cash flow statement and income statement should all be there with the rest of the financial statements. This is just another option, and for most people the easiest.

Keep In Mind....

When analyzing the financials of a company you are interested in, pay attention to the debt, liabilities, and free cash flow increases. All companies have debt and liabilities. Not all have sufficient cash flow.

Debt and liabilities can increase in a company. The free cash flow should increase as well. Look at the balance sheet and the cash flow statements. If the debt appears to be rising at a faster rate than the free cash flow, would you feel safe investing in this company at its current price? Would you give money to an individual who is increasing their debt, yet isn't taking home more money? Something to consider along with many other factors....

Other Stock Investing Metrics

Other Stock Investing Metrics

Price to Earnings Ratio(P/E Ratio)- This tells you the relationship between the price of the stock and its earnings(income the company keeps). For example, if a company has a P/E of 50, that means the price of the stock is 50 times its earnings, which may make it expensive to buy at that moment. The formula is as follows: **Market Capitalization divided by net income.**

Another way to interpret this is what you are willing to pay to earn a dollar on this stock. So if the P/E is 50, that means you are willing to pay $50 to earn $1x investing in this company.

No P/E for a stock most likely means it has no earnings.

The P/E ratio is a way to determine whether a company's stock price is a good deal. It's like comparing the price of a toy to how fun it is to play with.

Here's how it works:

- We take the current price of a company's stock
- We divide it by how much money the company earns for each share

The P/E ratio helps us understand:

- If a stock costs too much or too little
- How a company is doing compared to other similar companies
- What investors think about a company's future

Let's imagine two toy companies:

1. Fun Toys Inc.

   - Stock price: $10

   - Earnings per share: $1

   - P/E ratio: 10 ($10 ÷ $1 = 10)

2. Super Games Co.

   - Stock price: $20

   - Earnings per share: $2

   - P/E ratio: 10 ($20 ÷ $2 = 10)

Even though Super Games Co. has a higher stock price, both companies have the same P/E ratio. This means investors think they're equally good deals!

There's no one perfect P/E ratio. It depends on:

- *What kind of company it is*

- *How fast the company is growing*

For example, a fast-growing tech company might have a higher P/E ratio than a slow-growing food company.

The P/E ratio is helpful, but it doesn't tell us everything. Here are some things to remember:

1. It doesn't show how fast a company is growing

2. It can change quickly if the stock price changes a lot

3. Sometimes, it's hard to know exactly how much a company is earning

That's why investors often use other tools, along with the P/E ratio, to make decisions about stocks.

Price to Earnings Growth(PEG Ratio)- Based on the price to earnings ratio to a degree, this metric indicates the price of a particular stock in relation to its expected annual earnings per share growth. Unlike Price to Earnings, Price to Sales and Price to Book ratios which look backwards at a company, the PEG ratio looks for forward growth in a company. The lower the ratio, the better. If the ratio is around 1 or lower, this could indicate an undervalued company or stock. It is calculated by the P/E Ratio divided by the expected Earnings per share(EPS) growth annually.

To find the PEG ratio, we need to do these steps:

1. Find out how much one share of the company costs
2. Find out how much money the company makes per share
3. Divide the share price by the money made per share (this gives us the P/E ratio)
4. Find out how fast the company is growing
5. Divide the P/E ratio by the growth rate

A lower PEG ratio is usually better. Here's what different PEG ratios mean:

- PEG less than 1: The stock might be a good deal
- PEG equal to 1: The stock price is fair
- PEG more than 1: The stock might be too expensive

Let's look at two pretend companies:

1. Banana Corp:
   - Share price: $10
   - Money made per share: $1
   - Growth rate: 10%
   - PEG ratio: 1
2. Apple Inc:
   - Share price: $20
   - Money made per share: $2
   - Growth rate: 30%
   - PEG ratio: 0.33

Although Apple Inc.'s shares cost more, its PEG ratio is lower. This means the company's stock might be a better deal because it is growing faster.

Beta- Beta tells you how volatile a stock is in relation to the overall stock market. The stock market as a whole has a beta of 1. Any stock above 1 is more volatile, and the higher above 1 it is, the more volatile that investment. Any stock below 1 is less volatile. A volatile stock does not mean you should not necessarily invest in it. It just means it has higher and lower swings than the market. Conversely, a low beta does not mean you should go out and buy it, as it may not make you much money. Do your research.

If a stock has a beta of 1.2:

- When the market goes up 10%, this stock might increase about 12%.

- When the market drops 10%, this stock might drop about 12%.

If a stock has a beta of 0.8:

- When the market goes up 10%, this stock might only go up about 8%.

- When the market goes down 10%, this stock might only go down about 8%.

Investors use beta to help them decide how risky a stock is. If they want less risk, they might choose stocks with lower betas. They might select stocks with higher betas if they're okay with more risk.

Different types of companies often have different betas:

- Technology companies often have higher betas (riskier).

- Utility companies (like electric companies) often have lower betas (less risky).

Alpha- Alpha will tell you how the stock performs against the overall stock market in relation to how risky the stock may be. The stock market has an alpha of 0. If the alpha of the stock is above 0 or is a plus, that tells you it is currently outperforming the market relative to its risk. If it is below 0, or negative, that tells you it is underperforming the market.

Let's imagine two kids selling lemonade:

1. Sally makes $10 from her lemonade stand. Most lemonade stands in her neighborhood make $8. Sally has a positive alpha because she did better than the overall lemonade market.

2. Tommy makes $6 from his lemonade stand. Since most stands make $8, Tommy has a negative alpha because he didn't do as well as the overall lemonade market.

Price to Sales Ratio(P/S Ratio)- This tells you the relationship between the price of the stock and its revenue per share(money brought in from business activity). It describes how much someone must pay to buy one share of a company relative to how much one share generates in revenue. The lower the ratio, typically the better. Price to sales does not consider the actual earnings of the company, which is why many investors prefer the P/E ratio over the P/S ratio. The formula is as follows: **Market Capitalization divided by revenue**

If a company's stock costs $10 per share

And the company makes $5 in sales for each share

The P/S ratio would be $10 \div 5 = 2$

The P/S ratio helps us determine whether a company's stock is a good deal or too expensive.

*   A low P/S ratio might mean the stock is a good deal
*   A high P/S ratio might mean the stock is expensive

Let's say we have two candy companies:

1. Sweet Treats Co.
    *   Stock price: $20
    *   Sales per share: $10
    *   P/S ratio: $20 \div 10 = 2$

2. Candy Castle Co.
    *   Stock price: $30
    *   Sales per share: $5
    *   P/S ratio: $30 \div 5 = 6$

In this case, Sweet Treats Co. has a lower P/S ratio, which might mean it's a better deal than Candy Castle Co.

Price to Cash Flow Ratio(P/CF Ratio)- The price to cash flow ratio indicates the price of a company in relation to its operating cash flow. It is calculated by taking the price per share of the stock and dividing it by the cash flow per share. If a company has a P/CF Ratio of 15, then this means the price of the stock is 15 times the operating cash flow, or for every $15 you spend on the stock, you receive $1 in operating cash flow. The lower the ratio, the better. The formula is as follows: **Market Capitalization divided by operating cash flow**

The P/CF ratio is helpful because it looks at a company's actual cash flow, not just its paper profits. Sometimes, a company might seem to be losing money, but it actually has lots of cash coming in. The P/CF ratio helps us see that.

Let's say there's a lemonade stand. Each share of the stand costs $10, and the stand makes $2 in cash for each share. The P/CF ratio would be:

$10 ÷ $2 = 5

This means for every $1 of cash the stand makes, people are willing to pay $5 for a share.

What's a Good P/CF Ratio?

There's no perfect number, but generally:

- A low number might mean the stock is a good deal

- A high number might mean the stock is expensive

Remember, different types of businesses will have different typical P/CF ratios.

Price to Free Cash Flow Ratio(P/FCF Ratio)- The price to free cash flow ratio indicates the price of a company in relation to its free cash flow. Along with the price to earnings ratio, it is one of the most important ratios in analyzing a stock. Since free cash flow is not on a cash flow statement, you may have to do a little math to figure this one out. Once you figure out the current annual free cash flow of the company, the formula is as follows: **Market Capitalization divided by free cash flow.** The lower the number, the better.

- A low P/FCF number usually means the stock might be a good deal.

- A high P/FCF number might mean the stock is expensive.

Let's say a toy company has:

- Market value: $100

- Free cash flow: $10

   The P/FCF would be: 100 ÷ 10 = 10

This means the stock costs 10 times the amount of extra money the company has.

- *Always compare a company's P/FCF to those of other similar companies.*

- *Look at the P/FCF over time to see if it's improving.*

A Few Things to remember.....

Every metric has slight flaws; however they can be useful when analyzing a company. You may or may not want to use all of them. Use the ones that you personally find most important. Remember this is all for reference so don't get overwhelmed.

   Outside of Free Cash Flow, you don't really need to do any math to figure out these ratios. A viable brokerage account will have all of this easily accessible, as well as other valuations for the company you are interested in. Simply search for the stock or company, and go through all the information that they are providing on the company.

   Also, make sure you compare the company to its competitors and peers. Tech stocks will not operate like energy stocks. Compare apples to apples always. You can also do this in your brokerage account. Once you learn how to use your brokerage account, this all becomes fairly simple. Use this guide to help you. You should be doing very little if any math at all. These ratios and valuations should all be there for you.

   Below are more valuation metrics you should easily be able to find in your brokerage account under a tab showing the valuations of the company. Again, you shouldn't have to do any calculations to figure all of this out as it should already be present in your brokerage account. As a reminder, do not get too overwhelmed and use the valuations most important to you. You will want to compare these valuations to the valuations of a company's peers when doing your analysis. Recent news about the company should be

readily available as well. Also, you should be able to see analysts' thoughts on the stock you are looking to purchase. See what they think as well about the company, however don't make your decision solely based on what they think. They can be wrong as well. Always do your own research. Brokerage accounts have helped to simplify the investment process in many ways. Use them to your advantage.

Gross Profit Margin- Profit a company makes after paying off its cost of goods sold. A higher gross profit margin means a company has more funds available for research and development, marketing, or investment.

1. *First, you figure out how much money you made from selling your product. This is called "sales".*

2. *Then, you subtract how much it cost you to make the product. This is called "cost of goods sold".*

3. *What's left is your "gross profit".*

4. *To get the margin, you turn this into a percentage of your sales.*

Let's say you have a lemonade stand:

- *You sell 10 cups of lemonade for $1 each. Your sales are $10.*

- *It costs you 50 cents to make each cup (for lemons, sugar, and cups). Your total cost is $5.*

- *Your gross profit is $10 - $5 = $5*

- *Your gross profit margin is $5 ÷ $10 = 0.5 or 50%*

This means for every dollar you make from selling lemonade, you keep 50 cents as profit!

Gross profit margin helps business owners know if they're making enough money. If the number is too low, they might need to raise prices or find ways to make their product for less money.

Operating Profit Margin- Operating income (earnings before interest and taxes) divided by sales (or revenue). A higher operating margin shows the company is keeping costs under control.

Operating margin is a way to measure how well a company is doing at making money from its main business. It's like checking how good you are at running a lemonade stand.

To find the operating margin, we use this simple math:

Operating Margin = Money earned from main business ÷ Total money made from sales

The answer is usually shown as a percentage (%).

Operating margin helps us understand:

1. How good a company is at making money from what it sells

2. How well the company is being run

3. If the company is getting better or worse at making money over time

Let's say you have a lemonade stand:

- You make $100 from selling lemonade (total money made from sales)

- It costs you $60 for lemons, sugar, and cups (costs)

- So you earned $40 from your main business

Your operating margin would be:

$40 ÷ $100 = 0.4 or 40%

This means for every dollar you make selling lemonade, you keep 40 cents as profit.

A higher operating margin is usually better. It means the company is good at making money from its main business.

We can only compare operating margins between similar businesses. For example, it wouldn't make sense to compare a lemonade stand to a toy factory.

Net profit margin shows what part of each dollar you keep as profit. It's usually shown as a percentage.

Net profit margin helps us understand:

1. How well a company is doing

2. If the company is good at managing its money

3. How much profit the company makes from what it sells

Let's use our lemonade stand:

- *You sell 100 cups of lemonade at $1 each*
- *Your total money (revenue) is $100*
- *After paying for all your supplies, you have $25 left*
- *Your net profit margin would be 25%*

This means for every dollar you made selling lemonade, you got to keep 25 cents as profit!

A higher net profit margin usually means a company is doing well and making more money from what it sells.

Return on Equity- *Measures how much profit a company generates using money invested by shareholders. The higher the percentage, the better.*

Return on Equity, or ROE for short, is a way to measure how well a company is doing with its money.

To find the ROE, we divide two important numbers:

1. *How much money the company made (called net income)*
2. *How much money the owners put into the company (called shareholders' equity)*

It's like dividing how many cookies you baked by how many ingredients you used. The result tells you how good you are at making cookies!

ROE helps us understand:

- *How well a company is using its money*
- *If the company is good at making profits*
- *If the company's leaders are doing a good job*

Let's say you have a lemonade stand:

- *You made $10 from selling lemonade (net income)*
- *You started with $5 worth of your own lemons and sugar (shareholders' equity)*

Your ROE would be:

$10 ÷ $5 = 2 or 200%

This means for every $1 you put in, you got $2 back. That's pretty good!

- *A higher ROE usually means the company is doing better*
- *But it's best to compare ROE between similar companies*
- *ROE is just one way to look at how well a company is doing*

Return on Assets- *Measures how efficiently management uses its assets to generate earnings by showing how effective a company is in converting the money it has to invest into net income. The higher the percentage, the better.*

Return on Assets (ROA) is a way to measure how well a company uses the things it owns to make money.

To find the ROA, we use this simple math:

ROA = Net Income ÷ Total Assets

- *Net Income: This is how much money the company made after paying all its bills.*
- *Total Assets: Everything the company owns that has value, like buildings, machines, and money in the bank.*

A higher ROA number means the company is doing a good job using what it has to make money. It's like getting really good at using all your art supplies to make amazing pictures!

A lower ROA means the company could do better at using what it has. It's like having a bunch of toys but not playing with them very much.

Let's pretend we have two lemonade stands:

1. *Lily's Lemonade:*
   - *Net Income: $50*
   - *Total Assets: $500*
   - *ROA = 50 ÷ 500 = 0.10 or 10%*

2. *Tommy's Tasty Drinks:*

- Net Income: $40

- Total Assets: $800

- ROA = 40 ÷ 800 = 0.05 or 5%

Even though Tommy's stand made almost as much money as Lily's, Lily's stand has a better ROA because it used less stuff to make about the same amount of money.

ROA helps us understand which companies are good at using what they have. Remember, it's best to compare ROA between companies that do similar things. For example, you wouldn't compare how well a toy company uses its stuff to how well a farm uses its stuff - they're too different.

Return on Investment- Measures the amount of income derived from investment compared with the cost of the investment. The higher the percentage, the better.

Return on Investment, or ROI for short, is a way to figure out if the money you spend on something is worth it. It's like checking if you got a good deal!

Imagine you have a lemonade stand. You spend $5 on lemons, sugar, and cups. At the end of the day, you made $15 from selling lemonade. ROI helps you figure out how well your lemonade stand did.

To find the ROI, we use this simple math:

1. First, we find out how much money we made: $15 - $5 = $10

2. Then, we divide that by how much we spent: $10 ÷ $5 = 2

3. To make it a percentage, we multiply by 100: 2 × 100 = 200%

So, the ROI for your lemonade stand is 200%!

If the ROI is positive (above 0%), you made more money than you spent. That's good!

If the ROI is negative (below 0%), you lost money. That's not so good.

The higher the percentage, the better your investment did.

Examples of ROI in Business

1. *Buying seeds to grow vegetables in your garden to sell*
2. *Spending money on art supplies to make paintings to sell*
3. *Putting money in a bank that gives you interest*

BASIC STOCK ANALYSIS TERMS

Here are some definitions to help you as you learn about investing in stocks. Take your time in learning this information. Refer to it when needed.

Market Cap- The total market value of the Company;

Shares outstanding x current stock price

If a company has a market cap of **$1 trillion**, that means it would cost you **$1 trillion** dollars to purchase the company.

Shares Outstanding- The total amount of a company's stock currently held by all its shareholders

If a company increases its shares regularly, it may need more money

If a company decreases outstanding shares or buys back shares, that may be good. It may indicate they have cash AND you as a shareholder will own a higher percentage of the company

Alpha- Measures how a security performs against the market when adjusted for risk

A positive Alpha above zero means it outperforms.

A negative Alpha means it underperforms

Beta- A measure of how volatile a stock is in comparison to the overall market

The market as a whole has a value of 1. Any stock above 1 is more volatile than the market. Any stock under one is less volatile than the market

Earnings Per Share (EPS)- How much one share of a company's stock earns

Price to Earnings Ratio (P/E)- A measure of a stocks share price in relation to its annual income(Price divided by Earnings Per Share)

   *Generally the higher the P/E ratio, the riskier or more expensive the stock may be

Price to Book (P/B)- A measure of a stocks share price in relation to the equity shareholders have in a company (Price divided by Book Value)

   *Generally the lower the number, the better. A P/B value under 1 is usually a good sign

Dividend- A sum of money paid regularly (usually quarterly) by a company to its shareholders

Yield- A dividend expressed as a percentage of a current share price of a stock

Ex-Dividend Date- The day on which a company checks its records to identify shareholders of the company in order to payout dividends. Whoever owns shares of the company before the ex-dividend date will receive the next dividend payout

Average Volume- The average number of shares traded in a day on a given stock

INCOME STATEMENT

Revenue- Money generated from business operations of a company over a period of time

Cost of Goods Sold (COGS)- Direct costs of producing the goods or services sold by a company

Cost of Revenue- The total cost to produce and sell a product or service including costs of goods sold

Profit- Total income from all sources before deducting expenses(Revenue minus Cost of Goods Sold)

Gross Profit Margin- The profit left over after subtracting the cost of goods sold from the revenue measured as a percentage

   *How much of every dollar is kept by the company by percentage. A gross profit margin of 65% means that for every dollar the company brings in, they keep 65 cents in gross profit

*The higher the percentage, the better

Net Profit Margin- Measured as a percentage, how much profit is left after subtracting both the cost of goods sold AND all operating expenses

  *How much of every dollar is kept by the company by percentage in net profit

  *The Higher the percentage, the better, however this percentage will be lower than the gross profit margin

  *Most investors value the net profit margin over the gross profit margin as it is more specific

Net Income- Money a company has left after ALL expenses have been paid or deducted from revenue

BALANCE SHEET

Cash and Cash Equivalents- Value of a company's assets that are cash or can be converted into cash immediately

Total Current Assets- Assets of a company that will provide economic benefits to the company short term(1 year)

Total Assets- Total amount of assets owned by a company

Total Current Liabilities- A company's debt or obligations that must be paid to creditors within a year

Total Liabilities- The combined debts of a company

Total Liabilities/Total Assets(debt ratio)- How much debt a company has in comparison to its assets. Calculated by dividing the total liabilities by the total assets. The lower the %, typically the better. If a company's percentage is 30%, 30% of its assets are financed(debt) and 70% of its assets are owned by the shareholders

  The value of a company's TOTAL ASSETS should be greater than their TOTAL LIABILITIES

Debt to Equity Ratio(D/E)- How much debt a company has in comparison to the equity shareholders have in the business. Calculated by dividing total liabilities by total stockholders' equity. The higher the D/E ratio, the more a company relies on debt to finance the company.

If a company's total liabilities = $300,000,000, and its total stockholders' equity is $100,000,000, then the calculation would be $300,000,000 / $100,000,000 = 3.

*This means that the company has $3 of debt for every $1 of equity.

Common Equity/Total Shareholders' Equity- The amount shareholders have invested in the company(Assets minus Liabilities)

Liabilities and Shareholder's Equity- Must be the same as Total Assets in order for the balance sheet of a company to be balanced.

Earnings Before Interest, Taxes, Depreciation, Amortization (EBITDA)- A company's earnings from its core operations

CASH FLOW STATEMENT

Net Operating Cash Flow/Cash Generated from Operating Activities- Cash generated by a company's normal business operations

Property, Plant, Equipment(Capital Expenditures, Capex))- Money a company spends on physical assets to help grow the business

Net Investing Cash Flow/Net Cash Used In Investing- Cash a company uses for investments(stocks/securities, bonds, purchase of assets, equipment, etc.)

*If a company is constantly investing, this may appear as a loss on a cash flow statement

Net Financing Cash Flow/Net Cash Used In Financing- Cash movements between a company and its investors, owners and creditors. Cash used to finance a company including debts, equity and dividend payments

*If a company is getting rid of its debts, paying dividends or buying back shares, this may appear as a loss on a cash flow statement. This isn't a bad thing to many investors

Free Cash Flow- Cash that is generated that is "free" and "clear" of any and all obligations of the company

*FREE CASH FLOW DOES NOT APPEAR ON A CASH FLOW STATEMENT. YOU CAN CALCULATE THIS YOURSELF

(Cash from Operating Activities minus Capital Expenditures)

*If free cash flow is negative, it means a company is spending more than it makes.

*When there is no cash left over after all expenses and obligations, a company has negative free cash flow.

Remember, a cash flow statement is important because it provides insights into a company's or an individual's cash inflows and outflows over a specific period. Here's why a cash flow statement is important:

1. Assessing Liquidity: *The cash flow statement helps determine how much cash is available to cover immediate financial obligations.*

2. Understanding Operating Activities: *The cash flow statement breaks down cash inflows and outflows related to the core business operations. It shows how much cash is generated or used by the company's day-to-day activities, excluding financing and investing activities.*

3. Identifying Cash Sources and Uses: *The statement categorizes cash flows into operating, investing, and financing activities. This classification helps identify where cash is coming from (sources) and how it's being used (uses).*

4. Evaluating Profitability: *While the income statement shows the profitability of a company, the cash flow statement provides insights into the actual cash generated by the operations.*

5. Detecting Financial Issues: *A negative cash flow can indicate financial issues that need to be addressed.*

6. Investment Decisions: *Investors use the cash flow statement to assess a company's ability to generate cash and its financial stability. A company with strong positive cash flow might be more attractive to investors.*

7. Creditworthiness: *Lenders and creditors review cash flow statements to assess a borrower's ability to repay loans. Positive cash flow indicates the borrower's capacity to meet financial obligations.*

8. Tracking Financial Performance: *Over time, comparing cash flow statements allows you to track improvements or changes in fi-*

nancial performance, highlighting areas of growth and concern. The cash flow statement is an important tool for analyzing the financial health of a company.

WHAT IS A "GOOD" COMPANY?

How do you know a company is a "good" company? Many people will tell you they are purchasing a stock because it is a "good" company to invest in, but how could you possibly know that without ANY research? Here are some things to consider....

1. Can you tell if a person is healthy just by looking at them? Would a doctor just look at a patient and determine their health? Or would they perform blood work on the patient and check their weight, body fat percentage, cholesterol levels, blood pressure, heart rate, etc.? Wouldn't the doctor do research to determine the health of the patient? Just because someone is thin or athletic looking doesn't mean they are healthy. As an investor, shouldn't you do research to determine the health of the company you are investing in? Here is another example.

2. Can you tell if a person is wealthy or rich just by looking at them? Would a smart loan officer just loan money to a person just by looking at them? How do you know if someone is actually wealthy or rich? Wouldn't you go through their financials and assets/liabilities to determine their net worth if you were a loan officer? How many people look at a person with a big house, or a beautiful car and assume they are rich or in good financial standing? They could be in extreme debt and have a negative net worth. For all you know, YOU could actually be in better financial standing than they are. This is why doing some level of research is so important. You couldn't possibly know if a company is healthy unless you do the bloodwork of the company.

Many companies APPEAR to be good or healthy companies when in reality they are not. Just looking at the name of the company or what it appears to be doing and buying stock in it is no different than a doctor just believing a patient is healthy just by looking at them. As an investor, you are the doctor and the company is the patient. Not everyone who sees a doctor is in poor health, but you couldn't possibly know that without research.

*A helpful way to analyze the health of a company is to look at its Enterprise Value. The Enterprise value is the market capitaliza-

tion of the company plus the total debt minus its cash(Market cap + total debt - cash). The difference between the market cap and the enterprise value is basically the debt the company has. The higher the difference between the enterprise value and the market cap, the more debt the company is carrying without the cash to cover it. If the enterprise value is lower than the market cap, that is generally a good sign, as it signals the company has cash on hand. The enterprise value represents the cost to purchase a company including all of its shares AND the debt associated with the company.

Enterprise Value (EV) is a way to measure how much a company is worth. It's like finding out the price tag for an entire business!

To figure out Enterprise Value, we add up these things:

- The total value of all the company's shares (called market capitalization)
- All the money the company owes (its debts)
- Then we subtract any cash or savings the company has

Enterprise Value gives us a more complete picture of a company's worth than just looking at its stock price. It's especially useful when:

- One company wants to buy another company
- Investors want to compare different companies

Company A's Enterprise Value

Let's look at how we could find the Enterprise Value for Company A

1. First, we add up the value of all Company A's shares: $5.13 billion
2. Then we add Company A's debts: $2.998 billion
3. Finally, we subtract Company A's cash: $1.03 billion

So, Company A's Enterprise Value is about $7.098 billion!

Why not just use market value?

Market value only looks at the price of a company's shares. But Enterprise Value also considers:

- How much money the company owes
- How much cash the company has saved up

This gives us a better idea of the company's true worth.

*Return on Invested Capital(ROIC) is also a great metric to use. ROIC measures how well a company uses its capital to make profit off of investments. Basically, how well a company invests its money. It is shown as a percentage. Typically, an ROIC of 10% or higher is considered good for a company.

Return on Invested Capital (ROIC) measures how well a company uses its money to make more money. It's like planting seeds and seeing how many flowers grow.

To find ROIC, we use this simple math:

ROIC = Money made from investment ÷ Money invested

It's usually shown as a percentage, like 10% or 15%.

ROIC helps us know if a company is doing a good job with its money. If the ROIC is higher than what it costs the company to get money (like from loans), then the company is doing well.

Let's say a business invests $10. If they make $2 off of that investment, their ROIC would be:

ROIC = $2 ÷ $10 = 0.2 or 20%

This means for every dollar they invested, they made 20 cents.

ROIC can be used to compare different companies in the same industry. A company with a higher ROIC is often doing better than others. Again, a ROIC of 10% or higher is considered acceptable for a company.

ROIC is a helpful tool for understanding how well a company invests its money. It's like a report card for how competent a company is with its investments.

BELOW ARE MORE KEY METRICS YOU MAY CONSIDER.........

Current Ratio

The current ratio is a way to measure how well a company can pay its bills in the short term. It's like checking if you have enough money in your piggy bank to buy all the candy you want right now.

How to Calculate the Current Ratio

To find the current ratio, we divide two things:

1. Current assets: Things a company owns that can be turned into cash quickly (within a year)
2. Current liabilities: Bills and debts the company needs to pay soon (within a year)

The formula looks like this:

Current Ratio = Current Assets ÷ Current Liabilities

What the Current Ratio Tells Us

- If the ratio is 1 or higher: The company can likely pay all its short-term bills
- If the ratio is less than 1: The company might have trouble paying its bills soon

Examples of Current Ratio

Let's imagine two lemonade stands:

1. Lily's Lemonade:
   - Current assets: $100 (cash and lemons)
   - Current liabilities: $50 (money owed for cups)
   - Current ratio: 100 ÷ 50 = 2

Quick Ratio

The quick ratio is a simple but powerful tool that helps us understand how well a company can pay its bills in the short term. It's like checking if someone has enough money in their pocket to buy lunch today, not how much they have saved in the bank for next year.

Why is it Called the "Quick" Ratio?

It's called "quick" because it looks at assets that can be turned into cash quickly, usually within 90 days. These are things like:

- Cash in the bank
- Stocks and bonds that can be sold fast

- Money that customers owe the company (called accounts receivable)

How Does it Work?

The quick ratio compares these fast-to-cash assets to the bills the company needs to pay soon (called current liabilities). It's like comparing how much money you have in your piggy bank to how much you need to spend on groceries this week.

Why is it Important?

The quick ratio helps people understand if a company might have trouble paying its bills soon. This is important for:

- Investors who might want to buy part of the company

- Banks that might want to lend money to the company

- Suppliers who sell things to the company

Example of the Quick Ratio in Action

Imagine you have a lemonade stand. You have $10 in cash and $5 worth of lemons. Your quick assets are $15. If you owe $5 for the stand rental, your quick ratio would be 3 ($15 ÷ $5 = 3). This is good because you have 3 times more quick assets than bills to pay. You have $3 of liquid assets to cover every $1 dollar in current liabilities.

Long-Term Debt to Capitalization Ratio

The long-term debt to capitalization ratio is a way to measure how much debt a company has compared to its total available money. It's like looking at how much of a piggy bank is filled with borrowed money versus the owner's own savings.

The formula for calculating a company's long-term debt to total capitalization ratio is:

Long-term debt to total capitalization ratio = Long-term debt ÷ Total capitalization

Total capitalization is the sum of a company's total debt and total shareholders' equity.

How It Works

Imagine you have a big jar that represents all the money a company has to work with. This jar has three parts:

1. Long-term debt (money the company borrowed and needs to pay back after a long time)
2. Preferred stock (special shares of the company)
3. Common stock (regular shares of the company)

The ratio looks at how much of that jar is filled with long-term debt compared to everything else.

Why It's Important

This ratio helps people understand how risky it might be to invest in a company. Here's why:

- If the ratio is low: It means the company uses more of its own money to run the business. This is usually seen as less risky.
- If the ratio is high: It means the company borrows a lot of money to run the business. This can be riskier because the company has to pay back all that borrowed money.

Example

Let's say we have two lemonade stands:

1. Lemon Lovers: They borrowed $50 from their parents (long-term debt) and used $50 of their own savings (equity).
   - Their ratio would be: $50 ÷ ($50 + $50) = 0.5 or 50%
2. Citrus Squad: They borrowed $80 from their parents and used $20 of their own savings.
   - Their ratio would be: $80 ÷ ($80 + $20) = 0.8 or 80%

Citrus Squad has a higher ratio, which means they rely more on borrowed money. This could be riskier because they have to pay back more money.

Cash Flow Per Share

Cash flow per share tells us how much cash a company is making for each share of its stock. It's like looking at how much allowance each person in a family gets, but for a business.

Why is it Important?

Many experts think cash flow per share is more useful than earnings per share (EPS) when figuring out if a company is doing well. This is because:

1. It's harder to change or trick people with cash flow numbers.

2. It gives a clearer picture of how much real money the company is making.

How is it Calculated?

The formula for cash flow per share is:

(Money coming in from business - Money paid to special share-holders) ÷ Number of regular shares

Examples

Let's imagine we have a lemonade stand company:

1. If our lemonade stand makes $100, pays $20 to special share-holders, and has 10 regular shares, the cash flow per share would be:

   ($100 - $20) ÷ 10 = $8 per share

2. Now, if we make more lemonade and earn $150, still pay $20 to special shareholders, and still have 10 regular shares:

   ($150 - $20) ÷ 10 = $13 per share

This shows our lemonade business is growing and making more cash per share!

Why Do People Use This?

Cash flow per share helps show:

- How much cash a company is making

- If the company is getting stronger financially

- How well the company might do in the future

Remember, just like it's good to save some of your allowance, companies that have good cash flow often have money saved up to grow their business or handle tough times.

Book Value Per Share

Book Value Per Share (BVPS) is a way to measure how much a company is worth on paper for each share of its stock. It's like figuring out how much money each person would get if a company sold everything it owned, paid all its debts, and split the leftover money among its shareholders.

How to Calculate BVPS

To find the Book Value Per Share, we use this formula:

BVPS = (Total Equity - Preferred Equity) ÷ Total Shares Outstanding

Let's break this down:

- Total Equity: All the money the company owns
- Preferred Equity: Special shares that some people own
- Total Shares Outstanding: How many pieces the company is divided into

Why BVPS is Important

BVPS helps investors decide if a company's stock price is a good deal or not. If the BVPS is higher than the stock price, it might mean the stock is undervalued (cheaper than it should be).

Example of BVPS

Let's imagine a lemonade stand company:

- Total Equity: $1000
- Preferred Equity: $0
- Total Shares: 100

BVPS = ($1000 - $0) ÷ 100 = $10 per share

This means each share of the lemonade stand is worth $10 on paper.

Price to Tangible Book Value

Price to Tangible Book Value (PTBV) is a way to compare a company's stock price to the value of its physical stuff. It's like comparing the price tag on a toy to how much the toy's parts are actually worth.

What are Tangible Assets?

Tangible assets are things a company owns that you can touch or see. For example:

- Machines in a factory
- Trucks for delivery
- Buildings where people work
- Raw materials to make products
- Finished products ready to sell

Why is PTBV Important?

PTBV helps us understand if a company's stock price is fair compared to what the company actually owns. It's like checking if the price of a sandwich is fair based on the ingredients inside.

How to Calculate PTBV

To find the PTBV, we use this simple math:

PTBV = Price of one share of stock ÷ Tangible Book Value per share

The Tangible Book Value per share is found by:

1. Adding up all the company's tangible assets
2. Subtracting what the company owes (its debts)
3. Dividing that number by how many shares of stock exist

Example

Let's say a toy company has:

- Tangible assets worth $1,000,000
- Debts of $400,000
- 100,000 shares of stock

Tangible Book Value = $1,000,000 - $400,000 = $600,000

Tangible Book Value per share = $600,000 ÷ 100,000 = $6

If one share of this company's stock costs $12, then:

PTBV = $12 ÷ $6 = 2

This means the stock price is 2 times the tangible book value per share.

When is PTBV Useful?

PTBV is most helpful when looking at companies that own a lot of physical stuff, like:

- Car makers
- Oil companies
- Factories

It's not as useful for companies that make money from ideas or services, like software companies or social media platforms.

Remember, PTBV is just one tool to help understand a company's value. It's always good to look at other information too!

Dividend Payout Ratio

The dividend payout ratio is a way to measure how much money a company gives back to its owners (called shareholders) compared to how much money the company makes. It's like looking at how much of your allowance you spend versus how much you save.

How Do We Calculate It?

We can calculate the dividend payout ratio using this simple formula:

Dividend Payout Ratio = Dividends Paid ÷ Net Income

Let's break this down:

- Dividends Paid: This is the money the company gives to its shareholders.
- Net Income: This is how much money the company made in total.

Examples

1. Imagine a lemonade stand that made $100 (net income) and gave $25 to its owners (dividends).
   Dividend Payout Ratio = $25 ÷ $100 = 0.25 or 25%

2. A cookie company made $1000 and gave $500 to its shareholders.
   Dividend Payout Ratio = $500 ÷ $1000 = 0.5 or 50%

What Does the Ratio Tell Us?

- A low ratio (like 25%) means the company is keeping more money to grow or save.

- A high ratio (like 75%) means the company is giving more money back to its shareholders.

- If the ratio is 0%, it means the company isn't giving any money to shareholders.

- If it's 100%, the company is giving all its money to shareholders.

Why Is This Important?

The dividend payout ratio helps us understand if a company:

1. Is saving money to grow bigger

2. Is giving money back to its owners

3. Has enough money to keep paying dividends in the future

Remember, there's no "perfect" ratio. It depends on how old the company is and what its plans are for the future.

Again, there are SEVERAL metrics involved when analyzing a company. No company is perfect, and some metrics will be better than others. Make a list of the metrics you value most, and use those in your analysis of the company. Analyzing a company is not easy. It takes time. Are you willing to put in the time?

Metrics typically fall into one of four categories: Valuation, Profitability, Capitalization and Liquidity. Below are GENERAL simple rules to live by when analyzing and comparing companies you are interested in buying stock in:

Valuation Metrics- Measures the value of the stock in relation to its price

Examples: Price to Earnings, Price to Sales, Price to Cash Flow, Price To Free Cash Flow

*With Valuation metrics, generally speaking the lower the number or ratio, the better.

Profitability Metrics- Measures how much profit the company makes from running its business

Examples: Gross Profit Margin, Net Margin, Return on Assets, Return on Equity, Return on Invested Capital

*With Profitability Metrics, generally speaking the higher the number or ratio, the better.

Capitalization Metrics- Measures how much access to money and resources a company has in relation to its debts.

Examples: Debt to Equity, Total Debt to Total Assets, Long Term Debt to Equity

*With Capitalization Metrics, generally speaking the lower the number or ratio, the better.

Liquidity Metrics- Measures how much cash a company has or has access to

Examples: Current Ratio, Quick ratio, Cash ratio

*With Liquidity Metrics, generally speaking, the higher the number, the better.

When doing intense research on a company's stock, you can utilize your brokerage account, or websites such as marketwatch.com or yahoofinance.com or both. There are several others. Simply go to the website and search for the company by name or ticker symbol. Then do research by looking at the profile of the company, the financials, and the valuations. You can also compare the company you are interested in with other companies side by side. You can monitor stocks, mutual funds, and etfs on your phone in a basic stock app, and get alerts as well. Utilize all the tools you can at your disposal.

CHAPTER 8:
INVESTMENT STRATEGIES AND STOCK ANALYSIS

Quiz No: 8

Serial No	Question	Answer
1.	Money generated from business operations of a company is known as: A. Profit B. Revenue C. Total Assets D. Equity	
2.	A measure of how volatile a stock is in comparison to the overall market is known as: A. Beta B. Alpha C. EPS D. Standard Deviation	
3.	All of the following are liabilities except: A. Debt B. Payroll expenses C. Loans D. Cash	

4.	Portfolio investment should be based on the investor's A. Emotions B. Risk tolerance C. Opinion articles D. Friends and family	
5.	A strategy of investing in a stock or ETF in little amounts over time regularly known as: A. Hold On For Dear Life(HODL) B. Cash Flow Investing C. Portfolio Management D. Dollar Cost Averaging(DCA)	
6.	With the Net Profit Margin of a company, you want the percentage to be: A. High B. Low C. Balanced D. Decreased	
7.	Money a company has left after ALL expenses have been paid or deducted from revenue is known as: A. Gross Income B. Capital Expenditures C. Net Income D. Earnings before interest, taxes, depreciation, amortization	
8.	Money a company spends or invests back in its business is known as: A. Capital Expenditures B. Profit Margin C. Net Income D. Common Equity	

9.	On a company's balance sheet, liabilities and shareholders equity must be the same as: A. Total Liabilities B. Total Current Liabilities C. Total Assets D. Total Current Assets	
10.	Cash that is generated that is "clear" of any and all obligations of the company is known as: A. Positive cash flow B. Capital Expenditures C. Operating Cash Flow D. Free Cash Flow	

Key

1. B

2. A

3. D

4. B

5. D

6. A

7. C

8. A

9. C

10. D

FINAL THOUGHTS

*There is only one way in this world to become wealthy. OWNERSHIP. You can get rich through a variety of means, but to be truly wealthy, you must own something or many things that generate income. It's that simple.

Don't believe me? Research the 10 wealthiest people on earth. What is one thing that they all have in common?

Investing wisely gives you ownership over income producing assets. Chances are you will never be in the top 10 wealthiest people on earth. And that is ok, you don't need to be. However in order to build wealth, you must own something that generates income. What do you own that generates income, or has the potential to generate income? Investing helps to solve this problem.

*As Warren Buffet(one of the greatest investors in history) points out, if you love analyzing investments go for it. If you don't, simply dollar cost average into an Index Fund and invest that way.

*Anybody can pick a stock that does well with no research at all. That's called guessing. That is not true investing. You'll guess right sometimes, and wrong other times. Doing no research when picking a stock, or a rental property is leaving your investment to luck. There is good luck, and bad luck. You may be successful, but you may fail also. True investing requires giving yourself a margin of safety. When you are just guessing, there is no margin of safety involved.

*Remember, you are not in the predicting business. You are in the investing business.

*When buying stocks, remember there aren't many great companies. If most companies were "great", then they wouldn't be great, they would be average.

*Always be rational when the market is being irrational

*Have you ever heard the terms Bull market and Bear Market?

A bull market is a period of time in a financial market when assets rise continuously

A bear market is a period of time in a financial market when assets fall continuously

Bull markets typically last longer than Bear markets.

When should you be more aggressive in your investing? During a bull market, or a bear market?

*You can make money investing in a bear market(the storm). Even in a storm, people can make money. Think about it. In a torrential downpour, the person selling umbrellas and raincoat can make a lot of money, because they prepared for the storm. The same thing can happen if you as an investor are prepared for the economic storms that come with investing.

*Everyone makes money when the markets are doing well. Everyone is a "great" investor in a bull market. However, pay attention to those who can do well when there is great uncertainty in the markets. Stars don't shine bright during the light of day. They shine brightest in the darkness of night.

*Be careful listening to "predictions" that aren't really predictions. Many people predict the obvious, and when it eventually happens people believe that person to be an expert. Anyone "predicting" the market will go up or down is stating the obvious. Markets go up and down. Eventually they will be right at some point. A true prediction would be the day the market goes up or down, how long it lasts and the lasting impact. Of course, nobody can accurately "predict" this. If I "predicted" in July that winter will be from December to March, is that actually a prediction? Or would you be more impressed if I told you in July about a major snowstorm that will occur in winter to the day, time, and inches? And even if I predicted this event correctly, how many times can I accurately do this? Be wary of "predictions".

*The easiest way to begin investing is to buy an all market ETF or Mutual Fund. These investments invest in the ENTIRE stock market. Outside of bonds, if you want to start investing in something

that you can't screw up while you learn about investing, there are a few to choose from.

VTI(Vanguard), SCHB(Schwab), ITOT(IShares), SPTM(SPDR), FSKAX(Fidelity)

There are others. Do your research, look at the fund holdings, and the expense ratios.

Remember, some mutual funds carry investment minimums while ETFs generally do not.

Also remember, mutual funds trade only once a day(end of the day), while ETFs can be traded anytime.

Expense ratios are important. If you invest $1000 in an ETF, and the expense ratio is 0.03%, then that means you will pay $.30 cents a year to own the ETF. Not bad. The higher the expense ratio, the more you pay.

*When investing, always have a set of personal rules and boundaries that you apply to your investments. Would you play a game that didn't have a set of rules? One could argue that living by these rules is actually more important than having endless knowledge in investing.

*Be very careful listening to "experts". They are wrong plenty of times. They may also trick you into being the greater fool. It is known that articles and media will drive up the price of an asset to get you to buy it so that they can sell it to you at a higher price, making you the greater fool. Or, they will scare people off of an asset so they sell, driving down the price so they can buy it cheap and then run the price up again. In each instance, you are the greater fool. Gain knowledge in investing, have a solid plan with margin of safety and over time you will do well.

*Don't invest in something because everyone else is doing it. Most people are sheep. And the wolves in the market hunt the sheep. Do what is best for you.

*Prepare your investments for the storms, not the sunny days. Everyone plans their investments for when things are going well, but never for when things aren't. Look at your investments. If things don't go your way, will your investment still be a good investment?

Everyone wants the house on the beach until the flood waters hit. When the storm happens, will your house survive? Storms will happen in investing, as in life. Will your investment survive? Will you survive? Do you have a level of margin of safety? Maybe it's better to have a house that isn't as spectacular, but won't flood. If the investment can survive the hurricane, then it will have no problem on a sunny day.

What if you own a rental property, and the tenant doesn't pay the rent for 1 year? Can you cover the mortgage and expenses and survive?

Can the stock you invested in survive a long recession in the economy?

*PRICE AND VALUE MATTER- If I ask you why you are picking an investment, and your answer is "it's a good investment", you may be making a bad investment. You should be able to explain in detail why you are picking that investment. It doesn't mean you will be right, but you are more likely to be right if you have a valid explanation

So many times, people will tell me they want to buy stock in a company. I ask them why, and 90% of the time the answer is "because it's a good company." How do you know it's a good company? I ask, and they almost never have an answer(outside of someone else telling them so, or they read it somewhere). Always have an explanation for the investment you are making. If you can't explain it, maybe you shouldn't do it.

I then ask them if a Honda or a Toyota is a good car? They say yes. I then ask if they would pay $10,000,000 for one. They say absolutely not. Just because a company is a "good company" doesn't mean you should pay the going rate for it at that moment. It may be overpriced. A good stock or piece of real estate may be overvalued, or undervalued. DO YOUR RESEARCH!! I can't stress enough.....margin of safety, and the greater fool theory.

*Always look for good investments, at great prices.

*Anyone can easily pick a stock with no research that goes up over time. However, a true investor wants to maximize their return by purchasing at the best price possible.

*Be careful with stock splits. A stock split is when a company decides to increase its shares outstanding by dividing its existing stock. An example of a stock split would be a 2-1 split(if you own 10 shares of the stock, you would now own 20). The price of each share of the stock would decrease however you own more shares so your investment value remains the same. New investors falsely believe that with the stock split the price of the stock is cheaper, however it is not. It is just more affordable. If you buy a car for $50,000 and the dealership extends the loan from 60 months to 72 months to make the monthly payments lower, the monthly payments are more affordable however the price of the car is still $50,000. The car didn't become cheaper.

*Always research current news about any company you plan to invest in. Look for relevant news such as new products or innovations, or potential lawsuits against the company before you invest.

*Everyone should own a trademark, copyright, patent or a combination of all 3.

*When you trade time for money, you lose.

*Work hard for assets, not money. The right asset will work to get the money for you.

*Many high school students must take out loans for college. Many high school students do not have the funds for college. Why? Because their parents wasted their most valuable resource. TIME. If you are a parent of a young child, don't make that mistake. If you are a teenager, learn from this mistake. Here is something to look at....

If you put $5000 in an S&P 500 Index fund, and invested:

$200 a month consistently into that fund for:

18 years

with a 9% average return, compounded monthly, you would have:

$132,383.52Could this be useful for paying for college? Or helping your high school graduate start a business, or begin their adult life?

Is this really that complicated?

*You can own 1 of these 2 farms ....

Farm A

This farm has 1 Cow. It produces fantastic milk. People pay top dollar for the milk of this one cow. It can make you a tremendous amount of money.

Farm B

This farm has 50 cows. It produces good milk, but not as fantastic as the 1 Cow on Farm A. It makes you money as well, however not as much money as the single cow in Farm A.

Farm A = STOCK

Stocks are individual companies you are buying shares in. They can be risky. The stock could rise making you a lot of money, however if the company goes out of business you lose all your money. If your 1 cow dies, your farm is dead

Farm B = ETFs

ETFs are a basket of companies in an index or a sector. They are less risky than individual companies or stocks. If 5 of your 50 cows were to die, you still have 45 cows that can provide you milk to keep your farm alive. However, there is a chance your return may not be as good as an individual cow or stock.

*Remember, you can open your own brokerage account, but just understand the pros and cons:

Pros:

You have full control over what you invest in

Capital gains tax rather than Income Tax

No fees/Lower fees

No minimum distributions

Beneficiaries can receive control with no tax implications

You can match or possibly beat the market

Cons:

You have full control over what you invest in(this could be bad if you don't know what you are doing)

You have to actively manage it

Must stay educated in the market

May open yourself to more emotional investing.

   *Stocks vs Real Estate? Should you do just one, or can you do both? It's up to you.

Stocks

Easy to diversify

Can trigger emotions

Paper asset

Less headache

Easy to get out of a bad decision

Low cost of entry

Real Estate

Great against inflation

Less emotion involved day to day

Tangible asset

Cash Flow

Hard to get out of a bad decision

High cost of entry

   *Do you have a will? Have you established a trust for your kids? How will you pass down your wealth and protect it for your chil-

dren or beneficiaries? Protecting your wealth is as important as creating it if you want to build generational wealth. Talk to a lawyer who specializes in this.

Do you have life insurance? Life insurance is not an investment, but it is another wealth building tool for future generations......

*Be cautious reading opinion articles and media. Opinions aren't facts. Everyone has an opinion. Everyone isn't right. Do your own research

*If you plan to get into an investment, you should always have a plan to get out of that investment as well

*For the majority of people, investing consistently and periodically in an Index Fund is probably the best form of investment. However for those of you looking to branch out, ESPECIALLY if you have time to your advantage, do not limit yourself once you learn more about investing.

*In investing, new news isn't new.......it's just new to you

*If your investment is based off of chance, you are not investing. You are gambling

*Did you know that in many of the world's religions, investing is actually your religious duty? Don't believe me? Do your research. Several passages from the most popular book on earth(the Bible) discuss this.

*A credit score shows how good you are at making banks money. Your net worth shows how good you are at making yourself money. Can you think of one way to increase your net worth?(Here's a hint.....it's in the title of this book).

*Which is more important to you, your first name or your last name? Your answer to this question will determine if you plan to build generational wealth.

LASTLY.....ALWAYS DO YOUR OWN RESEARCH!

This book is just a simple introduction to the world of investing. There are many things about investing that couldn't possibly all be covered in this book. Please continue to read, study and learn about investing. It is a lifelong course that never ends. This book is simply to provide information, not advice. I do not know you or what is best for you, therefore I cannot advise you.

QUOTES TO HELP YOU ON YOUR INVESTING JOURNEY

Remember these famous quotes to get you through your investing journey......

*The more you **LEARN**, the more you **EARN***

*Your **NETWORK** is your **NET WORTH***

Discipline is Freedom

Everyone wants to get to heaven, but nobody wants to die

Price is what you pay; Value is what you get

Youth is wasted on the young

Never hate what you want to be

Two things in life are irreplaceable: People that you love, and Time

You can't build wealth losing money

If the outcome ain't income, then how come?

Always have a plan in life, but don't expect life to go as planned

Do you have a plan, or do you have hope?

If you took all the wealth in the world and distributed it equally to everyone, it would eventually go back to the wealthy

You can't be an exceptional person doing what the average person does

Things are good, until they are not

What's good for the lion isn't good for the gazelle

The longer things are good, the more nervous you should be

You can't predict the future, but you can prepare for it.

Own or be owned

Don't give up what you want most, for what you want now

Stupid people make wealthy people wealthier

Excuses make today easy but tomorrow hard; Discipline makes today hard, but tomorrow easy

It is not guaranteed you will be wealthy through investing. It is guaranteed you will not become wealthy without investing

Forecasts tell you about the forecaster.....they tell you nothing about the future

It's great to learn from your mistakes. It's even better to learn from the mistakes of others.

AFTERWORD

As an investor, I've lost plenty of money(usually due to emotion and undisciplined behaviors). However these "losses" were actually lessons. I've learned(and am still learning) from these lessons. These lessons are what prompted me to create this guide for those who are new to investing. Investing for beginners can be a daunting task, but understanding a few key principles can set you on the right path.

Investing is important for beginners because it offers a pathway to build wealth and achieve financial goals over time. It allows your money to grow through compounding, where your initial investment earns returns that then generate more returns. By investing early, you can take advantage of this compounding effect. Additionally, investing helps you beat inflation, which erases the purchasing power of your savings. It's an opportunity to diversify your assets and potentially earn higher returns than traditional savings methods. However, it's crucial to educate yourself and make informed decisions to manage risks effectively.

For Your Children

> *"What the wise do in the beginning, fools do in the end."-*
> *Warren Buffet*

Investing for children is important for several reasons:

1. Long-Term Growth: *Starting early allows investments to grow over a longer period, potentially harnessing the power of compounding, where your earnings generate further earnings.*

2. Financial Security: *Investments can provide a financial safety net for important life events like education, buying a home, or starting a business.*

3. Education Funding: *Investing for children can help cover the costs of higher education, reducing the burden of student loans and ensuring access to quality education.*

4. Teaching Financial Literacy: *Involving children in investment decisions can help teach them about financial responsibility, budgeting, and the value of saving and investing.*

5. Wealth Transfer: *Investments can serve as a means to transfer wealth to the next generation, helping ensure a better financial future for your children and even grandchildren.*

6. Estate Planning: *Proper investments can be part of a broader estate planning strategy, helping to ensure assets are passed on efficiently.*

7. Retirement Benefits: *Investing for children early can free up resources in your later years, potentially providing a more comfortable retirement. If your child has their own investments when they become adults they are less likely to ask you for help in starting their lives which may take away from your retirement.*

Referring to the earlier quote, investing for your children at the beginning of their lives is a wise decision. Continually waiting to invest for your children, one could argue, is a foolish one.

For Yourself

"You don't have to be smarter than the rest. You just have to be more disciplined than the rest."- Warren Buffet

Investing for yourself is important for several reasons:

1. Financial Independence: *Investing allows you to build wealth over time, which can lead to greater financial independence and the ability to achieve your goals without relying solely on a paycheck.*

2. Long-Term Goals: *Investing helps you work toward long-term goals such as retirement, buying a home, starting a business, or pursuing other aspirations that require substantial funds.*

3. Inflation Protection: *Investing can help your money outpace inflation, ensuring that the purchasing power of your savings doesn't diminish over time.*

4. Diversification: *Through investing, you can spread your funds across various assets, reducing the risk associated with putting all your money in one place.*

5. Passive Income: *Certain investments, like dividend-paying stocks or real estate, can generate passive income streams, providing financial stability and additional funds.*

6. Retirement Planning: *Investing early and consistently for retirement can lead to a more comfortable retirement, allowing you to maintain your desired lifestyle even after you stop working.*

7. Emergency Fund: *Building investments can serve as an emergency fund, providing a financial cushion to handle unexpected expenses or life events.*

8. Lifestyle Improvements: *Investments can help you afford experiences, hobbies, and opportunities that enrich your life and contribute to your well-being.*

9. Legacy Planning: *Investing can help you leave a financial legacy for your loved ones, ensuring that your assets are distributed according to your wishes.*

For The Future

> *"Someone's sitting in the shade today because someone planted a tree a long time ago."- Warren Buffet*

Investing for the future is important for several reasons:

1. Long-Term Financial Security: *Generational wealth provides a safety net that ensures financial stability for your family members not only in the present but also for future generations.*

2. Education Opportunities: *Having access to generational wealth can facilitate quality education for your descendants, opening doors to better career opportunities and improved quality of life.*

3. Reduced Financial Stress: *Generational wealth can alleviate financial stress for families by providing resources to handle unexpected expenses, medical emergencies, or other life challenges.*

4. Wealth Transfer: *It allows you to pass down assets and resources to your heirs, enabling them to start with a stronger financial*

foundation and have more opportunities for growth than you did.

5. Entrepreneurial Ventures: *Generational wealth can provide the capital necessary for your descendants to pursue entrepreneurial endeavors, fostering innovation and business growth.*

6. Homeownership: *It can help your family members afford homeownership, providing stability that can appreciate over time.*

7. Retirement Security: *Generational wealth can contribute to comfortable retirements for your descendants, allowing them to enjoy their later years without financial strain.*

8. Investment in the Future: *By creating generational wealth, you're investing in the future success and well-being of your family, enabling them to achieve their goals and aspirations.*

9. Legacy Preservation: *It allows you to leave a lasting legacy, not just in terms of financial assets, but also in terms of values, traditions, and a sense of identity.*

10. Social Mobility: *Generational wealth can promote upward social mobility, breaking cycles of poverty and providing a foundation for your family to improve their socioeconomic status.*

11. Economic Empowerment: *Having access to generational wealth empowers your descendants to make choices based on aspirations rather than financial limitations.*

Investing for future generations is critical to building generational wealth. Referring to the quote by Warren Buffet, it is up to you to plant the tree now that will grow to provide shade for your future generations.

Investing should never be something you do alone. Connect together with other like-minded investors. Share ideas. Go over different investments. Discuss investing. You may see something they don't see, and they may see something you don't see. Encourage each other. Challenge each other. Build an investment network. Remember, your network is your net worth. I created C.O.I.N.(The Community Outreach Investment Network) for this purpose. It allows for investors to learn and connect with other like-minded individuals to collectively grow their wealth. Visit the website at coinforlife.com.

Lastly, remember that investing is a long-term endeavor. It requires patience, discipline, and lifelong learning. Regularly monitor your investments, stay informed about market trends, and be prepared to adjust your sxtrategy as needed. Try to stay away from hype and predictions that are found all over the media, the internet, and among people you know. Always control your emotions. Build a solid foundation, and drown out the noise about investing. Have a plan and a foundation, and stick to it with adjustments when necessary. By starting early, diversifying your portfolio, and staying committed to your goals, you can lay a solid foundation for a successful investing journey. Always remember, in order to build wealth, ***INVESTING IS THE BEST THING!***

ACKNOWLEDGEMENTS AND THANK YOU'S

Thank you to my family, especially Natacha, Shauna, Céline, and DeVante Boyce.

Special thank you to my parents, Mark and Marlene, for getting me started on the path of investing. This would not have been possible without you. Thank You.

www.ingramcontent.com/pod-product-compliance
Lightning Source LLC
Chambersburg PA
CBHW060922120626
46557CB00003B/847